Springer Series
on Family Violence

Albert R. Roberts, PhD, Series Editor

Allen J. Ottens, PhD, received his doctorate from the University of Illinois–Urbana. He is currently Associate Professor of Counseling at Northern Illinois University and a licensed clinical psychologist in Illinois. He worked as a psychologist at Cornell University's Psychological Services Center and at the Counseling and Student Development Center at Northern Illinois University. One of his areas of professional interest is crisis intervention on the college campus.

Kathy Hotelling, PhD, ABPP, received her doctorate from the University of Missouri–Columbia. She is the Director of the Counseling and Student Development Center at Northern Illinois University in DeKalb. She is board certified in Counseling Psychology. She has published, consulted, and presented extensively regarding women's mental health issues.

Sexual Violence on Campus

Policies, Programs, and Perspectives

Allen J. Ottens, PhD, and
Kathy Hotelling, PhD, ABPP, Editors

 Springer Series on Family Violence

Springer Publishing Company, Inc.
536 Broadway
New York, NY 10012-3955

Acquisitions Editor: Bill Tucker
Production Editor: Jeanne W. Libby
Cover design by Susan Hauley

02 03 04/5 4 3 2

Library of Congress Cataloging-in-Publication Data

Sexual violence on campus : policies, programs, and perspectives / Allen J. Ottens and Kathy Hotelling, editors
    p. cm.—(Springer series on family violence)
   Includes bibliographical references and index.
   ISBN 0-8261-1374-5
   1. Sexual harassment in universities and colleges—United
States.   2. Sexual harassment—United States—Prevention.
3. Women college students—Crimes against—United
States.   4. Male college students—United States—Psychology.
I. Ottens, Allen J. II. Hotelling, Kathy. III. Series.
LC212.862 .S52 2001
378.1'958—dc21

                             00-030140
                             CIP

Printed in the United States of America

Contents

Contributors

Ron Binder, EdD
Director of Greek Affairs
University of North Carolina
CB 5100
Chapel Hill, NC

Nina Cummings, MS
Cornell University
Gannett Health Center
10 Central Avenue
Ithaca, NY

Barbara Fouts, PsyD
Staff Psychologist
Counseling & Student Develop-
    ment Center
Northern Illinois University
DeKalb, IL

Francesca Giordano, PhD
Associate Professor
Department of Counseling,
    Adult, and Health Education
Gabel Hall
Northern Illinois University
DeKalb, IL

Jamie R. Funderburk, PhD
Clinical Assistant Professor
    and Counseling
    Psychologist
Counseling Center
301 Peabody Hall
University of Florida
Gainesville, FL

Tim Marchell, PsyD
Director of Substance Abuse
    Services
Cornell University
Gannett Health Center
10 Central Avenue
Ithaca, NY

Douglas Pearson, PhD
Assoc. Vice President for
    Student Affairs
University of West Florida
Office of Student Affairs—
    Building 21
11000 University Parkway
Pensacola, FL

Jayne Schuiteman, PhD
Assistant Professor
Women's Studies/Women's
  Resource Center
Michigan State University
332 Union Building
East Lansing, MI

Beverly Tuel, PhD
Director
Gay, Lesbian, Bisexual,
  Transgender Resource
  Center
University of Colorado
CB 103
Boulder, CO

Jeff O'Brien, MS
Center for the Study of Sport
  in Society
Northeastern University
716 Columbus Avenue
Suite 161 CP
Boston, MA

Joan Zorza, JD
25 Sutton Place South #8D
New York, NY

Introduction

Colleges are grappling with the massive problem of relationship and sexual violence. Date and acquaintance rape and physical and psychological abuse are its most common manifestations. What to do about violence and abuse has taken many forms, including installing security systems in buildings and on grounds, sponsoring campus-wide prevention workshops, instituting tougher policies and sanctions, targeting programs toward "high risk" student groups, and disseminating information about rape and helping resources.

Several years ago, the Higher Education Center for Alcohol and Other Drug Prevention (1995) in Newton, Massachusetts published a guide to help campus program coordinators prevent acquaintance rape. Besides discussing in detail the components of a comprehensive prevention program, the guide offered examples of programs and innovative interventions that were contributed from staff at numerous universities across the country.

Several praiseworthy examples have been gleaned from the guide and are presented below. They illustrate how the entire campus community—faculty, Greeks, athletes, women's groups, and others—can be mobilized to address acquaintance rape.

- In the Fall of 1990, a number of students at Brown University, frustrated with the lack of an effective disciplinary system for sexual assault cases, began writing the names of men on bathroom walls who they claimed had assaulted or sexually harassed them. The rape list gained national attention after students invited the New York Times to send a reporter to the campus. The result was tremendous controversy and embarrassment for the school's administration. As a result, the president hired a consultant and formed a task force to address the problem. The result was the creation of the Sexual Assault Peer Education (SAPE) program and a mandatory orientation session for all first-year students. In addition, in the spring of 1991, the school expelled one student, suspended another for two years, and put a third on probation for four years, all for sexual misconduct. (pp. 26–27)

- The Interfraternity Council at Pennsylvania State University developed a mandatory sexual assault education program for all new fraternity members. In groups of about 70 students each, between 600 and 700 pledges attend the program each year. Conducted by the coordinator of Greek life and the sexual assault prevention coordinator from the Center for Women Students, the program relies on trained students to lead small-group discussions following a film of a simulated fraternity party. The University of Maine's Greek Peer Educator Program recruits one member from every fraternity and sorority. After a semester-long training course, members offer a mandatory workshop for pledges entitled, "Liquor, Law and Lust" which focuses on alcohol, risk management, and sexual assault. (p. 34)

- At the Colorado School of Mines, the varsity football coach decided to act before a problem arose. After hearing how college coaches at other schools had come under fire because of their players' drinking and assaultive behavior, he asked the staff at the Student Development Center to provide a workshop on acquaintance rape for the players. Diana Doyle, Director of Student Development, remembers that "we were also doing a separate alcohol awareness program with a FIPSE [Fund for the Improvement of Postsecondary Education] grant, and, seeing how alcohol and sexual assaults were related, we decided to address both problems together in a specially developed workshop. . . . " (p. 36)

- Portland State University in Oregon decided to target faculty who teach courses that have some relationship to the problem of sexual assault, such as sociology, psychology, and health education instructors. Peer-led workshops were given in more than 20 classes during a single semester in 1994;

during the entire year, 1,500 out of 10,000 students participated in at least one of the workshops. (p. 39)

- A few schools, such as Muskingum College and UCLA, offer
women courses in defending themselves against rape. At
UCLA, the school contracts with the Los Angeles Commission
on Assaults Against Women to provide certified instructors
to teach free Saturday workshops for students, faculty, and
staff. While much of the focus is on preventing stranger rape,
typically these courses also provide techniques women can
use to prevent assaults by acquaintances, including techniques for defusing situations in which men start to become
aggressive or violent. These courses also stress the role
alcohol plays in reducing women's ability to assess dangerous situations and take effective action to prevent or escape
them. (p. 39)
- When Myra Hindus was first hired by the University of Connecticut to run its Women's Center, she was told that there
was no time during new student orientation to fit in an activity on acquaintance rape. With the help of media attention
to the problem and her own persistence, she was eventually
given permission to provide a session. Although she wanted
to put on a skit, she was told that was too serious, so she
compromised on a 60-minute session consisting of a video
and follow-up discussion offered ten times over the seven-
day orientation period. Students now rate the session as one
of the best orientation events they attend. (p. 42)
- At the University of Maine, Sandra Caron, a faculty member
who teaches courses in human sexuality and family studies,
initiated an acquaintance rape prevention program called
Athletes for Sexual Responsibility that relies exclusively on
varsity athletes as workshop facilitators. Her goal was "to
capitalize on the high visibility of athletes, and their ability
to set standards for behavior for other students, to use them
as role models for appropriate social and sexual behavior."
Caron also believes that using athletes makes it possible
to help change campus norms about sexual behavior and
drinking. (p. 53)

Besides these relatively large-scale initiatives, there are other
less public, less well-publicized efforts where constituents of the

campus community are confronted with the realities of sexual and relationship violence. These are the very private, emotionally charged moments when fate taps a faculty or staff person or student on the shoulder and designates her or him as "it"— the one who is asked to respond to the victim(s) of sexual violence and its aftermath. Examples are legion, but almost any faculty or staff person would be familiar with these hypothetical encounters:

. . . a university health service physician providing medical assistance and counseling to a student who delayed for two weeks a visit to the service because she had been uncertain whether to define as rape a male acquaintance's sexual exploitation of her.

. . . an influential member of the faculty, a male who is "out" and who is regarded by the gay community as a campus advocate, being asked to lend his support to a student who had been harassed in a residence hall.

. . . a teaching assistant consulting with a staff member of the university counseling center regarding an essay—a literal plea for help, actually—written by a freshman woman who had been raped at a fraternity party over the Labor Day weekend during a Rush Week event.

. . . a campus security officer, tipped off by an anonymous caller about a "young woman in distress," entering an off-campus apartment and finding a victim passed out on a bed after having ingested an illegal "date-rape" drug.[1]

. . . the college's judicial officer offering counsel to a sophomore woman who is unsure whether to bring charges against an assailant.

. . . a male friend requesting help at the office of student affairs because he feels overwhelmed trying to act as peacemaker to a cohabiting couple whose arguments are escalating in ferocity.

---

[1]For a chilling real life parallel to this hypothetical example, see Cichon (2000) who recently reported that State College police discovered in a fraternity house three unconscious female Pennsylvania State University students who had overdosed on the increasingly common, yet hazardous, drug, gamma hydroxybutyrate (GHB).

The chapters that follow provide insights, interventions, and recommendations about preventing and responding to sexual violence on campus. In fact, the reader will find that many of the issues captured in the preceding vignettes are discussed at length by our chapter contributors. The authors provide multiple perspectives that encompass broad, systemic primary prevention approaches all the way to counseling strategies for the individual survivor of that violence.

The chapter authors have many years of experience in "frontline" positions as student affairs professionals, faculty, and counselors/therapists in higher education settings. Collectively, they espouse an attitude that sexual violence on campuses can only be addressed through using creative interventions, heightening awareness, working proactively, and involving as many constituents as possible—from campus and from the local community.

OUTLINE OF THE BOOK

Professor Allen Ottens in chapter 1 begins with a discussion of the extent of the problem of sexual and relationship violence on campus. A major thesis of this chapter is that in order to deal with perpetrators' motivation to abuse others, the university must identify where in the campus social context opportunities exist for sexual exploitation and understand the personological characteristics of the individuals at highest risk for taking advantage of them.

In chapter 2, Dr. Tim Marchell and Ms. Nina Cummings, staff members at Gannett Health Center of Cornell University, provide an overview of the connection between alcohol use and sexual violence on the college campus. From a prevention standpoint, Marchell and Cummings point out the limitations of the traditional "individual approach" to responsible drinking. Instead, they recommend targeting the many environmental factors impacting students' drinking behavior. The "social norms" approach is one potentially useful environmental intervention that corrects students' overestimations of the actual drinking behavior of their peers. With an established, accurate normative baseline for drinking behavior, would-be perpetrators of sexual assault will find it more difficult to use alcohol exploitively.

Joan Zorza, Esq., a noted legal expert on drug-facilitated rape, provides timely information in chapter 3 about the properties and effects of illegal sedating substances that are being introduced at an alarming rate onto campuses. She makes pertinent recommendations for treating the survivors of drug-facilitated sexual assaults and for prosecuting the perpetrators.

Feminist scholars have made paradigm-shifting contributions to our understanding of power and control in relationships. In chapter 4, Professor Jayne Schuiteman of Michigan State University demonstrates how women's studies/feminist scholarship can establish linkages with campus efforts to combat sexual violence. She suggests how feminist perspectives can inform university policy and preventive programming. Gender inclusiveness in educational programming is given particular emphasis as a means for deterring sexual assault among such high-risk groups as male athletes and fraternity members.

Dr. Barbara Fouts is intimately involved in implementing through the residence halls a sexual assault prevention program for all freshmen at Northern Illinois University. In chapter 5, she and Ms. Jenny Knapp describe the key components of the program as well as how it has been designed to match the unique needs within the NIU campus community. This chapter is relevant for student development professionals who are planning to initiate such a program.

Fraternity and sorority communities are some of the largest, most highly visible, and well-organized student groups on campus. They are also regarded as groups at higher risk for sexual assault involvement. Components of a comprehensive effort against sexual assault—including educational programs and policy formation—are topics of chapter 6. Dr. Ron Binder, Director of Greek Affairs at the University of North Carolina at Chapel Hill, is the chapter author.

Mr. Jeffrey O'Brien, Director of the Mentors in Violence Prevention (MVP) Program at Northeastern University, describes in chapter 7 his sexual assault prevention work with student-athletes. Undergirding MVP is the unique bystander approach that empowers men to work collaboratively and responsibly to deter assault.

Professor Francesca Giordano of Northern Illinois University adopts a developmental strategy (chapter 8) for understanding and addressing anger within the relationships of cohabiting college students. Student affairs professionals need to be cognizant of violence within this group since cohabiting students are at the highest risk for relationship violence.

Chapter 9 addresses the prevalence and patterns of sexual assault against (and by) gay, lesbian, and bisexual students, as well as important considerations for survivors of assault and for campus prevention efforts. Dr. Beverly Tuel of the University of Colorado at Boulder also describes innovative programs developed by the GLBT Resource Center where she is Director.

Chapter 10 deals with the sensitive issue of how sexual assault cases are handled through the judicial affairs process. From his experience in the Dean of Students Department at Florida State University, Dr. Douglas Pearson provides us with invaluable information for protecting the rights of victim and alleged perpetrator. Dr. Pearson walks the reader through the steps for dealing with a sexual assault violation on campus and gives us "insider" insights into resolving points of conflict between the rights of the victim and the charged student.

Helping women survive sexual assault is a critical tertiary prevention effort. In chapter 11, Dr. Jamie Funderburk of the University of Florida presents various group interventions and alternative paths toward recovery. Her insights into group counseling for survivors derive from her experience at the Center for Sexual Assault and Abuse Recovery and Education on the University of Florida campus.

In chapter 12, Dr. Kathy Hotelling, Director of the Counseling and Student Development Center at Northern Illinois University, shares summary remarks and suggests future directions from her perspectives as clinician and student development specialist.

REFERENCES

Cichon, F. (2000, April 10). "Police find drugs in Penn State fraternity." *The Digital Collegian.* [On-line]. Available: www.collegian.psu.edu/archive/2000/04/04-10-00tc

Higher Education Center for Alcohol and Other Drug Prevention (1995). *Preventing alcohol-related problems on campus: Acquaintance rape.* Newton, MA: Author. [On-line]. Available: www.edc.org/hec/pubs/acqrape.html

CHAPTER 1

The Scope of Sexual Violence on Campus

Allen J. Ottens

Amanda had it figured out. Tonight she was going to teach her former boyfriend, Pete, a much deserved lesson. She and Pete had had a tumultuous ten month relationship, punctuated by several episodes of infidelity on his part. Each time he cheated on her, Amanda, swayed by his promises of turning over a new leaf, took him back. Then, three weeks ago to her surprise, he abruptly terminated the relationship, saying he'd had enough of being "stuck on a short leash." When she tearfully appealed for a second chance of her own, Pete, unmoved, offered no consolation. "I have only two words for you," he said. "It's over."

The lesson, as Amanda conceived it, was to be played out tonight at Rooster's, a popular off-campus club. Pete, a Rooster's regular, would be enticed by the club's T.G.I.F. 99¢ shot-and-beer special. Amanda also expected that another fellow would be there, too. This was Nick, a popular and socially "smooth" (some would say "too smooth") member of ABC fraternity, who had made previous attempts in the past to date Amanda while she was staying faithful to Pete. It seemed to Amanda a pretty good bet that she could get Nick to pick her up at the club, where they

1

could spend some time drinking and dancing, and then conspicuously leave together, under Pete's nose.

Amanda's Friday night plan unfolded perfectly. As she predicted, both Pete and Nick were at the club, and it took only minutes to attach herself to Nick. They danced together and shared several drinks. Through the din, Amanda managed to give Nick the basics of her retaliation strategy. He caught on to it quickly—not just to Amanda's desire to get even but also to something about this transparent ploy that left her in a vulnerable position—and he suggested that for greater effect they make out while on the dance floor.

Around 11:30 p.m., Nick proposed they leave Rooster's for a party that was now in full swing at the ABC house. But before they drove over there, would it be OK to stop at his apartment, maybe roll a joint of marijuana, and get a case of beer that he promised to bring to the party? "That's great. Let's go," she said as they exited with a flourish past Pete.

At the apartment, Nick retrieved his little bag of marijuana but couldn't find any rolling papers. While he hunted, Amanda munched on a few leftover cookies. "Damn," he said, as he emerged from the back bedroom, "I thought my roommate had some!" "Well, it's not that big a deal," Amanda said. "You can get some papers at the party." She made two steps toward the door, when Nick reached out for her wrist and pulled her back.

She was jarred by the force of his grip. "Hey, where are you going?" he asked. Amanda gave him a puzzled look. "You got me pretty worked up at Rooster's," Nick said, "and I thought we should finish what we started." Nick took his other arm and swung it around Amanda's waist and pushed her onto a lumpy couch. Amanda was now vividly aware that Nick's playfulness had suddenly transformed into malevolent coercion. Her initial efforts to extricate herself were met with muscular resistance. "Come on," Nick snarled, "quit being such a prick teaser!"

Despite Amanda's repeated pleas to stop, Nick had begun to touch her in sexually invasive ways. Somehow Amanda managed to pry one arm loose. She was just able to reach the lamp table behind the couch to tip the table over. Table and lamp crashed to the floor, distracting Nick enough for her to wriggle out from underneath him.

It is possible to understand Nick's motivation to initiate acquaintance rape as the result of an intersection of a multitude of factors. Let's examine several. One factor could have been Nick's appraising the situation in such a way ("she was asking for it") as to minimize his degree of culpability. Another factor could be something within Nick's psychological make-up; that is, once he understood that Amanda had shown him a vulnerable facet of herself, he aggressively worked to take advantage of it. It is also likely that Nick was emboldened by the ease with which he could take advantage of the ambiguity of the social situation that presented itself. Given Nick's personality tendency to exploit opportunities to his own advantage, his motivation to rape was further abetted by myths about women and rape and by the ambiguity of the situation.

Speaking to the specific problem of acquaintance rape, Lonsway (1996) argued that deterrence as a prevention strategy is doomed to fail. "True" prevention, she averred, must target the perpetrators; or, in the case of rape, it means addressing "men's *motivation to rape*" (p. 232, italics preserved).

It is our contention that significantly impacting the motivation to abuse and rape requires: (a) identifying where in the campus social context windows of opportunity exist for the exploitation of intimates; (b) an understanding of the psychological factors of the perpetrators; and (c) the implementation of interventions that reduce the perpetrators' opportunity to exploit and to get away with it. Stated a bit differently, *I argue that protective social conventions moderating the college dating/"partying" scenes are so easily circumvented, that implicit rules governing students' intimate relationships are so ambiguous, and that colleges' administrative policies and proclamations may be capriciously applied, allowing individuals with certain personality tendencies to see enormous opportunity for engaging in exploitive behavior.* These loopholes need to be closed down.

In this chapter I address such issues as: where are significant ambiguities and exploitable opportunities found, how do certain victimizers exploit them, and what are characteristics of the victimizers? Before tackling these topics and to establish a context, I begin with an overview of the extent of sexual violence on campus as well as the costs incurred to those involved.

THE EXTENT OF THE PROBLEM

An overview of statistics pertaining to campus rates of sexual assault, physical and emotional abuse, and the psychological costs to victims suffices to bring one to the conclusion made a decade and a half ago that sexual aggression is common, normative, and embedded in the structure of intimate relationships (Burkhart & Stanton, 1986).

RATES OF SEXUAL AGGRESSION

Perhaps the most cited study of sexual aggression and victimization among college students was conducted by Koss, Gidycz, and Wisniewski (1987). In their ambitious research, Koss and her colleagues surveyed over 6000 students at 32 U.S. colleges. Their data revealed the unconscionably high incidence and prevalence rates of sexual violence perpetrated against the women respondents. For example, almost 54% of the women reported experiencing some form of sexual victimization (rape, attempted rape, sexual coercion) since age 14. Of the college men surveyed, 25% admitted to some type of sexually aggressive behavior, which, as the data analysis revealed, was not enough to account for the number of victimizations claimed by the women. Koss et al. calculated from their data a victimization rate of 83 per 1000 women who, within just the 6 month period preceding the survey, reported a sexual experience that met legal definitions for rape and attempted rape. Perhaps the most woeful findings were that 57% of the rapes occurred on a date, and 84% of the women raped knew their assailants, thus countering the notion that stranger rape is the greatest risk for women.

Using different sampling procedures, survey instruments, or definitions of what constitutes sexual aggression, and at times limiting their study to a specific institution, many other researchers have uncovered rates of dating violence that are alarmingly consistent. Following on the heels of the Koss et al. (1987) research, Miller (1988) surveyed women students at North Carolina State University and found that 27% of the sample reported having been physically or psychologically pressured into intercourse.

In a study that included over 900 women at a large midwestern university, Frintner and Rubinson (1993) found that over 21% reported being involved in at least one incident of sexual assault, attempted sexual assault, or sexual abuse since their arrival on campus. Finley and Corty (1993), at another midwestern school, concluded from their survey results that " . . . by the time they were in the junior and senior years, about a third of the women reported having been victim [of forced sexual assault] and about a third of the men reported being perpetrators" (p. 116). Hazarding a "best guess" based on their review of the extent of dating violence, Sugarman and Hotaling (1991) estimated that "about 28% of dating individuals were involved in intimate violence at some point in their careers" (p. 104). Similarly, estimates cited by researchers of the incidence and prevalence rates for sexual assault at U.S. institutions are in the 15 to 25% range (e.g., Frintner & Rubinson, 1993; Malamuth, Sockloskie, Koss, & Tanaka, 1991; Schwartz & DeKeseredy, 1997).

PHYSICAL ABUSE

Although there exists a parallel line of investigations into the scope of physical violence in college students' intimate relationships, we realize that it is easy to artificially bifurcate physically abusive and sexually assaultive behaviors. Relatively few studies have examined the comorbidity of both aggressive acts against dating partners. One noteworthy example of this type of research was reported by Hannan and Burkhart (1993) from their study of 266 Auburn University male undergraduates. Over half the men admitted to engaging in physically or sexually aggressive behavior against a dating partner. About one third of these men (17% of the entire sample) reported committing both types of aggression. Hannan and Burkhart's study suggests that not only is there a "relatively high" degree of comorbidity between physical and sexual assault, but that these dual perpetrators may represent a distinct group of especially violent men. Results such as these lead us to agree with Kurz (1998), who argued that physical violence must be considered with related types of violence, including rape and sexual harassment.

It was Makepeace's (1981) landmark study at Bemidji State University that brought overdue attention to the problem of "courtship violence." Makepeace found that over 21% of his respondents had been involved in some type of dating violence. Matthews (1984) replicated this study at the University of Massachusetts, where he found almost 23% of his sample had experienced direct violence (e.g., pushing, hitting, throwing objects) in a dating relationship. A few years later, Sugarman and Hotaling (1989) reviewed over 40 dating violence studies and estimated that about 40% and 33% of female and male college students, respectively, used violence at some time in their dating careers. Moreover, cohabiting couples whose relationships are often marked by both emotional commitment and jealous possessiveness appear to have a higher rate of assault and more severe violence than either married or dating couples (Sugarman & Hotaling, 1991). More recently, at the University of Maine, Stacy, Schandel, Flannery, Conlon, and Milardo (1994), using items from the Conflict Tactics Scale, focused on violence in one's most recent relationship. In their sample of undergraduates, they found that 21% admitted to committing an act of violence (e.g., slapping, kicking, weapon threat), which was double the rate found 10 years earlier at this university.

While studies have revealed the reciprocity of violence in male-female relationships (e.g., Lo & Sporakowski, 1989; Bookwala, Frieze, Smith, & Ryan, 1992; Ellis & Frieze, 1995), it is believed that female college students are generally not the initiators of that physical violence. DeKeseredy and his colleagues (cited in Currie, 1998), from their research at Canadian universities, found that a substantial amount of violence used by women was in self-defense. This evidence led the researchers to reject the "mutual combatant" theory between males and females. In the study cited above, for example, Stacy et al. (1994) found that only 13% of their female respondents admitted to initiating the physically abusive behavior.

SEXUAL VIOLENCE "TRANSPLANTED" ONTO CAMPUS

By the time students reach college age, many are steeped in the conventional wisdom (myths) that justify violent behavior against romantic partners. Rape-supportive attitudes have been shown to be common among high-schoolers (e.g., Davis, Peck, & Storment, 1993), with boys tending to be more accepting of rape myths than girls (Blumberg & Lester, 1991; Feltey, Ainslie, & Geib, 1991). Approximately 15 to 20% of high school students have had at least one exposure to violence with a dating partner (Bergman, 1992; Smith & Williams, 1992). Adolescents have also been exposed to countless models of sexual aggression either in their family-of-origin or through the media. Grimly, cohorts of future college freshmen have learned that even the Oval Office is an arena for sexual exploitation. The result is that many 18-year olds bring to campuses motivations for sexual exploitation and beliefs about what one can get away with in a sexual encounter. Their experiences as victims or victimizers also come with them.

Research has amply documented the extent of this transplanted pain and dysfunction. For example, in a survey of over 900 women from four colleges, Harrington and Leitenberg (1994) found that 25% had been victims of sexual aggression since age 16. When Muehlenhard and Linton (1987) surveyed more than 700 undergraduates, they found that over 70% of the women and 50% of the men reported at least one incident of unwanted sexual activity, ranging from kissing to sexual intercourse, during their high school careers. Thirty-three percent of the female students screened by Gidycz, Hanson, and Layman (1995) at a large midwestern university reported experiencing either a rape or attempted rape after age 14 but prior to participation in the study. Coffey, Leitenberg, Henning, Bennet, and Jankowski (1996) found that those college women in their sample who had witnessed physical conflict between parents before age 16 were twice as likely after 16 to have experienced dating violence than women who had never witnessed such conflict.

Given such unsettling research findings, I urge those in higher education who establish partnerships with public school districts to develop prevention programs that target sexually aggressive behaviors and rape-supportive attitudes. These programs can't begin soon enough.

"HIDDEN" EXPRESSIONS OF CAMPUS SEXUAL VIOLENCE

Campus sexual violence is traditionally regarded as male against female violence within romantic or intimate contexts. The real census of victims and victimizers, however, must be captured with a much larger net. Such violence pervades the campus social structure. For example, Rickgarn (1989) publicized the plight of resident assistants (RAs). These student employees of the university are often subjected to stressful sexual harassment (e.g., inappropriate touching, sexual slurs) that frequently goes unreported. Palmer (1996) pointed out that many RAs are thrust into the emotional turmoil presented by sexually assaulted residents in crisis. The deleterious psychological impact on the RAs in these instances goes largely unrecognized.

Another "hidden," less well-understood dimension of sexual violence on campus occurs in gay, lesbian, bisexual, and transgendered relationships. Although a topic of discussion within the GLBT campus communities, the problem is only now coming under empirical investigation. In a recent study (Bowman & Morgan, 1998) performed at a mid-sized public university, it was found that rates of physical and verbal violence were higher in lesbian respondents compared to heterosexual respondents; gay men, however, consistently reported less such violence than either lesbians or heterosexuals.

Even in the larger U.S. society, research on same-sex relationship violence is in its early stages, but estimates reveal the magnitude of this phenomenon. Elliott (1996) reviewed findings from several preliminary studies that indicated 17 to 46% of gays and lesbians have experienced a physically violent same-sex relationship. In their literature review, Stahly and Lie (1995) concluded that battering appears to occur at a higher rate in lesbian couples than in heterosexual relationships. Island and Letellier (1991) estimated conservatively that 500,000 gay men are battered each year.

Significantly, same-sex intimate violence has represented a challenge to the prevailing feminist theory of sexual victimization because it fails to take into account that such violence could occur (Letellier, 1994). Renzetti (1998) has pointed out that the familiar sociocultural and contextual factors such as heterosexism and gender inequality are proving insufficient to account for the totality of intimate violence. Instead a multidimensional perspective on intimate violence is being proposed that takes into consideration both the *sociocultural* variables (e.g., patriarchal

values, sex-role socialization patterns) and the *psychological* variables (e.g., narcissistic, antisocial, or borderline personality characteristics) of the abuser (e.g., Coleman, 1994; Hamberger, 1994;
Letellier, 1994; Renzetti, 1998).

Later in this chapter I shall describe how this same perspective
has value for understanding campus sexual violence: that the
social and cultural contexts on campus present ambiguities and
windows of opportunity that are exploited by individuals with
certain psychological characteristics.

THE COSTS INCURRED

Sexual and physical aggression against college women exacts an
incalculably high price. If college is a place for healthy risk-taking
and for personal, social, and vocational maturation, then rape
and abuse represent blows to the search for self-identity and life
roles (Stith, Jester, & Bird, 1992). Acquaintance rape may leave the
victim feeling socially stigmatized and ostracized—even unable to
talk about the assault lest she be disbelieved (Benson, Charlton, &
Goodhart, 1992). Not only may she fail to label the assault as a
rape (Koss et al., 1987; Schwartz & Leggett, 1999), she may delay
seeking treatment (Sorensen & Brown, 1990) or underuse professional sources of help (Sugarman & Hotaling, 1991).

Physical and sexual abuse have deleterious psychological sequelae on the victim. Compared to nonabused women, victims
of physical aggression have been shown to have significantly
higher scores on a measure of depression (Witt, 1989), as well
as poorer psychological adjustment (Coffey et al., 1996). Compared to college women who had experienced only one incident
of physical violence in a dating relationship, women who were
subjected to on-going incidents of such violence were found to be
at much higher risk of allowing more instances of male-controlling
behavior and less likely to end the relationship (Follingstad, Rutledge, Polek, & McNeill-Hawkins, 1988). In a real sense, on-going
exposure to physical violence and controlling behaviors by a
male work to make the victim more "victimizable."

Date and acquaintance rape leave their victims with a complicated recovery picture. Shapiro and Schwarz (1997), for example,

studied samples of women at the University of Connecticut and found that women who had been date raped had significantly more trauma symptoms (e.g., anxious arousal, dissociation) and lowered sexual self-esteem than those who had not been raped. A very serious complication is the greater self-blame that acquaintance rape victims, as opposed to stranger rape victims, are likely to levy against themselves (Koss, Dinero, & Seibel, 1988). This self-blame has been shown to be associated with postassault depression (Frazier, 1990), as well as symptoms of fear and anxiety and slower recovery time (Katz, 1991). It must also be kept in mind that quite a few women come to college with histories of childhood or adolescent sexual assault experiences. These women tend to be at higher risk for being sexually revictimized by a college date or acquaintance (Gidycz, Coble, Latham, & Layman, 1993; Gidycz et al., 1995; Sanders & Moore, 1999). Hence, college personnel should be particularly sensitive and aware of the needs of these previously victimized women and be prepared to provide outreach and preventive services to them.

An often overlooked cost to the victim is sexual violence's impact on her academic performance. Frintner and Rubinson (1993) found that 37.1% (23 women) of the sample who experienced a sexual assault reported a decrease in grade point average after the incident. Ten other women reduced their course load, and three others suspended their studies for varying lengths of time. Bohmer and Parrot (1993) did not report actual figures; however, they claimed to have heard " . . . story after story of individuals transferring or dropping out of school altogether after an assault" (p. 41). From their anecdotal evidence, Bohmer and Parrot claimed that the likelihood of transferring or dropping out increases if the university fails to take the victim's allegations seriously or when the assailant remains on campus.

The institution, too, pays a price. Reports of stranger or acquaintance rapes hurt any university's marketing and public relations strategies. Bohmer and Parrot (1993) pointed out that universities that fail to consistently enforce behavior code policies or that lack such policies leave themselves exposed to civil liability. Bohmer and Parrot also rightly argue that students' ethical or moral development will not be enhanced if the university itself does not fulfill its moral and ethical responsibilities in cases of sexual violence. I believe strongly that by silencing inquiry, by discounting the seriousness of the problem, by responding inconsistently to sexual violence cases, and by failing to promulgate (or enforce) policies, the university fails in its most basic mission: to provide a nourishing learning environment free from intimidation and bias.

Finally, the perpetrators of sexual assault risk sanctions such as suspension, expulsion, and arrest by local authorities. As Capraro (1994) reminds us, sexual assault is " . . . a behavior linked in men's minds to larger systems of attitudes, values, and modalities of conduct that constitute masculinity" (p. 22). Unfortunately, many men remain unconscious of the link to these "larger systems." Perpetrators fail to label their rape as rape and to empathize with their victims. They also lack self-reflectivity. Perpetrators may be largely unconscious of their motives to control, dominate, and exploit and of the socialization pressures (e.g., attachment difficulties, homophobia, gender role strain) attendant to such motives. By dint of this unconsciousness, perpetrators fail to achieve *perspective*. Sadly, it is the victims, not the perpetrators, who truly understand through their experience what has transpired.

HOW SEXUALLY ASSAULTIVE COLLEGE MALES FIND EXPLOITABLE OPPORTUNITIES

Traditional-age college students are a high-risk group for sexual violence. Both sociocultural and psychological factors have been identified as contributors to the risk. Sex role socialization patterns and society's double messages about sexuality and violence are examples of the former; adolescents' uncertainty about their identities and beliefs in personal invincibility are two psychological factors (Roark, 1987).

I agree with Coleman (1994), Lettelier (1994), and Renzetti (1998) that sexual violence is best understood by taking into account *both* sociocultural and individual psychological factors. College campuses are environments where intimate relationships are often fluid, where expectations governing such relationships are ambiguous, and where sufficient opportunity—even tolerance—exists for sexual abuse. Also on campuses are individuals with certain personality characteristics who may be willing to exploit those opportunities. What I shall discuss in this section are several of the prominent campus-culture "windows of opportunity" that perpetrators of intimate violence successfully exploit. These are: (a) the scripting of college dating, (b) rape-supportive myths within the college culture, (c) the role of alcohol, and (d) institutional laxity.

DATING "RULES"

Schwartz and DeKeseredy (1997) coined the phrase "courtship patriarchy," referring to a system of rules where, " . . . the male under many circumstances is entitled to sex provided by the female" (p. 62). One way in which courtship patriarchy has been shown to be played out is in Holland and Eisenhart's penetrating ethnographic study of young women at two southern colleges. They documented the women's intense efforts and pressure to become attached to the right male. Holland and Eisenhart (1990) described the pressure of being on a "sexual auction block," a position fraught with great risk:

> Hypothetically, an unattractive woman had to settle for the "nerds," men as unattractive as she was. Her other option was to go out with a more attractive man and put up with bad treatment commensurate with the discrepancy in their attractiveness. In either case, being on the sexual auction block was risky for the woman because men often did things—from ignoring them to sexually assaulting them—that in the logic of the cultural system indicated that the women were not particularly attractive and were therefore lower status. (p. 212)

What these researchers made explicit was an implicit dating rule embedded in the campus courtship patriarchy that a young woman could expect maltreatment by a "more attractive" male. It is my contention that such a rule is known by *virtually all* students on campus but represents an opportunity that only *some* males will choose to exploit.

One of the most common tacit rules governing dating behavior, as Schwartz and DeKeseredy (1997) noted, is the males' entitlement to sex as the dating becomes steady. Another way in which courtship patriarchy is played out is through unwritten dating rules pertaining to monetary expenditures and sexual favors. Muehlenhard and Linton (1987), speaking to the exploitable power disparity between men and women, noted that sexual aggression is more likely in situations where the men initiated the dates, paid for them, and provided the transportation. That implicit rules governing such sexual entitlement hold powerful sway was demonstrated by the research of Sandberg, Jackson, and Petretic-Jackson (1987). In their sample of over 400 undergraduates, 48% reported that sexual activity was expected of them if a dating partner paid for dinner or a movie.

Contemporary college students overwhelmingly reject sexual assault or rape as acceptable behaviors, but a surprisingly sizeable minority, both male and female, believe that certain dating situations allow for "justifiable aggression" (Cook, 1995). For example, 36% of Cook's sample of 546 students expected a woman to be assaulted in a situation where she first consented to sex and then reneged or when she was stoned or drunk.

My argument is that assaultive men can "work" these implicit rules and expectations governing ambiguous dating situations and will take advantage of women's situational dependency. Underscoring our argument of the importance of unwritten do's and don't's is the observation by Bohmer and Parrot (1993) that freshmen women are often sexually victimized during their first weeks of college " . . . before they know the social 'rules' " (p. 26).

RAPE-SUPPORTIVE MYTHS

Rape myths have been defined as " . . . attitudes and beliefs that are generally false but are widely and persistently held, and that serve to deny and justify male sexual aggression *against women* (Lonsway & Fitzgerald, 1994, p. 134, italics preserved). There are a host of rape myths (e.g., "only strangers can commit rape," women have an unconscious desire to be raped," "when women dress provocatively, they are asking for sex"), and a high acceptance level of them exist in the general population, varying according to place, time, and cultural group (Lonsway & Fitzgerald, 1994). Those with the highest potential for rape myth acceptance are individuals who are least exposed to rape awareness information, have a victim-blaming mind set, and harbor stereotypical sex role expectations (Hinck & Thomas, 1999). One consistent finding is that males are more accepting of the myths than females (Anderson, Cooper, & Okamura, 1997).

Two important functions of rape myths are to shift the blame for sexual assault onto the victim and to exert control over women (Lonsway & Fitzgerald, 1994). Therein, perpetrators of sexual assault can find an open door to exploitation.

Through their wide acceptance, rape myths represent a type of conventional wisdom. Not only can college males who are inclined to force sex use rape myths to justify their use of violence against women (Osland, Fitch, & Willis, 1996), but through them, the men can convince themselves they are acting normally (Schwartz & DeKeseredy, 1997). Should a sexual assault incident be brought to the attention of a campus security officer or administrator who also holds myths about rape, it may be dismissed, discounted, or half-heartedly pursued. Moreover, since many victims have been socialized to buy into rape myths and other sex-role stereotypes, they may be reluctant to label the assault as rape or feel too ashamed to report it.

We can see that when rape myths are embedded in the assumptions governing students' intimate relationships, perpetrators of sexual assault will find justifications for their behavior and can expect to avoid significant blame, guilt, and consequences.

ALCOHOL

Although it has been estimated that upwards of one half of all sexual assaults involve alcohol consumption by the perpetrator and/or the victim (Abbey, Ross, McDuffie, & McAuslan, 1996; Muehlenhard & Linton, 1987; Williams & Smith, 1994), alcohol is regarded not as the cause but rather as a facilitator of or excuse for the assaults. Our view is that the role of alcohol in college sexual assaults is complex, but that in virtually every instance it

1999). There are even conflicting findings whether fraternity members hold more rape-supportive myths. The questions are actually difficult to answer given problems in sampling procedures (see Koss & Cleveland, 1996), with variability across different campuses, team sports, and fraternity chapters. To me, the more important issue is whether the institution is showing leniency or favoritism to the fraternity members or athletes who are perpetrating assaults against women. Unfortunately, there is a literature replete with examples of fraternity members receiving inconsequential penalties for sexual assaults, eluding sanctions altogether, or having the sanctions overturned (see Martin & Hummer, 1989; Sanday, 1990; Schwartz & DeKeseredy, 1997).

In their study of male athletes in college and professional ranks, Benedict and Klein (1997) found a "dramatic difference" in rape conviction rates favoring the athletes (31%) compared to the rate in a national sample (54%). Benedict and Klein attributed some of this favoritism to what they termed "The Jock Safety Net," which involves access to sharp legal counsel, delaying legal tactics, and characterization of the victims as consenting liars. The stance taken by coaching staffs is critical in influencing the attitudes and behaviors of athletic team members. During their study of judicial affairs offices, Crosset, Ptacek, McDonald, and Benedict (1996) discovered that some significant decreases in sexual assaults occurred following changes in coaching staffs. To these researchers (1996), "This suggests that changes in coaching regimes may have a significant effect on the team's social milieu and thus on athletes' behavior outside of sport" (p. 176). Moreover, without the cooperation of the coaches, efforts to establish and legitimize campus rape prevention programs for male athletes may fail (Parrot, Cummings, Marchell, & Hofher, 1994).

SUMMARY

In the above section I have highlighted where perpetrators of sexual violence can find windows of opportunity within the context of the campus culture. As I argued, these perpetrators not only are aware the loopholes exist but also how to use them effectively. The perpetrators of sexual violence on campus are aided by the fact that the opportunities for exploitation—the keg party, sex-role stereotyping, dating conventions, the "protective" coach—do not, on the surface, appear especially sinister. It should be kept in mind, too, as Hoffman (1992) pointed out, that the majority of men on campus don't rape or harass women. What we also need to understand are the psychological characteristics of those who perpetrate sexual violence. The next section of the chapter addresses that topic.

PERSONALITY CHARACTERISTICS OF SEXUALLY AGGRESSIVE STUDENTS

In summarizing the results of their study on personality characteristics of sexually coercive college men, Rapaport and Burkhart (1984) noted that the general cultural context of college tends to condone sexual behavior, but for this to turn coercive and aggressive requires the potentiating effect of characterologic features of the perpetrator. I agree with this perspective, as well as Renzetti's (1998) that understanding intimate violence requires a multidimensional perspective involving both sociocultural and psychological variables. Thus, in this section I address the issue of the personality characteristics of individuals at highest risk for perpetrating sexual exploitation.

Although an exhaustive review of this literature is beyond the scope of this chapter, one can see that various researchers and clinicians have attempted to construe the behaviors and attitudes exhibited by sexual aggressors (e.g., lying, dependency, lack of empathy, evasion of responsibility, manipulative behavior, use of force) as features associated with various personality disorders. Berkowitz, Burkhart, and Bourg (1994) made the important point that such research has revealed various personality characteristics that may predispose men to sexual violence, but the characteristics themselves are not necessarily indicative of diagnosable psychopathology. Moreover, research is establishing that the personalities of the perpetrators may have been effected deleteriously by inadequate attachment experiences during early childhood. Examples of work in this field will also be presented.

One line of research with college men has focused on connecting sexual aggression (e.g., using verbal threats, alcohol, and force against women) with the hypermasculine, or macho, personality. Not a psychological disorder per se, hypermasculinity, as Lisak and Roth (1990) suggested, amounts to a self-presentation based on rigid beliefs about manliness and male-female relationships that compensates for insecurity about one's masculinity. As one aspect of their study of 15 college men who were self-reported (but never arrested) rapists or attempted rapists, Lisak and Roth assessed the men on the Femininity subscale of the California Psychological Inventory (CPI). They found that, compared to control subjects, the rapists/attempted rapists evidenced lower scores, an indication of their holding more hypermasculine attitudes. Low scorers on this subscale may be viewed as "masculine and opportunistic in interpersonal relations" (p. 272), qualities that Lisak and Roth linked to previous research profiling date rapists. The rapists/attempted rapists were also found to show more hostility toward women, feel more deceived by women, and have stronger dominance motives than the control group.

Kosson, Kelly, and White (1997) linked psychopathy-related traits to sexually aggressive behavior in college males. Kosson et al. cited prior research identifying psychopathy as a two-dimensional construct: one component associated with callous, remorseless exploitation of others (high narcissism), and the other with an unstable, antisocial lifestyle (low socialization). Kosson et al. hypothesized that both components of psychopathy would contribute either independently or interactively in the prediction of various indices of sexual violence. A final sample of 378 college men completed a battery of instruments, including the Socialization (So) scale from the CPI and the Narcissistic Personality Inventory (NPI). About 40% of the sample reported committing at least one type of sexually aggressive behavior—few of which could meet the legal definition of rape—such as using force and threats and exploiting an intoxicated person. Men with both low So and high NPI scores (i.e., those most resembling psychopaths) were found to report a higher absolute frequency of sexual aggression than any other sample subgroup. Moreover, each measure uniquely predicted at least one type of sexual aggression. For example, low So scores were predictive of exploitation of intoxicated persons; high NPI scores predicted abuse of status.

Although Kosson et al. (1990) cautioned that their findings linking psychopathic traits and types of sexual violence are only preliminary, they do support the earlier work of Rapaport and Burkhart (1984). These researchers administered an assessment battery consisting of personality measures and coercive sexuality to almost 200 male undergraduates. Rapaport and Burkhart (1984) found that the personality measures most useful for predicting the amount of sexually coercive behaviors were the Responsibility (Re) and So scales from the CPI. Low scores on these scales "... reflect personal characteristics of immaturity, irresponsibility, and lack of a social conscience and have been traditionally associated with delinquency and antisocial behavior" (p. 220).

Utilizing a large ($n = 2652$) sample, Malamuth et al. (1991) studied characteristics of sexually and nonsexually aggressive college men. They found that the sexually aggressive men evidenced high levels of sexual promiscuity and hostile masculinity, a construct consisting of exaggerated masculinity characteristics and narcissistic tendencies. The nonsexual aggression, characterized by such behaviors as yelling and hitting, was found to be largely a function of hostile masculinity. Malamuth et al. saw parallels between their findings and previous research suggesting that hostile men who perpetrate nonsexual aggression tend to be very dependent on their partners and socially isolated.

Dutton (1998), whose own work has focused on physically abusive men, presented the results of a study performed by one of his graduate students on young college males who had been in intimate heterosexual relationships. The subjects first were assessed with various tests, including the Borderline Personality Organization (BPO) Scale, and then they listened to audiotapes of couples arguing. According to Dutton, BPO is characterized by primitive defenses, identity disturbances, and difficulty with reality-testing. The high-BPO males tended to display a "blaming mindset" toward the woman on the tape as well as more negative attitudes toward women and much self-reported anger. After experiencing these male students, Dutton commented that, "Some of the college men we assessed are the abusive husbands of the future. They have inchoate abusive personalities" (p. 91).

Personality characteristics of the perpetrators of physical abuse are noted to play a role in same-sex relationships. Coleman

(1994), for example, observed that many of the lesbian batterers in her clinical practice display personality structures indicative of borderline, narcissistic, and antisocial personality disorders. Based on their clinical interviews, Marrujo and Kreger (1996) identified a number of psychological characteristics of the primary aggressor in abusive lesbian relationships. These characteristics included pathological jealousy, controlling and manipulative behavior, and sense of entitlement. Although the observations of Coleman and Marrujo and Kreger were not specifically of college women, student affairs workers need to be cognizant that this type of abuse may exist on their campuses and to be prepared to assist the partners of these relationships. It should be kept in mind that the personality features of the batterer should not be indicative of GLBT relationships as abnormal or unhealthy lifestyles (Istar, 1996).

AN ATTACHMENT CONNECTION

Research is establishing the importance of the quality of early childhood attachment experiences as a factor in subsequent behavior toward intimates. Based on the work of Bowlby (1969, 1977), attachment theory holds that it is on early experiences with caregivers that one forms an "internal working model" that guides expectations of the quality and availability of nurturing from subsequent attachment figures. Attachment relationships are of importance across the lifespan. Adults are influenced to think and behave toward their intimate partners in ways that are reflective of experiences with childhood attachment figures (Ainsworth, 1989).

Hazen and Shaver (1987) devised an instrument to assess three styles of adult attachment. Bartholomew and Horowitz (1991) subsequently classified individuals (mostly college students) into a four-category model according to prototypical attachment style: *securely attached* (characterized by valuing and maintaining close intimate relationships); *dismissing* (characterized by independence, restricted emotionality, and downplaying of relationship importance); *preoccupied* (characterized by dependence, overinvolvement, and emotionality in relationships); and *fearful* (characterized by distrust of others, insecurity, and fear of rejection). As might be inferred from the prototype characterizations, the nonsecure attachment styles contain features of dysfunctional personality styles such as dependent, schizoid, and histrionic.

Very preliminary research findings suggest that forging a connection between sexual violence and college students' attachment style is a topic for fruitful study. For example, in a study of 144 dating couples at Texas A & M University, Simpson (1990) found that participants exhibiting a secure attachment style had relationships characterized by interdependence, trust, satisfaction, and commitment. Relationships of those with insecure styles exhibited just the opposite characteristics. Levy, Blatt, and Shaver (1998) found that securely attached and nonsecurely attached undergraduates differ in their descriptions of parents. Fearful participants, for example, described their parents as "relatively punitive and malevolent" (p. 407). Brennan and Shaver (1998), in a large nonclinical sample of college students, found significant associations between attachment styles and personality disorders, with fearful individuals appearing to be the most troubled with regard to personality disorders.

In work with court- and self-referred assaultive men, Dutton, Saunders, Starzomski, and Bartholomew (1994) found that fearful, and to a lesser extent, preoccupied, attachment styles were significantly correlated with measures of anger, borderline personality organization, jealousy, and emotional abusiveness. According to Dutton (1998), the term "fearful" is a misnomer because the hallmark of these men is their behavioral and emotional expression of anger. In their efforts to reduce anxiety about abandonment, fearfully attached men try to control their female partners.

SUMMARY

As revealed through psychological assessments or clinical observations, perpetrators of sexual assault display behaviors and personality features often associated with personality disorders. This research must be interpreted with caution. Scores on personality inventories or a history of sexually aggressive behavior, by themselves, are not sufficient evidence of a personality disorder under common diagnostic classification systems (e.g., DSM-IV; American Psychiatric Association, 1994).

My view is that intimate violence is better understood by taking into account both sociocultural and psychological variables that pertain to the perpetrator. From a sociological perspective, Schwartz and DeKeseredy (1997) explained college men's perpetration of sexual assault as stemming from a male peer support system that facilitated their objectives of domination and conquest of women. We believe that further research into the attachment histories and personality styles of all sexually exploitive college students could provide insights into antecedents of that need to dominate and conquer.

REFERENCES

Abbey, A., McAuslan, P., & Ross, L. T. (1998). Sexual assault perpetration by college men: The role of alcohol, misperception of sexual intent, and sexual beliefs and experiences. *Journal of Social and Clinical Psychology, 17,* 167–195.

Abbey, A., Ross, L. T., McDuffie, D., & McAuslan, P. (1996). Alcohol and dating risk factors for sexual assault among college women. *Psychology of Women Quarterly, 20,* 147–169.

Ainsworth, M. D. S. (1989). Attachment beyond infancy. *American Psychologist, 44,* 709–716.

American Psychiatric Association (1994). *Diagnostic and statistical manual of mental disorders* (4th ed.). Washington, DC: Author.

Anderson, K. B., Cooper, H., & Okamura, L. (1997). Individual differences and attitudes toward rape: A metanalytic review. *Personality and Social Psychology Bulletin, 23,* 295–315.

Bartholomew, K., & Horowitz, L. M. (1991). Attachment styles among young adults: A test of a four-category model. *Journal of Personality and Social Psychology, 61,* 226–244.

Benedict, J., & Klein, A. (1997). Arrest and conviction rates for athletes accused of sexual assault. *Sociology of Sport Journal, 14,* 86–93.

Benson, D., Charlton, C., & Goodhart, F. (1992). Acquaintance rape on campus: A literature review. *Journal of American College Health, 40,* 157–165.

Bergman, L. (1992). Dating violence among high school students. *Social Work, 37,* 21–27.

Berkowitz, A. D., Burkhart, B. R., & Bourg, S. E. (1994). Research on college men and rape. In A. D. Berkowitz (Ed.), *Men and rape: Theory, research, and prevention programs in higher education* (pp. 3–19). New Directions for Student Services, No. 65. San Francisco: Jossey-Bass.

Blumberg, M. L., & Lester, D. (1991). High school and college students' attitudes toward rape. *Adolescence, 26,* 727–729.

Boeringer, S. B. (1999). Associations of rape-supportive attitudes with fraternal and athletic participation. *Violence Against Women, 5,* 81–90.

Bohmer, C., & Parrot, A. (1993). *Sexual assault on campus: The problem and the solution.* New York: Lexington Books.

Bookwala, J., Frieze, I. H., Smith, C., & Ryan, K. (1992). Predictors of dating violence: A multivariate analysis. *Violence & Victims, 7,* 297–311.

Bowlby, J. (1969). *Attachment and loss: Vol. I. Attachment.* New York: Basic Books.

Bowlby, J. (1977). The making and breaking of affectional bonds. *British Journal of Psychiatry, 130,* 201–210.

Bowman, R. L., & Morgan, H. M. (1998). A comparison of rates of verbal and physical abuse on campus by gender and sexual orientation. *College Student Journal, 32,* 43–51.

Brennan, K. A., & Shaver, P. R. (1998). Attachment styles and personality disorders: Their connection to each other and to parental divorce, parental death, and perceptions of parental caregiving. *Journal of Personality, 66,* 835–878.

Burkhart, B. R., & Stanton, A. L. (1986). Sexual aggression in acquaintance relationships. In G. Russell (Ed.), *Violence in intimate relationships* (pp. 43–65). Englewood Cliffs, NJ: Spectrum.

Capraro, R. L. (1994). Disconnected lives: Men, masculinity, and rape prevention. In A. D. Berkowitz (Ed.), *Men and rape: Theory, research, and prevention programs in higher education* (pp. 21–33). New Directions for Student Services, No. 65. San Francisco: Jossey-Bass.

Coffey, P., Leitenberg, H., Henning, K., Bennet, R. T., & Jankowski, M. K. (1996). Dating violence: The association between methods of coping and women's psychological adjustment. *Violence and Victims, 11,* 227–238.

Coleman, V. E. (1994). Lesbian battering: The relationship between personality and the perpetration of violence. *Violence and Victims, 9,* 139–152.

Cook, S. L. (1995). Acceptance and expectation of sexual aggression in college students. *Psychology of Women Quarterly, 19,* 181–194.

Crosset, T. W., Ptacek, J., McDonald, M. A., & Benedict, J. R. (1996). Male student-athletes and violence against women: A survey of campus judicial affairs offices. *Violence Against Women, 2,* 163–179.

Currie, D. H. (1998). Violent men or violent women? Whose definition counts? In R. K. Bergen (Ed.), *Issues in intimate violence* (pp. 97–111). Thousand Oaks, CA: Sage.

Davis, T. C., Peck, G. Q., & Storment, J. M. (1993). Acquaintance rape and the high school student. *Journal of Adolescent Health, 14,* 220–224.

Dutton, D. G. (1998). *The abusive personality.* New York: Guilford.

Dutton, D. G., Saunders, K., Starzomski, A., & Bartholomew, K. (1994). Intimacy-anger and insecure attachment as precursors of abuse in intimate relationships. *Journal of Applied Social Psychology, 24,* 1367–1386.

Elliott, P. (1996). Shattering illusions: Same-sex domestic violence. In C. M. Renzetti & C. H. Miley (Eds.), *Violence in gay and lesbian domestic partnerships* (pp. 1–8). Binghamton, NY: Haworth Press.

Ellis K., & Frieze, I. (1995). Assaultive girlfriends. APA *Monitor,* September, 1995.

Feltey, K. M., Ainslie, J. J., & Geib, A. (1991). Sexual coercion attitudes among high school students: The influence of gender and rape education. *Youth and Society, 23,* 229–250.

Fine, M. (1989). The politics of research and activism: Violence against women. *Gender & Society, 3,* 549–558.

Finley, C., & Corty, E. (1993). Rape on campus: The prevalence of sexual assault while enrolled in college. *Journal of College Student Development, 34,* 113–117.

Follingstad, D. R., Rutledge, L. L., Polek, D. S., & McNeill-Hawkins, K. (1988). Factors associated with patterns of dating violence toward college women. *Journal of Family Violence, 3,* 169–182.

Frazier, P. A. (1990). Victim attributions and post-rape trauma. *Journal of Personality and Social Psychology, 59,* 298–304.

Frintner, M. P., & Rubinson, L. (1993). Acquaintance rape: The influence of alcohol, fraternity membership, and sports team membership. *Journal of Sex Education and Therapy, 19,* 272–284.

Gidycz, C. A., Coble, C. N., Latham, L., & Layman, M. J. (1993). A sexual assault experience in adulthood and prior victimization experiences: A prospective analysis. *Psychology of Women Quarterly, 17,* 151–168.

Gidycz, C. A., Hanson, K., & Layman, M. J. (1995). A prospective analysis of the relationships among sexual assault experiences. *Psychology of Women Quarterly, 19,* 5–29.

Hamberger, L. K. (1994). Domestic partner abuse: Expanding paradigms for understanding and intervention. *Violence and Victims, 9,* 91–94.

Hannan, K. E., & Burkhart, B. (1993). The topography of violence in college men: Frequency and comorbidity of sexual and physical aggression. In L. C. Whitaker & J. W. Pollard (Eds.), *Campus violence:*

Kinds, causes, and cures (pp. 219–237). Binghamton, NY: Haworth Press.

Harrington, N. T., & Leitenberg, H. (1994). Relationship between alcohol consumption and victim behaviors immediately preceding sexual aggression by an acquaintance. *Violence and Victims, 9,* 315–324.

Hazan, C., & Shaver, P. (1987). Conceptualizing romantic love as an attachment process. *Journal of Personality and Social Psychology, 52,* 511–524.

Hinck, S. S., & Thomas, R. W. (1999). Rape myth acceptance in college students: How far have we come? *Sex Roles, 40,* 815–832.

Hoffman, F. L. (1992). Gender paradoxes in college student development. In L. C. Whitaker & R. E. Slimak (Eds.), *College student development* (pp. 193–214). New York: Haworth Press.

Holland, D. C., & Eisenhart, M. A. (1990). *Educated in romance: Women, achievement, and college culture.* Chicago: University of Chicago Press.

Istar, A. (1996). Couple assessment: Identifying and intervening in domestic violence in lesbian relationships. In C. M. Renzetti & C. H. Miley (Eds.), *Violence in gay and lesbian domestic partnerships* (pp. 93–106). New York: The Haworth Press.

Island, D., & Letellier, P. (1991). *Men who beat the men who love them: Battered gay men and domestic violence.* Binghamton, NY: Haworth Press.

Katz, B. L. (1991). The psychological impact of stranger versus nonstranger rape on victims' recovery. In A. Parrot & L. Bechhofer (Eds.), *Acquaintance rape: The hidden crime* (pp. 251–283). New York: Wiley.

Koss, M. P., & Cleveland, H. H. (1996). Athletic participation, fraternity membership, and date rape. *Violence Against Women, 2,* 180–190.

Koss, M. P., Dinero, T. E., & Seibel, C. A. (1988). Stranger and acquaintance rape: Are there differences in the victims' experience? *Psychology of Women Quarterly, 12,* 1–24.

Koss, M. P., Gidycz, C. A., & Wisniewski, N. (1987). The scope of rape: Incidence and prevalence of sexual aggression and victimization in a national sample of higher education students. *Journal of Consulting and Clinical Psychology, 55,* 162–170.

Kosson, D. S., Kelly, J. C., & White, J., W. (1997). Psychopathy-related traits predict self-reported sexual aggression among college men. *Journal of Interpersonal Violence, 12,* 241–254.

Kurz, D. (1998). Old problems and new directions in the study of violence against women. In R. K. Bergen (Ed.), *Issues in intimate violence* (pp. 197–208). Thousand Oaks, CA: Sage.

Letellier, P. (1994). Gay and bisexual male domestic violence victimization: Challenges to feminist theory and responses to violence. *Violence and Victims, 9,* 95–106.

Levy, K. N., Blatt, S. J., & Shaver, P. R. (1998). Attachment styles and parental representations. *Journal of Personality and Social Psychology, 74,* 407–419.

Lisak, D., & Roth, S. (1990). Motives and psychodynamics of self-reported, unincarcerated rapists. *American Journal of Orthopsychiatry, 60,* 268–280.

Lo, W. A., & Sporakowski, M. J. (1989). The continuation of violent dating relationships among college students. *Journal of College Student Development, 30,* 432–439.

Lonsway, K. A. (1996). Preventing acquaintance rape through education: What do we know? *Psychology of Women Quarterly, 20,* 229–265.

Lonsway, K. A., & Fitzgerald, L. F. (1994). Rape myths: In review. *Psychology of Women Quarterly, 18,* 133–164.

Makepeace, J. (1981). Courtship violence among college students. *Family Relations, 30,* 97–102.

Malamuth, N. M., Sockloskie, R. J., Koss, M. P., & Tanaka, J. S. (1991). Characteristics of aggressors against women: Testing a model using a national sample of college students. *Journal of Consulting and Clinical Psychology, 59,* 670–681.

Marrujo, B., & Kreger, M. (1996). Definitions of roles in abusive lesbian relationships. In C. M. Renzetti & C. H. Miley (Eds.), *Violence in gay and lesbian domestic partnerships* (pp. 23–33). New York: The Haworth Press.

Martin, P. Y., & Hummer, R. A. (1989). Fraternities and rape on campus. *Gender & Society, 3,* 457–473.

Matthews, W. J. (1984). Violence in college couples. *College Student Journal, 18,* 150–158.

Miller, B. (1988). Date rape: Time for a new look at prevention. *Journal of College Student Development, 29,* 553–555.

Muehlenhard, C. L., & Linton, M. A. (1987). Date rape and sexual aggression in dating situations: Incidence and risk factors. *Journal of Counseling Psychology, 34,* 186–196.

Norris, J., & Cubbins, L. A. (1992). Effects of victim's and assailant's alcohol consumption on judgments of their behavior and traits. *Psychology of Women Quarterly, 16,* 179–191.

Osland, J. A., Fitch, M., & Willis, E. E. (1996). Likelihood to rape in college males. *Sex Roles: A Journal of Research, 35,* 171–183.

Palmer, C. J. (1996). Violence and other forms of victimization in residence halls: Perspectives of resident assistants. *Journal of College Student Development, 37,* 268–278.

Parrot, A., Cummings, N., Marchell, T. C., & Hofher, J. (1994). A rape awareness and prevention model for male athletes. *Journal of American College Health, 42,* 179–184.

Pollard, J. W., & Whitaker, L. C. (1993). Cures for campus violence, if we want them. *Journal of College Student Psychotherapy, 8*, 285–295.

Rapaport, K., & Burkhart, R. B. (1984). Personality and attitudinal characteristics of sexually coercive college males. *Journal of Abnormal Psychology, 93*, 216–221.

Renzetti, C. M. (1998). Violence and abuse in lesbian relationships: Theoretical and empirical issues. In R. K. Bergen (Ed.), *Issues in intimate violence* (pp. 117–127). Thousand Oaks, CA: Sage.

Rickgarn, R. L. V. (1989). Violence in residence halls: Campus domestic violence. In J. M. Sherrill & D. G. Siegel (Eds.), *Responding to violence on campus* (pp. 29–40). New Directions for Student Services, No. 47. San Francisco: Jossey-Bass.

Roark, M. L. (1987). Preventing violence on college campuses. *Journal of Counseling and Development, 65*, 367–371.

Sanday, P. R. (1990). *Fraternity gang rape.* New York: New York University Press.

Sanday, P. R. (1996). Rape-prone versus rape-free campus climates. *Violence Against Women, 2*, 191–208.

Sandberg, G., Jackson, T. L., & Petretic-Jackson, P. (1987). College students' attitudes regarding sexual coercion and aggression: Developing educational and preventive strategies. *Journal of College Student Personnel, 28*, 302–311.

Sanders, B., & Moore, D. L. (1999). Childhood maltreatment and date rape. *Journal of Interpersonal Violence, 14*, 115–124.

Schwartz, M. D., & DeKeseredy, W. S. (1997). *Sexual assault on the college campus: The role of male peer support.* Thousand Oaks, CA: Sage.

Schwartz, M. D., & Leggett, M. S. (1999). Bad dates or emotional trauma? *Violence Against Women, 5*, 251–271.

Shapiro, B. L., & Schwarz, J. C. (1997). Date rape: Its relationship to trauma symptoms and sexual self-esteem. *Journal of Interpersonal Violence, 12*, 407–413.

Simpson, J. A. (1990). Influence of attachment styles on romantic relationships. *Journal of Personality and Social Psychology, 59*, 971–980.

Smith, J. P., & Williams, J. G. (1992). From abusive household to dating violence. *Journal of Family Violence, 7*, 153–165.

Sorensen, S. B., & Brown, V. B. (1990). Interpersonal violence and crisis intervention on the college campus. In H. L. Pruett & V. B. Brown (Eds.), *Crisis intervention and prevention* (pp. 57–66). New Directions for Student Services, No. 49. San Francisco: Jossey-Bass.

Stacy, C. L., Schandel, L. M., Flannery, W. S., Conlon, M., & Milardo, R. M. (1994). It's not all moonlight and roses: Dating violence at the University of Maine, 1982–1992. *College Student Journal, 28*, 2–9.

Stahly, G. B., & Lie, G-W. (1995). Women and violence: A comparison of lesbian and heterosexual battering relationships. In J. C. Chrisler & A. H. Hemstreet (Eds.), *Variations on a theme: Diversity and the psychology of women* (pp. 51–78). Albany, NY: State University of New York Press.

Stith, S. M., Jester, S. B., & Bird, G. W. (1992). A typology of college students who use violence in their dating relationships. *Journal of College Student Development, 33,* 411–421.

Sugarman, D. B., & Hotaling, G. T. (1989). Dating violence: Prevalence, context, and risk markers. In M. A. Pirog-Good & J. E. Stets (Eds.), *Violence in dating relationships: Emerging social issues* (pp. 3–32). New York: Praeger.

Sugarman, D. B., & Hotaling, G. T. (1991). Dating violence: A review of contextual and risk factors. In B. Levy (Ed.), *Dating violence: Young women in danger* (pp. 100–118). Seattle: Seal Press.

Ward, S. K., Chapman, K., Cohn, E., White, S., & Williams, K. (1991). Acquaintance rape and the college coed scene. *Family Relations, 40,* 65–71.

Williams, J. G., & Smith, J. P. (1994). Drinking patterns and dating violence among college students. *Psychology of Addictive Behaviors, 8,* 51–53.

Witt, V. (1989). Premarital abuse: What is the effect on the victim? *Journal of College Student Development, 30,* 339–344.

CHAPTER 2

Alcohol and Sexual Violence Among College Students

Tim Marchell and Nina Cummings

Heavy alcohol consumption has long been part of the campus culture of many American colleges and universities. A Cornell fight song penned around 1905 provides a glimpse into the role of alcohol on campus at that time:

> "Tell them just how I busted
> lapping up those high, highballs.
> We'll all have drinks at Theodore Zincks
> when I get back next fall."
> ("Give my Regards to Davy")

Although college drinking, historically, has been viewed by many as a relatively innocent rite of passage, there is evidence that it is a rite that too often results in negative consequences for drinkers such as poor academic performance, public misconduct, and health problems. Furthermore, it is recognized that heavy drinking also contributes to a host of "second-hand" problems, those that affect persons other than the drinker. In particular, alcohol is often a factor in various forms of interpersonal violence. This chapter examines the role of alcohol in sexual violence committed by college men against college women and explores strategies for reducing the prevalence of such alcohol-related aggression. Recent research suggests the need to examine sexual coercion by women against men, including the use of alcohol and drugs as a coercive tactic (Larimer, Lydum, Anderson, & Turner, 1999). Because of the prevalence of men's sexual aggression against women—and its associated consequences—the present discussion focuses on this form of violence.

ALCOHOL, OTHER DRUGS, AND SEXUAL ACTIVITY ON CAMPUS: PREVALENCE AND PATTERNS

In 1997, the alcohol-poisoning deaths of Scott Krueger, a first-year student at the Massachusetts Institute of Technology, and Benjamin Wyne, a first-year student at Louisiana State University, focused the national media spotlight on what is often called "binge" or high-risk drinking on college campuses. In both cases, the young men died after consuming large quantities of alcohol as part of fraternity hazings. In conjunction with these tragedies, data from national surveys that documented the level of drinking on campuses received considerable media attention. Frequent news reports between 1997 and 1999 indicated that alcohol-related deaths and overall drinking levels among college students were on the rise. The number of alcohol-related deaths occurring annually among college students, however, is unknown because there is presently no central database for tracking these incidents. Furthermore, data from the University of Michigan's Monitoring the Future Study (MTFS) suggest that from 1980 to 1997 the rate of alcohol consumption by American college students remained relatively constant, with slight decreases on some measures (Johnston, O'Malley, & Bachman, 1998).

Levels of alcohol consumption vary considerably among college students, an important point to consider when developing strategies for reducing alcohol-related sexual violence. According to the 1997 Core Alcohol and Drug Survey (Presley, Leichliter, & Meilman, 1998), 16% of students are nonusers of alcohol. Eighteen percent are considered infrequent users, drinking between one and six times a year. A total of 43% are categorized as moderate users (drinking between once/month and once/week), and 24%

are classified as frequent users (drinking between three times per week and every day). Consistent with the MTFS findings, the Core Institute data from 1995 to 1997 show that approximately 4 in 10 students engage in high-risk drinking (drinking 5 or more drinks in a sitting at least once within a 2-week period). Half of those did so three or more times within a 2-week period. In addition to the use of alcohol, the 1997 Core survey found that 34% of students reported using marijuana, and 14% reported that they had used an illegal drug other than marijuana at least once in the past year (Presley, Leichliter, & Meilman, 1998). The most commonly used of those drugs were hallucinogens (10%) and amphetamines (9%) (J. Leichliter, personal communication, January 22, 1999).

Certain groups are more prone to heavy drinking than others. Males drink significantly more than females (Johnston, O'Malley, & Bachman, 1998). White (non-Hispanic) students drink more than their non-White peers (Wechsler, Dowdall, Davenport, & DeJong, 1995), with Asian-American and African American students having the lowest rates of drinking among the primary racial/ethnic groups on campuses (Presley, Meilman, & Cashin, 1996). Members of fraternities and sororities engage in high-risk drinking at higher rates than nonmembers, and members who live in their chapter house also drink more than members who live elsewhere (Enos & Pittayathikhun, 1996). Athletes also engage in higher levels of high-risk drinking compared to nonathletes (Wechsler, Austin, & DeJong, 1995), and the highest level of drinking on campus is found among athletes affiliated with fraternities (Meilman, Leichliter & Presley, 1999).

Several studies connect alcohol use and sexual activity on college campuses. The 1995 National College Health Risk Behavior Survey reported that 86% of college students had sexual intercourse and more than one-third had had six or more partners during their lifetime (Centers for Disease Control, 1997). According to the Core Institute, 66.7% of college students report having had sexual intercourse in the past year (Presley, Meilman, & Leichliter, 1999). One study found that 35% of students have engaged in some form of sexual activity because of alcohol, and 18% reported having had sexual intercourse due to drinking (Meilman, 1993). In another study, 22% of college men and 13% of college women reported that their last sexual encounter occurred under the influence of alcohol or other drugs (Centers for Disease Control, 1997). The social environment of many students includes language about sex and alcohol that illustrates the role that alcohol sometimes plays in fostering brief sexual encounters. For example, "beer goggles" make potential partners look more attractive and increase the likelihood of "hooking up."

Data on Alcohol and Sexual Violence

Evidence linking alcohol and sexual violence is found in studies of alcohol use and in the sexual aggression literature. These studies examine the use of alcohol by men who report engaging in sexual aggression as well as use by women who report having been victimized. Alcohol plays a dual role in men's expression of sexual violence. When self-administered, it may be believed to heighten sexuality; or it may be provided to women as a coercive tactic. Although there is growing concern about the risk of sexual assaults in which a man incapacitates a woman with a psychoactive substance such as Rohypnol or gamma hydroxybutyrate (GHB), alcohol can be considered the most widely used "date rape drug."

In a national study, Koss (1988) found that 15% of college women reported experiencing completed nonconsensual sexual intercourse and 12% reported experiencing attempted nonconsensual sexual intercourse since the age of 14. Of these women, at least 55% indicated that they have been drinking (and/or using other drugs) prior to the assault. Muehlenhard and Linton (1987) found that 21% of women who experienced sexual aggression on a date reported being intoxicated, and 32% reported having been "mildly buzzed" when the incident occurred. Thus a total 53% of the women were under the influence of alcohol at the time they were victimized.

In Koss's (1988) national sample, 8% of the men indicated that since age 14 they had attempted or completed nonconsensual sexual intercourse through the use of force, threat of force, or provision of alcohol or other drugs to a woman. Seventy-four percent of these men indicated that they had consumed alcohol or other drugs prior to the assault. Muehlenhard and Linton

(1987) found that of men who acknowledged engaging in sexual aggression on a date, 26% indicated that they had been intoxicated, and 29% had been "mildly buzzed" at the time of the incident. Thus, a total of 55% were under the influence of alcohol when they committed the aggression. The 1997 Core survey found that 5% of college men acknowledged that they had taken "advantage of someone sexually" during the past year while under the influence of alcohol or other drugs. Reports by women provide further information about the frequency of sexual aggression by men who are under the influence of alcohol. The 1993 College Alcohol Study found that since the beginning of that academic year 26% of women had experienced unwanted sexual activity by a student who had been drinking (Wechsler et al., 1996). In the same study, 2% of women indicated that in the past year they had been victims of a sexual assault or date rape committed by someone who had been drinking.

Data suggest that provision of alcohol or other drugs to a woman is a frequent coercive tactic used by men. Koss (1988) found that since age 14, 5% of men had attempted nonconsensual intercourse by giving a woman alcohol or other drugs, and 4% indicated having had nonconsensual intercourse using this tactic. In a study of 129 male college athletes, 16% of respondents indicated at least once in their lifetime they had sexual intercourse with a woman against her wishes by giving her more alcohol or other drugs than she could handle (Marchell, 1998).

A limitation of self-reports of sexual aggression that involve alcohol is that they may reflect underreporting due to a combination of reasons. For example, the perpetrators may not perceive the sexual activity as aggressive, their memories may be clouded by alcohol use, they may believe they were entitled to the sexual activity, or they may be unaware of their partner's inability to consent.

THE ROLE OF ALCOHOL IN A MODEL OF SEXUAL AGGRESSION

During the past 20 years, considerable research has attempted to identify the primary factors that contribute to sexual aggression. Unfortunately, attempts to develop adequate etiological models have proven difficult: sexual offenders are markedly heterogeneous, with the exception that the vast majority is male. The emerging consensus is that sexual aggression is determined by a multiplicity of variables that interact in complex ways (Prentky & Knight, 1991).

One cluster of variables concentrates on perpetrator characteristics such as personality, physiology, socialization, beliefs, and attitudes (Hall & Hirschman, 1991; Malamuth, Sockloskie, Koss, & Tanaka, 1991). Based on review of the experimental literature, Seto and Barbaree (1995) present a model describing the disinhibitory effects of alcohol on perpetrators. Other research (Harney & Muehlenhard, 1993) examines similar variables in women that may increase their risk of victimization. Still other studies focused on the situational variables and misrepresentation of intent associated with sexual aggression (Abbey, 1991; Richardson & Hammock, 1991). Berkowitz (1992) proposed an integrated model of variables related to perpetrators, victims, and social contexts.

In a national sample of college students, Malamuth et al. (1991) concluded that sexual aggression is most strongly associated with the interaction of two variables among men—hostile masculinity and frequency of sexual intercourse. Those men who have high levels of hostile masculinity are more likely to engage in sexual aggression if they have frequent opportunities to do so. To the extent that alcohol increases the likelihood of sexual encounters, it therefore may also increase the likelihood of sexual assaults.

In addition to hostile masculinity, other cognitive patterns have been associated with sexual aggression by men. These include rape-supportive attitudes such as adversarial sexual beliefs, acceptance of interpersonal violence (Burt, 1980), and assumptions about women who consume alcohol (Abbey, 1991). Some view women who drink as "fair game" for coercive sexual advances (Abbey, 1991; Parks & Miller, 1997; Testa & Parks, 1996). Furthermore, men often mistakenly believe that a woman who is extremely intoxicated can consent to sex, whereas some state laws stipulate that severe intoxication, under certain circumstances, precludes an ability to give consent.

Men's expectancies about the effects of alcohol may increase the likelihood of sexual violence (Abbey, 1991). Men often expect to feel more powerful, sexual, and aggressive after consuming alcohol (Brown, Goldman, Inn, & Anderson, 1980), and these expectations can lead to greater physiological and psychological sexual arousal. When men believe they have been drinking alcohol, they may be more sexually aroused and more responsive to rape scenarios (Wilson & Lawson, 1976; Wilson & Niaura, 1984). The provocative sexual images (e.g., women in bikinis dancing around men) in alcohol advertisements that target men contribute to the positive expectancies that men have about alcohol's presumed sexuality-enhancing effect. The Core survey (1997) found that 49% of college men and women believe that alcohol facilitates sexual encounters.

As a central nervous system depressant, alcohol in even moderate amounts can impair cortical functions such as reasoning and impulse control. Such disinhibition may increase the expression of otherwise restrained sexually aggressive impulses. In addition, college men who are classified as alcohol dependent or alcoholic may experience significant personality changes during periods of intoxication, including episodes of sexual violence. Approximately 15% of college males indicate that during the past year they have thought that they might have a problem with alcohol or other drugs (Presley et al., 1999), although it is not known what proportion of those are alcoholic. One estimate suggests that approximately 16% of 18- to 20-year-old males (and 6% of 18- to 20-year-old females) may have alcoholism (Williams, Stinson, Parker, Harford, & Noble, 1987).

As alcohol interferes with thought processes, it may increase a man's misperceptions of a woman's sexual intent. Studies suggest that men, even when not affected by alcohol, are more likely than women to misinterpret verbal and nonverbal cues as indicating a desire for sex (Abbey, McAuslan, & Ross, 1998). This difference may reflect both social conditioning and physiological differences. For example, young men are often taught to interpret resistance by women as a tacit indication of willingness to have sex. In addition, recent neuro-imaging research suggests that the brains of adolescent males often do not activate in ways that enable them to identify correctly the emotion represented in the facial expression of another person (Hotz, 1998). Thus a young man may see a woman's expression of fear and believe it means something else. If he is consuming alcohol, the likelihood may increase that he will misinterpret a woman's intentions and desires and attempt sexual contact despite a lack of consent by the woman.

In addition to interfering with a man's ability to perceive a woman's sexual intent accurately, alcohol may also lead to a general decrease in concern for consequences for self or others. Even if a man accurately perceives that a woman is not giving consent, under the influence of alcohol he may be less likely to care about her objections. He also may be more likely to deny that his behavior is coercive or violent or to rationalize that what he is doing is not harmful to the woman. Such an interaction of alcohol and defense mechanisms may play a role in cases in which a man who is intoxicated assaults a woman and then later asks her for a second date.

Sexually violent men may use their own alcohol consumption as a justification for their behavior (Scully & Marolla, 1984). In addition, some research suggests that a man who rapes may be viewed by others as bearing less responsibility if he was intoxicated at the time of the assault (Richardson & Campbell, 1982). Sexually aggressive men who believe that alcohol minimizes their legal responsibility may premeditate their assaults and intentionally become intoxicated to minimize their sense of culpability. Other men may not plan to engage in sexual aggression, but do so impulsively and subsequently rationalize that they were not responsible for their behavior because they were drunk. Men in educational workshops are often surprised to learn that their state law does not reduce a perpetrator's culpability for an assault if he was intoxicated at the time.

The role of alcohol in sexual aggression among men who engage in both sexual and physical (nonsexual) aggression compared to those who commit sexual aggression only is not clear. Erway and Burkhart (1993) found that among 261 college males, 17% engaged in sexual and physical aggression, 25% engaged in sexual aggression only, 11% engaged in physical aggression only, and 47% did not engage in aggression. A major finding of this study was that men who were sexually and physically aggressive formed a socially and clinically distinct group (Erway, 1990). In contrast to men who were sexually aggressive only, physically aggressive only, or nonaggressive, these men who more strongly endorsed

violent attitudes demonstrated attraction to controlling, domi-
nant, and aggressive sexual behaviors and reported more acts
of aggression against women. Men in this group may be more
likely to use actual force during an assault. In comparison, men
who are sexually aggressive only may be more likely to use less
overtly violent tactics to achieve sexual intercourse. The extent
to which alcohol is used as a coercive tactic by these subgroups
of sexually aggressive men is an issue for further research.

ALCOHOL AND GROUP DYNAMICS

In addition to the effect of alcohol on a lone perpetrator, alcohol
also contributes to the likelihood of group violence against
women. The risk of a group sexual assault ("gang rape") may
increase when men are intoxicated partly because they are less
able to exercise reasoning skills that are required to challenge
potentially dangerous group dynamics. Processes such as the
"outgroup homogeneity effect" (O'Sullivan, 1991) and "group-
think" (Janis, 1982; O'Sullivan, 1991) that may increase the likelihood of group sexual assault may be more likely to occur when
men are intoxicated. Groups of men may also conspire to give
alcohol to a woman to minimize her resistance to their sexual
advances. For example, some groups will hold parties at which
they serve women punch spiked with tasteless grain alcohol as
a means of rapidly intoxicating them.

Data suggest that perpetrators of group sexual assaults are
often members of fraternities or athlete teams (O'Sullivan, 1991),
the two demographic groups with the highest levels of alcohol
consumption among college males (Meilman et al., 1999). In one
study, 3% of male athletes at a midsize state university acknowledged having had group sex with a woman against her wishes
(Marchell, 1998). Twenty-nine percent, however, reported that
they had group sex with a woman who willingly participated.
However, it is unknown to what extent these men accurately
perceived the woman's participation as "willing." A woman who
engages in group sex against her wishes may exhibit no resistance
or may appear to consent because of intimidation or dissociation.
This phenomenon may also occur when a lone perpetrator as-

saults a woman, but the circumstances of a group sexual assault may increase the likelihood of distorted perceptions on the part of the offenders. For example, in group sexual assaults some perpetrators may enter the situation after the victim, as a means of survival, has ceased resisting. Hence, a man arriving after the onset of the assault may be more likely to perceive the victim as a willing participant, particularly if his perceptions are distorted by alcohol. Such dynamics are compounded by the beliefs of some men that having sex with one man indicates a woman's willingness to have sex with others.

COMMENTARY ON ALCOHOL AND RESPONSIBILITY FOR SEXUAL VIOLENCE

It is important to underscore that alcohol use by men neither causes nor excuses sexually aggressive behavior. Although alcohol may contribute to the likelihood that a man will engage in sexual violence, it is not a prerequisite for aggression against women. Many men become intoxicated and never assault women, while many other men assault women when not using alcohol or other drugs. As noted above, Malamuth et al. (1991) suggest that a common denominator in sexual violence is hostility toward women. Alcohol, therefore, may function as a catalyst of men's violence against women, but its role should be considered secondary to the attitudes and cultural practices that foster and tolerate such behavior. If alcohol (and other drugs) were eliminated from society, men would continue to assault women, albeit likely in decreased numbers.

WOMEN'S ALCOHOL USE AND THE RISK OF SEXUAL ASSAULT

Someone who is sexually assaulted is never responsible for the abuse, even if intoxicated at the time. The legal and moral responsibility for sexual assault lies with the perpetrator of the act. Consuming alcohol, however, increases the risk of being sexually assaulted and having experiences that, while not rising to the level of criminal offense, are nonetheless sexually traumatic. In general, intoxication increases the likelihood of unplanned and unwanted sexual encounters, thereby increasing the risk of sexually transmitted diseases and unwanted pregnancies as well as sexual aggression.

Physiological differences between sexes may contribute to the risk of sexual assault for women. When drinking equivalent amounts of alcohol, women generally will become more affected than men for a combination of reasons. Women tend to have a higher percentage of body fat than men and therefore have less water in their bodies to dilute the alcohol consumed. Compared to men, women also have lower levels of alcohol dehydrogenase, an enzyme that helps metabolize alcohol. In addition, because women on average are smaller than men, the same amount of alcohol produces higher concentrations in women's bodies. Therefore, women who drink "head to head" with men will likely become substantially more impaired. Drinking games (e.g., "Beer pong," "Kings," and "Quarters") in which players often consume several drinks within a short period can lead to much more rapid intoxication in women than men.

Even at relatively low blood alcohol content levels, women in a social setting may be less likely to exercise caution and normal risk-reduction behaviors. As they become increasingly impaired, women's ability to perceive cues that may otherwise alert them to a risk in their environment decreases. Intoxication also interferes with women's ability to communicate assertively and to employ physical defenses.

Women who are sexually assaulted while intoxicated are often blamed for contributing to the assault. Indeed, they may blame themselves. Moreover, if they are severely intoxicated at the time of the assault, they may have little or no memory of the event. If a woman reports the assault to authorities, the credibility of her claim may be questioned if she was drinking prior to the incident. Furthermore, an underage drinker may be reluctant to report an assault out of fear of legal consequences for her drinking behavior. These factors often prevent women from seeking the help they need, thereby exacerbating the impact of the assault.

REDUCING THE INCIDENCE OF ALCOHOL-RELATED SEXUAL VIOLENCE

Prevention philosophies in both the sexual assault and alcohol and other drug (AOD) fields have evolved considerably in recent years. Early approaches to reducing sexual assault employed crime prevention strategies such as improved lighting, escort services, security phones, and self-defense techniques. These strategies reflected the widespread but erroneous views that women are more likely to be assaulted by strangers than acquaintances. More recently, efforts have focused on educating women about how to reduce the risk of being victimized, particularly by someone they know.

Traditional efforts to reduce alcohol-related sexual violence have fallen into two categories. The first is sexual assault education programs for men and women that focus on the role of alcohol in the social dynamics leading to assault. Secondly, AOD prevention strategies address sexual assault as one of the negative consequences related to substance use. In both the sexual assault and substance abuse prevention fields, a common strategy has been to educate men and women about the impact of alcohol on communication in sexual situations.

The effectiveness of traditional educational efforts to reduce alcohol-related sexual assault is unclear because few strategies have been empirically evaluated for their effect on behavior of either women or men. Hanson and Gidycz (1993) found that after participating in a sexual assault education program that highlighted the role of alcohol in acquaintance rape, women who had no history of sexual violence reported changes in dating behavior and a lower incidence of sexual assault compared to control participants. The study did not find a decreased incidence of sexual assault among women with a history of sexual victimization. Another study evaluating the effect of an educational presentation that included information on the role of alcohol in sexual assault found significant changes in attitudes among participants compared to controls (Schwartz & DeKeseredy, 1997). The changes were greater in magnitude among women than men, and the changes for men disappeared after 1 month.

Two primary factors have contributed to a shift that increasingly focuses sexual assault prevention strategies on men. First has been the growing recognition that men are fundamentally responsible for the sexual violence they perpetrate and that significant reductions in sexual assault will not occur until men change their behavior. Second, research suggests that because there are few female-related variables that can predict sexual assault, there is likely an upper limit on the number of risk-reduction strategies that women can employ (Hanson & Gidycz, 1993). Consequently, education programs targeting men have emerged during recent years (e.g., Berkowitz, 1994; Katz, 1995; Parrot, Cummings, & Marchell, 1994). These programs have employed a variety of strategies, including education about the role of alcohol in sexual assault. For example, some programs explore the impact of intoxication on sexual dynamics and the legal responsibility for behavior engaged in while under the influence of alcohol. Little research, however, exists to guide program development efforts with men (Burkhart, Bourg, & Berkowitz, 1994). Moreover, because sexual violence is largely a consequence of institutional systems, societal attitudes, and behaviors that define masculinity (Capraro, 1994), significant cultural changes are required before prevention strategies will have a widespread effect.

ALCOHOL AND OTHER DRUG PREVENTION

Historically, AOD prevention has focused on increasing individuals' knowledge about the risks of heavy drinking to themselves, including sexual assault. Messages such as "Know when to say 'when' " (often supported by the alcohol industry) place responsibility for drinking and any negative consequences that may arise from it on the individual drinker. Despite decades of warning college students about the hazards that may result from alcohol, the "individual" approach has had little impact on levels of drinking and associated consequences.

In contrast to the individual model, a promising new model for AOD prevention has emerged in recent years. The new paradigm in AOD prevention posits that drinking levels and related problems among students can be decreased through a long-term, comprehensive effort aimed at changing the environment in which students make choices about drinking (DeJong et al., 1998). The environmental model provides a framework for organizing existing practices that influence behavior and for identifying which dimensions of the environment offer opportunities for further intervention. In this context, educational interventions are seen as necessary but not sufficient to bring about fundamental change in the campus drinking culture.

Examples of environmental factors that affect student drinking include:

- perceived social norms (social environment)
- availability and price of alcohol (economic environment)
- enforcement of alcohol policies and laws (judicial/legal environment)
- availability of alcohol-free social options (recreational environment)
- course schedules and requirements (educational environment)

The environmental model is shaped by public health theory and therefore seeks to improve the physical, social, cultural, and institutional forces that influence health, while acknowledging that "health-related behavior is affected through multiple levels of influence: intrapersonal factors, interpersonal processes, institutional factors, community factors and public policy" (DeJong et al., 1998, p. 9). To the extent that alcohol increases the likelihood of sexual violence, environmental prevention efforts that reduce high-risk drinking may also help to reduce the incidence of sexual violence.

PRACTICAL STRATEGIES FOR AN INTEGRATED MODEL OF AOD-RELATED SEXUAL ASSAULT PREVENTION

Although environmental management is a guiding principle in current AOD prevention, a comprehensive approach includes education and intervention practices as well. Cornell University's AOD prevention strategy includes a student assistance program

(SAP) that seeks to identify and intervene with students who engage in high-risk drinking or other drug use. The SAP includes a network of staff (e.g., residence life staff, chaplains, minority affairs staff, academic counselors, financial aid counselors, judicial administrators, athletics department staff, fraternity/sorority advisors) and faculty who are trained to reach out to students who are unlikely to self-refer to the health care system on campus. This training includes an introduction to the BASICS (Brief Alcohol Screening and Intervention for College Students) model developed by the University of Washington's Addictive Behaviors Research Center (Dimeff, Baer, Kivlahan, & Marlatt, 1999). This harm-reduction strategy has been shown to be effective in reducing consumption among students with histories of high-risk drinking (Dimeff et al., 1999). In addition, the model facilitates referral of students with severe alcohol problems to abstinence-based programs.

Educational methods that target the link between alcohol and sexual violence are an important part of a comprehensive AOD prevention effort as well as sexual assault programming. At Cornell and other schools, sexual assault educators have developed interactive theater presentations that dramatize the dynamics of sexual violence, including the role that alcohol plays. For example, Cornell has offered the program "How to Get What You Want and Not More Than You Bargained For" to new students during orientation since 1986. Originally written by the Cornell Advocates for Rape Education, a collaborative group of faculty, staff and students, the program demonstrates the interplay between alcohol consumption and rape and allows the audience to question the behaviors, gender expectations, and alcohol use depicted in the scene. As performers enact a dating scene that ends with a rape, audience members become caught up in the familiar dynamics of attraction, dating, and sexual expectations. After the rape scene, the actors remain in role to answer questions from audience members about what happened and why. The program addresses peer influence in two ways: (a) during the performance, the audience observes the effects of peer pressure on the characters and how it impacts their drinking at a party, and (b) the interactive nature of the program encourages students in the audience to challenge each other when rape supportive or victim-blaming comments are made.

Increasingly, AOD educators are also addressing sexual assault issues in the context of alcohol programming. The Higher Education Center on Alcohol and Other Drug Prevention offers a free publication entitled *Preventing Alcohol-Related Problems on Campus: Acquaintance Rape* (Finn, 1997) that describes guidelines for reducing alcohol-related sexual assault. Another resource available at little cost to colleges and universities is the interactive computer program *Alcohol 101*. Developed by the University of Illinois with funding from the alcohol industry-supported Century Council, the program can be either used by individuals at a computer or projected for use in a group presentation. The program includes two segments on alcohol and sexual assault.

One of the most promising initiatives in AOD prevention is known as the "social norms" approach. This strategy is based on the phenomenon known as "pluralistic ignorance" in which individuals incorrectly perceive that the attitudes or behaviors of their peers are different from their own (Miller & McFarland, 1987). In the case of alcohol consumption, for example, many students overestimate the amount that their peers drink (Perkins, Meilman, Leichliter, Cashin, & Presley, 1999). This overestimation creates "imaginary peers" to which students tend to conform their behavior (Perkins & Berkowitz, 1986).

Social norms interventions are designed to correct students' misperceptions by providing them with accurate information on campus drinking norms as measured by self-report surveys. The social marketing techniques used to communicate social norms messages have been pioneered at Northern Illinois University, the University of Arizona, Western Washington University, Hobart College, and William Smith College. At each of these institutions, significant reductions in high-risk drinking have been associated with sustained social norms efforts. In 1999, Cornell University began implementation of an ongoing media campaign that informs the community that most students drink in moderation or not at all: "Most Cornell students (62%) have zero to three drinks when they party." This message is communicated through newspaper advertisements, posters, and table tents in dining halls and is projected in classrooms while students are arriving for class. Over 4000 mini-Frisbees with "Zero-3" printed on them were distributed to each student arriving in the university residence halls at the beginning of the year. At Hobart and William Smith Colleges, faculty members Wesley Perkins and David Craig have developed strategies for conducting a social norms campaign electronically. Via screen savers and a program called "Campus Factoids," students receive positive normative messages about alcohol embedded within other campus facts of interest to the student population.

Although social norms marketing seeks to correct individual's misperceptions about alcohol use, this approach can be considered an environmental strategy in that perceptions are social phenomena as well as individual attributes. The collective perceptions of students constitute part of the social environment at a college or university. Moreover, the social norms approach employs media and interpersonal methodologies that themselves become part of the social milieu on campus.

Social norms strategies may be applicable to other behaviors for which there is a misperception of norms. For example, students often overestimate how often their peers have sexual intercourse (Berkowitz, 1999). Similarly, students in workshops at Cornell frequently overestimate the proportion of students at the university that drank alcohol the last time they had sex. This observation suggests that if such a misperception were corrected, the percentage of students who engage in sex under the influence of alcohol may decrease. If such a decrease were achieved, it might contribute to a decrease in sexual assaults and other sexually related trauma.

In addition to overestimating the level of high-risk behavior, students may also underestimate the level of healthy, protective behaviors employed by their peers. At the University of Arizona, a social norms campaign aims to reduce the level of alcohol students consume in sexual situations. The campaign message also seeks to correct the misperception of the level of sexual activity among students: "Half of U of A students are sexually active. When asked about their best sexual experience, most of them report drinking one or less per hour or not drinking alcohol at all" (Johannessen, 1999).

Berkowitz (1999) has proposed possible applications of social norms theory to a range of health-related problems and issues of social justice, including sexual assault prevention with men. To the extent that misperceptions of peer norms may be a factor in the etiology of sexual assault, correcting them may contribute to a reduction in sexual violence. Studies suggest that college men tend to underestimate the extent to which other men are uncomfortable with language or behavior that objectifies or demeans women (Berkowitz, 1994: Kilmartin, Conway, Friedberg, McQuoid, & Tschan, 1999). In addition, Schewe (1999) found that while most college men would not enjoy forcing a woman to be sexually intimate, they believed that the majority of their peers would enjoy doing so. Such misperceptions may keep men from challenging attitudes and behaviors that they find objectionable. To the extent that such misperceptions can be corrected, men may be more likely to express their intolerance of sexist attitudes and coercive behaviors. In the absence of overt peer disapproval, sexually aggressive men may be more likely to commit sexual assaults.

Methods for correcting misperceptions related to sexual assault may include media and interpersonal strategies. For example, antiviolence consultant Jackson Katz has developed group programs that complement the social norms approach by challenging men to move from being bystanders to interveners in violence against women. In addition, his video *Tough Guise: Media Images and the Crisis in Masculinity* (Katz, 1999) explores the role of alcohol in cultural constructs of masculinities that may reward boys and men for antisocial behavior.

The social norms approach is a potential bridge between AOD prevention and efforts to reduce sexual assault. Similarly, the language of the environmental model used in AOD prevention may be useful to professionals whose primary goal is to reduce sexual assault. As feminist scholars have argued, sexual aggression is the culmination of a complex constellation of sociocultural and situational variables. Therefore, it is important to base strategies on an analysis of the social, economic, political, legal, educational, and physical dimensions of a campus-community environment that may foster sexual violence by college men.

SUMMARY

Alcohol and other drug use are associated with a high percentage of sexual assaults committed by men against women as well as other traumatic sexual experiences among college students. The substance most commonly involved in sexual violence is alcohol. Alcohol use by men can increase the likelihood of perpetrating sexual violence, particularly for those with individual characteristics, such as hostile masculinity, that are associated with sexual aggression. To the extent that alcohol increases the likelihood of sexual activity among men with such characteristics, it may further increase the probability of sexual aggression. For women, alcohol consumption is associated with an increased likelihood of being sexually assaulted. Regardless of the level of AOD consumption by either perpetrator or victim, the legal and moral responsibility for the assault lies with the offender. While alcohol may serve as a catalyst for sexual assault, it does not account for sexual aggression independent of sociocultural forces that foster men's violence against women. Methods for decreasing AOD-related sexual assault include environmental strategies aimed at reducing overall AOD use and specific interventions that seek to reduce heavy drinking in sexual situations. The social norms approach to prevention has been associated with reductions in heavy drinking and holds promise as a sexual assault prevention strategy for men.

REFERENCES

Abbey, A. (1991). Acquaintance rape and alcohol consumption on college campuses: How are they linked? *Journal of American College Health, 39*(4), 165–169.

Abbey, A., McAuslan, P., & Ross, L. T. (1998). Sexual assault perpetration by college men: The role of alcohol, misperception of sexual intent, and sexual beliefs and experiences. *Journal of Social and Clinical Psychology, 17,* 167–195.

Berkowitz, A. (1992). College men as perpetrators of acquaintance rape and sexual assault: A review of the research. *Journal of American College Health, 40,* 175–181.

Berkowitz, A. D. (1994). A model acquaintance rape prevention program for men. In A. D. Berkowitz (Ed.), *Men and rape: Theory, research, and prevention programs in higher education* (pp. 35–42). New Directions for Student Services, No. 65. San Francisco: Jossey-Bass.

Berkowitz, A. (1999). Applications of social norms theory to other health and social justice issues. In H. W. Perkins (Ed.), *The social norms approach to prevention.* Manuscript in preparation.

Brown, S. A., Goldman, M. S., Inn, A., & Anderson, L. R. (1980). Expectations of reinforcement from alcohol: Their domain and relation to drinking patterns. *Journal of Consulting and Clinical Psychology, 48,* 419–426.

Burkhart, B., Bourg, S., & Berkowitz, A. D. (1994). Research on men and rape: Methodological problems and future directions. In A. D. Berkowitz (Ed.), *Men and rape: Theory, research, and prevention programs in higher education* (pp. 67–71). New Directions for Student Services, No. 65. San Francisco: Jossey-Bass.

Burt, M. R. (1980). Cultural myths and support for rape. *Journal of Personality and Social Psychology, 38,* 217–230.

Capraro, R. L. (1994). Disconnected lives: Men masculinity and rape prevention. In A. D. Berkowitz (Ed.), *Men and rape: Theory, research, and prevention programs in higher education* (pp. 21–33). New Directions in Student Services No. 65. San Francisco: Jossey-Bass.

Centers for Disease Control (1997). *Youth risk behavior surveillance: National college health risk behavior survey—United States, 1995* [on-line] (Available <http://www.cdc.gov/nccdphp/dash/MMWR/ss4606.htm>).

DeJong, W., Vince-Whitman, C., Colthurst, T., Cretella, M., Gilbreath, M., Jacobs, J., Rosati, M., & Zweig, K. (1998). *Environmental management: A comprehensive strategy for reducing alcohol and other drug use on college campuses.* Newton, MA: The Higher Education Center for Alcohol and Other Drug Prevention.

Dimeff, L. A., Baer, J. S., Kivlahan, D. R., & Marlatt, A. G. (1999). *Brief alcohol screening and intervention for college students: A harm reduction approach.* New York: Guilford.

Enos, T., & Pittayathikhun, T. (1996). Alcohol and other drug prevention: A bulletin for fraternity & sorority advisers. In *The Higher Education Center for Alcohol and Other Drug Prevention* [on-line] (Available: <http://www.edc.or/hec/pubs/greek.htm>).

Erway, K. (1990). *Comorbidity of sexual and physical aggression in college males: Toward defining a typology of violence toward women.* Unpublished doctoral dissertation, Auburn University, Auburn, Alabama.

Erway, K., & Burkhart, B. (1993). The topography of violence in college men: Frequency and comorbidity of sexual aggression and physical aggression. *Journal of College Student Psychotherapy, 8,* 219–237.

Finn, P. (1997). *Preventing alcohol-related problems on campus: Acquaintance rape.* Newton, MA: The Higher Education Center for Alcohol and Other Drug Prevention.

Hall, G. C. N., & Hirschman, R. (1991). Toward a theory of sexual aggression: A quadripartite model. *Journal of Consulting and Clinical Psychology, 59,* 662–669.

Hanson, P. A., & Gidycz, C. (1993). Evaluation of a sexual assault prevention program *Journal of Consulting and Clinical Psychology, 61,* 1046–1052.

Harney, P. A., & Muelenhard, C. L. (1991). Factors that increase the likelihood of victimization. In A. Parrot & L. Bechhofer (Eds.), *Acquaintance rape: The hidden crime* (pp. 159–175). New York: Wiley.

Hotz, R. L. (1998, July 16). Scientists find teens' brains don't work like parents'. *The Seattle Times* [on-line] (Available: <www.seattletimes. com/news/healthscience/htm198/teen_071698.html>).

Janis, I. L. (1982). *Groupthink* (2nd ed.). Boston: Houghton-Mifflin.

Johannessen, K. (1999, July). *The University of Arizona social norms media campaign.* Paper presented at the National Conference on the Social Norms Model: Science-Based Prevention, Big Sky, MT.

Johnston, L., O'Malley, P., & Bachman, J. (1998). National survey results on drug use from the monitoring the future study 1975–1997. (No. 98-4346) National Institute on Drug Abuse, National Institutes of Health Publication.

Katz, J. (1995). Reconstructing masculinity in the locker room: The mentors in violence project. *Harvard Educational Review, 65*(2), 163–174.

Katz, J. (Featured contributor), & Jhally, S. (Executive director). (1999). *Tough guise: Media images & the crisis in masculinity* [videotape]. (Available from Media Education Foundation, 26 Center Street, Northampton, MA 01060).

Kilmartin, C., Conway, A., Friedberg, A., McQuoid, T., & Tschan, T. (1999, April). *Social conformity and sexism in all-male peer groups.* Paper presented at the Virginia Psychological Association Spring Conference, Virginia Beach, VA.

Koss, M. P. (1988). Hidden rape: Sexual aggression and victimization in a national sample of students in higher education. In A. Burgess (Ed.), *Rape and sexual assault II* (pp. 3–25). New York: Garland Publishing.

Larimer, M. E., Lydum, A. R., Anderson, B. K., & Turner, A. P. (1999). Male and female recipients of unwanted sexual contact in a college student sample: Prevalence rates, alcohol use, and depression symptoms. *Sex Roles, 40*(3/4), 295–308.

Malamuth, N. M., Sockloskie, R. J., Koss, M. P., & Tanaka, J. S. (1991). Characteristics of aggressors against women: Testing a model using a national sample of college students. *Journal of Consulting and Clinical Psychology, 59,* 670–681.

Marchell, T. (1998). *Sexual and physical aggression against women by male college athletes.* Unpublished doctoral dissertation. The California School of Professional Psychology at Alameda.

Meilman, P. W. (1993). Alcohol-induced sexual behavior on campus. *Journal of American College Health, 42,* 27–31.

Meilman, P., Leichliter, J., & Presley, C. (1999). Greeks and athletes: Who drinks more? *Journal of American College Health, 47,* 187–190.

Miller, D. T., & McFarland, C. (1987). Pluralistic ignorance: When similarity is interpreted as dissimilarity. *Journal of Personality and Social Psychology, 53,* 298–305.

Muelenhard, C. L., & Linton, M. A. (1987). Date rape and sexual aggression in dating situations: Incidence and risk factors. *Journal of Counseling Psychology, 34,* 186–196.

O'Sullivan, C. S. (1991). Acquaintance gang rape on campus. In A. Parrot & L. Bechhofer (Eds.), *Acquaintance rape: The hidden crime* (pp. 140–157). New York: Wiley.

Parks, K. A., & Miller, B. A (1997). Bar victimization of women. *Psychology of Women Quarterly, 21,* 509–525.

Parrot, A., Cummings, N., & Marchell, T. (1994). *Rape 101: Sexual assault prevention for college athletes.* Holmes Beach, FL: Learning Publications.

Perkins, W., & Berkowitz, A. (1986). Perceiving the community norms of alcohol use among students: Some research implications for campus alcohol education programming. *International Journal of the Addictions, 21*(9/10), 961–976.

Perkins, W., Meilman, P., Leichliter, J., Cashin, J., & Presley, C. (1999). Misperceptions of the norms for the frequency of alcohol and other drug use on college campuses. *Journal of American College Health, 47,* 253–258.

Prentky, R. A., & Knight, R. A. (1991). Identifying critical dimensions for discriminating among rapists. *Journal of Consulting and Clinical Psychology, 59,* 643–661.

Presley, C. A., Leichliter, J. S., & Meilman, P. W. (1998). *Alcohol and drugs on American college campuses: A report to college presidents.* Carbondale, IL: Core Institutes, Southern Illinois University at Carbondale.

Presley, C. A., Meilman, P. W., & Cashin, J. R. (1996). *Alcohol and drugs on American college campuses: Use, consequences, and perceptions of the campus environment, Vol. IV: 1992–1994.* Carbondale, IL: Core Institutes, Southern Illinois University at Carbondale.

Presley, C. A., Meilman, P. W., & Leichliter, J. S. (1999). *1998 statistics on alcohol and other drug use on American campuses.* Carbondale, IL: Core Institutes, Southern Illinois University at Carbondale.

Richardson, D., & Campbell, J. L. (1982). The effect of alcohol on attributions of blame for rape. *Personality and Social Psychology Bulletin, 8,* 468–476.

Richardson, D. R., & Hammock, G. (1991). Alcohol and acquaintance rape. In A. Parrot & L. Bechhofer (Eds.), *Acquaintance rape: The hidden crime* (pp. 83–95). New York: Wiley.

Schewe, P. (1999). [Empathy induction]. Unpublished raw data.

Scully, D., & Marolla, J. (1984). Convicted rapists' vocabulary of motive: Excuses and justifications. *Social Problems, 31,* 530–544.

Schwartz, M. D., & DeKeseredy, W. S. (1997). *Sexual assault on the college campus.* Thousand Oaks, CA: Sage.

Seto, M. C., & Barbaree, H. E. (1995). The role of alcohol in sexual aggression. *Clinical Psychology Review, 15,* 545–566.

Testa, M., & Parks, K. (1996). The role of women's alcohol consumption in sexual victimization. *Aggression and Violent Behavior, 1,* 217–234.

Wechsler, H., Dowdall, G. W., Davenport, A., & DeJong, W. (1995). Binge drinking on campus: Results of a national study (HEC 203). Newton, MA: The Higher Education Center for Alcohol and Other Drug Prevention.

Wechsler, H., Austin, B., & DeJong, W. (1996). Secondary effects of binge drinking on college campuses (HEC 205). Newton, MA: The Higher Education Center for Alcohol and Other Drug Prevention.

Williams, G. D., Stinson, F. S., Parker, D. A., Harford, T. C., & Noble, J. (1987). Demographic trends, alcohol abuse and alcoholism: 1985–1995. *Alcohol Health and Research World, 11*(3), 80–83, 91.

Wilson, G. T., & Lawson, D. M. (1976). Expectancies, alcohol and sexual arousal in male social drinkers. *Journal of Abnormal Psychology, 85,* 587–594.

Wilson, G. T., & Niaura, R. (1984). Alcohol and the disinhibition of sexual responsiveness. *Journal of Studies on Alcohol, 45,* 219–224.

CHAPTER 3

Drug-Facilitated Rape

Joan Zorza *

In the past few years, a number of newspaper stories (e.g., Carpenter, 1999; Croft, 1999), and articles in legal weeklies (e.g., Campagne, 1997; Ingram, 1998) have publicized alarming reports about rapists administering drinks laced with intoxicating substances to their intended victims who are thereby rendered incapable of protesting or resisting the attacks. In some instances, the victim cannot remember ever having been raped. These reports are obviously terrifying because we understand how easy it is for someone to "spike" a drink and how the victim of the drugging is prey to being raped. Such date rape drugs are a rapist's dream come true, making almost any woman a potential victim who is unlikely to be credible witness against the rapist.

DRUG-FACILITATED RAPE: A PARTICULARLY TERRIFYING CRIME

There are other factors that contribute to making drug-facilitated rape an especially troubling type of sexual assault. Contrary to

*I would like to thank Bob Nichols, Esq., Assistant State Attorney, Broward County State Attorneys Office, Sex Crimes Unit, Ft. Lauderdale, FL for his helpful comments.

myth, most rapes are premeditated (Hall, Hirschman, Graham, & Zaragoza, 1993; Koss et al., 1994), or at least the result of taking advantage of an opportunity (Allison & Wrightsman, 1993), with most rapists seeking women who are vulnerable (Foley & Davies, 1983). However, any rapist who administers drugs to the victim has clearly premeditated the crime and made his victim far more vulnerable and defenseless. The victim of a drug-facilitated rape almost always faces far worse consequences than is experienced for other rapes because she can never know exactly what happened and how badly she was violated. This makes any drug-facilitated rape a felony of the worst sort, a crime that should never be tolerated, minimized, or excused.

Drugged victims present a terrifying picture after the rape, staggering around with little idea of what happened. If they do have memories, they are likely to be fleeting—30 seconds here, 45 seconds there, often hours apart with no recollection of what happened in between. Sometimes the only reason that they suspect they were raped was that they regained consciousness wearing little or no clothing, found themselves in a strange room, and had no idea how they got there. Then again, they may have regained consciousness with their clothing mostly intact, but one or more articles of clothing may be missing or on backwards. It is not uncommon for victims to have unexplainable injuries, particularly bruises consistent with falling against knees, nose, or hands. If gamma hydroxybuterate (GHB) or Rohypnol were administered, there may be surprisingly limited trauma to vagina or rectum. However, victims in these terrible rapes may be more likely than other rape victims to have become infected with a sexually transmitted disease, HIV infection included, because drug-facilitated rapes often involve multiple perpetrators and longer periods of exposure to semen and blood. Victims are also less likely to obtain speedy and appropriate medical attention.

There is also relatively little public awareness of date-rape drugs, and this adds another frightening dimension to the problem. However, it is evident that many rapists know about and have access to these dangerous drugs and are administering them to their intended victims, particularly to women they know and date. Many drugs are used for their sedating effects, including benzodiazepines, barbiturates, hypnotics, tranquilizers, and ketamine (used mainly in veterinary medicine). Little about date rape drugs has yet to appear in the professional literature or case law. Regarding the former, one exception is the latest edition of *Our Bodies, Ourselves for the New Century: A Book By and For Women* (Boston Women's Health Book Collective, 1998), a sourcebook that is likely to reach many women on campus, but this reference contains only two brief warnings about Rohypnol.

A recent check of law review articles found only two that mention Rohypnol and none that addresses the drug GHB. Herring's (1996) article is mainly about international drug smuggling, and the second article ("The Date Rape Drug," 1997) noted the difficulties in prosecuting Rohypnol cases. A search for cases pertaining to either drug yielded but two. In *Commonwealth v. Stilley* (1997), the defendant unsuccessfully appealed his conviction and 5-year probation sentence for simple assault, terroristic threats, false imprisonment, and criminal mischief after administering GHB to his former girlfriend. In the second case, *Gorman v. Grand Casino of Louisiana* (1998), the plaintiff customer alleged that a security guard of the casino administered a date rape pill to her.

Not only does drug-facilitated rape in this country have a sinister history, but prosecution efforts are often stymied by the nature of the crime. Starting in 1958 a few law cases discussed rapes committed by doctors and other medical professionals having lawful access to drugs who administered them to patients to rape them. Although few of these doctors were ever prosecuted, those convicted were dealt with fairly harshly compared to other rapists of the time. Yet, among the successfully prosecuted medical cases (see, e.g., *Frank v. Superior Court and People,* 1989; *People v. Ing,* 1967; *Rhine v. State,* 1958; *State v. Lough,* 1995; *State v. Morowitz,* 1986), conviction usually occurred only after several women courageously came forward to relate a similar pattern of abuse by the same treating medical professional. Typically, the cases were unclear about which drug had been used. The inability to identify the drugs continues be a prominent issue because victims are frequently too intoxicated to seek help during the relatively brief interval when tests might detect the substance.

RAPE-FACILITATING DRUGS ON CAMPUS

In some parts of the country, rape-facilitating drugs are already readily available, and over time are likely to become widespread.

College and university administrators should not assume that just because these drugs are not now a problem on their campuses that they will not appear at some point in the future. In many instances, students will contaminate their campus community by bringing drugs back from a vacation or from their hometown. Some date-rape drugs can be produced in campus laboratories, and others are easily concocted in residence hall rooms. For example, GHB can be quickly and inexpensively mixed in any bathtub. Drugs might be accessible to those working at the campus health center, veterinary clinic, or off-campus health facility.

There is also the very real risk that the Internet can be a vehicle for infiltrating rape-facilitating drugs onto campus. A recent case in Michigan has brought this threat into the public eye. Two men, one from Florida and the other from Colorado, were charged with selling GHB "kits" for $200 over the Internet. State agents from Michigan went to the Website and purchased the kits which contained the chemicals needed to make GHB as well as step-by-step manufacturing instructions that were so easy even "a third-grader could have put them together." The men were likely to be extradited to Michigan to face charges ("Men charged," 1999).

Literature is beginning to shed light on the use of rape-facilitating drugs in fraternities. There is documentation of women being lured into fraternities as part of initiation rituals and sometimes being drugged to lower their resistance and reduce their credibility as potential witnesses (Martin & Hummer, 1989; Schwartz & DeKeseredy, 1997). Recently, many fraternities have been hosting parties with a "candy in your drink" theme. There are numerous reports, however, that the "candy" at the bottom of the free drink is actually replaced with a date-rape drug, incapacitating the victim who is later raped in the fraternity (B. Nichols, personal communication, April 30, 1999).

ALCOHOL, THE MOST COMMON RAPE-FACILITATING DRUG

Alcohol remains the most often used date rape drug both on and off campus. Surveys find that it is not uncommon for college women to have been forced to engage in sexual intercourse against their will when they were unable to resist because of alcohol or, less often, drugs. Schwartz and Pitts, for example, (1995) found that this happened to 17.1% of the college women they surveyed. It is not surprising that alcohol has been implicated in so many campus sexual assault, given that college students spend more on alcohol than they do on books, soda, coffee, tea, milk, and juice combined (Brody, 1999).

Alcohol can also be a date-rape drug when used solely by the perpetrator. Alcohol is often consumed to provide an excuse for the drinker's behavior (Valliere, 1997), and although inebriation may not provide a legal defense (B. Nichols, personal communication, April 30, 1999), it may cause the offense to be treated less seriously. However, the role of alcohol in actually inducing violent or criminal behavior is less clear, so that any correlation between drinking and misbehaving may be largely based on societal expectations and the rapist's expectations about alcohol's effects (Valliere, 1997).

Prosecution Problems

When alcohol is used as a rape-facilitating drug, it poses a particular problem if victims wish to prosecute the perpetrators. The problem occurs when victims who are aware of the alcoholic content of a beverage voluntarily drink it to the point of inducing a blackout, thereby impairing their memories of what had happened at the time of the nonconsensual sexual activity (Zorza, 1999). Alcohol blackouts often cause a complete loss of memory, but they do not necessarily impair the drinker's functioning, so that she may have appeared "normal" to others. If the victim cannot remember what happened because of a blackout, she cannot testify that she never consented to what happened, that she resisted or tried to fend off the perpetrator, or that the perpetrator overpowered her will. Unless there is a witness who can supply one of these essential pieces of information, no rape conviction is possible. An all too common result is that when the victim is a competent adult who voluntarily ingested such quantities of alcohol (or other drugs) that she cannot remember what happened, it is unlikely that a prosecutor would bring forward a rape or sexual assault case. Likewise, were such a case brought forward, it is even less likely that a jury would convict the perpetrator or that a conviction would be upheld if appealed (Zorza, 1999).

However, a voluntary intoxication scenario might still not prevent the victim from successfully bringing a campus disciplinary action if the alcohol use violated campus rules. It is also possible she might be able to obtain a civil protection order in court against the perpetrator in a state that permits dating partners to seek such relief; such relief is granted on the lesser standard of preponderance of evidence. If she was under the age of consent when the events took place, a criminal court could try the perpetrator for statutory rape. Similarly, a conviction should be possible when the victim was otherwise an incompetent adult.

Other than these limited exceptions or when a third party can testify as to the victim's lack of consent, the campus security officer, prosecutor, rape crisis advocate, or counselor can only point out these loopholes in the law to her. In addition, her helper should gently inform her that continued use of alcohol (or other intoxicating substances) to the point of blackout puts her at risk for further sexual assaults by unscrupulous individuals, and that subsequent victimizations are usually more upsetting than the first (Koss & Harvey, 1991; Rhode, 1997). If she has used large quantities of alcohol or drugs on previous occasions, the person assisting her should discuss options for alcohol or substance abuse treatment, even if she is in denial about having a problem (Zorza, 1999).

TYPES OF RAPE-FACILITATING DRUGS INFILTRATING CAMPUSES

Rohypnol (flunitrazepam) makes people who ingest it so incapacitated they are unable to resist a rapist or call for help. Victims commonly experience difficulty in moving their arms or legs, and their thinking is likely to be confused and impaired. Hence, the victim may appear to be drunk. Not only does Rohypnol slur a person's speech and make it difficult to walk, but the drug may impair the person's judgment or make the person less inhibited. Rapists like Rohypnol's qualities because as it is currently manufactured, it is tasteless, odorless, colorless, and soluble in any liquid. Potential victims cannot detect it. The drug's fast-acting effects begin within minutes and last for many hours, typically peaking about 2 hours after ingestion (Zorza, 1998).

Another drug popular with rapists is GHB. GHB has unique effects. It depresses the central nervous system while acting as a stimulant to the brain, actually exciting the brain into seizure mode (Mitchell, 1998; Zorza, 1998). It also has a tendency to exaggerate the feeling of intoxication, often causing the victim to feel enhanced sexual desire (Zorza, 1998). Such feelings, especially when they cause a victim to initiate or participate in sexual activity, are almost certain to leave the victim feeling more depressed and culpable. Curiously, the seriousness of the drug's effects are quickly forgotten, making drug abusers, those administering it, and possibly even date-rape victims somewhat oblivious to the drug's danger, thus increasing the risk for continued use.

Ketamine, a drug used primarily by veterinarians as an anesthetic, is a powerful sedative that also causes nausea, amnesia, hallucinations, and low blood pressure. On the street, it is known as Special K or K (Gess & Alberg, 1998). It is quite expensive, costing from $100 to $200, but it can be purchased legally by veterinarians for $7. It can be snorted, injected, mixed in drinks, or smoked (American Prosecutors Research Institute, 1999). Because it is believed to produce a better high than phenylcyclidine (PCP) or LSD and its effects last an hour or less, it is often a very popular "party drug." Since it is currently controlled only in California, Connecticut, New Mexico, and Oklahoma, few law enforcement agencies collect data on its abuse, except when "drunk" drivers are stopped and found to be using it.

PCP can cause muscle rigidity, seizures, and delerium (Volavka, 1995). Like cocaine and amphetamines, PCP can cause intoxication, paranoia, and delusional disorders, and it has the potential to cause belligerence and assaultiveness. The latter two propensities seem to make these drugs less likely choices to facilitate rape and more useful for the rapist himself (Rivinus & Larimer, 1993).

The two sections that follow address Rohypnol and GHB in greater detail. I conclude the chapter with two other sections that contain suggestions for how college and university staff can respond to, prevent, and treat drug-facilitated rape.

ROHYPNOL AND OTHER BENZODIAZEPINES

The benzodiazepines were first synthesized in the 1950s and have largely replaced the more dangerous barbiturates (Rivinus &

Larimer, 1993). They affect a different area of the brain than barbiturates, acting as central nervous system depressants that produce "drunk effects." Most are disinhibitors (Mitchell, 1998; Zorza, 1998). They are often prescribed to aid sleeping. The generic names of the benzodiazepines usually end with the syllables "lam" or "pam." The drug family includes diazepam (or Valium), lorazepam (Ativan), flunitrazepam (Rohypnol), triazolam (Halcion), and alprazolam (Xanax). Except in Canada, where Halcion is often used as a rape-facilitating drug, Rohypnol has received by far the most attention (Mitchell, 1998). The effects of these and most date-rape drugs are often so similar that chemical analysis is the only way to know which drug was administered.

ROHYPNOL'S EFFECTS

Rohypnol is one of the strongest benzodiazepines, having seven to ten times the potency of Valium by weight and four to eight times that of Halcion (Zorza, 1998). Rohypnol has a very strong anterograde amnesia effect when first used (Mitchell, 1998). Starting about 30 minutes after ingestion and, depending on the amount, for approximately the next 8 hours, Rohypnol causes muscles to relax, psychomotor performance to slow, and blood pressure to drop, followed by sleepiness and often amnesia (Zorza, 1998). The Office of National Drug Control Policy (1998) noted that some of Rohypnol's side-effects can include headaches, dizziness, nightmares, memory impairment, and tremors. Long-term use often leads to physical dependence and the need for medically supervised withdrawal.

Because of the drug's amnesic effects, a rape victim may be unable to remember what happened to her or who her attacker was. Consequently, the victim may never call the police or rape center or seek medical care. Complicating matters, if there were any witnesses, they probably assumed that the victim was drunk or consented to the sexual demands.

It is a popular drug among drug users who take it orally, snort it, or inject it. Consumption of Rohypnol with alcohol or other drugs can be deadly (Zorza, 1998), yet drug users may use Rohypnol alone or take it with alcohol or marijuana to enhance their effects. It is also self-administered to ease the withdrawal symptoms of heroin, crack, or cocaine.

AN ILLEGAL SUBSTANCE EASILY OBTAINED

It has never been legal to possess or manufacture Rohypnol in the United States. However, it is legally manufactured in Mexico and several other countries by the Swiss pharmaceutical company, Hoffman-La Roche, for sale outside of the United States. Physicians in 80 countries may legally prescribe Rohypnol as a short-term treatment for sleep disorders. In fact, it is the most prescribed prescription sedative in Europe, with over one million doses used per night (B. Nichols, personal communication, April 30, 1999). Although it is not legal to prescribe or sell Rohypnol in Canada, it can be imported in limited amounts for personal use when legally prescribed by a foreign physician. Since the late 1970s, abuse of Rohypnol has been reported in Europe, and more recently throughout the world.

Most of the supply of Rohypnol in the United States comes from South America and Latin America, especially Colombia and Mexico, where it is manufactured and can be purchased over the counter. The primary states of entry are Florida and Texas. Underscoring the dramatic availability of Rohypnol, in the southern part of Florida, the main point of entry, it is estimated that the number of children who will take Rohypnol may soon equal the number who use marijuana (B. Nichols, personal communication, April 30, 1999).

Street Names

On the street, Rohypnol is known by many names, including: circles, date-rape drug, dulcitas, forget me drug, forget-pill, la rocha, lunch money drug (because of its low price), Mexican Valium, mind erasers, minuses or negatives (referring to the 1-mg tablet's markings) or pluses (the 2-mg tablet's markings), pappas or potatoes (referring to the ingester's mental capacity while under the influence), pingus, poor man's quaalude, R-2, reynolds, rib, ro, roachies, roapies, robutal, rochas dos, roche, roofies, rope, rophies, rophy, roples, row-shay, ruvies, ruffles, trip-and-fall, and wolfies (Zorza, 1998).

Problems with Identification

Hoffman-La Roche sells Rohypnol as a tablet in an attractive bubble packaging with a foil backing, which fools many into thinking it is a harmless drug. Furthermore, because Rohypnol has never been legal in the United States, law enforcement officials cannot easily identify it from the photographs in the Physician's Desk Reference or other drug identification sources (Herring, 1996). Those sources list only legal medications.

In October 1997, in response to the widespread misuse of Rohypnol, Hoffman-La Roche agreed to add a blue color-releasing agent to Rohypnol tablets so that the drug is more likely to be detected. In addition, the manufacturer agreed to reformulate the tablets so that they will not dissolve as quickly in liquids and will leave particles at the surface of a beverage, signaling that something has been added (Ledray, Simmelink, Pharris, & Valentine, 1999). However, before actually making these changes, the drug manufacturing company has to obtain approval for the new reformulation in each of the 80 countries where Rohypnol is legally marketed, so that the change may be significantly delayed (Mitchell, 1998).

Penalties for Possession, Distribution, and Use

Simple possession of the drug in the United States is punishable by up to 3 years in prison as well as a fine. Under federal law, administering Rohypnol to another person without his or her knowledge and with intent to commit a crime or violence (including rape) is punishable by up to 20 years in prison. In addition, a number of states (e.g., Florida, Idaho, Minnesota, New Mexico, North Dakota, Oklahoma, Pennsylvania) have placed Rohypnol under Schedule I control (stiffer than under federal law), subjecting those who possess or distribute it to state penalties as well (B. Nichols, personal communication, April 30, 1999; Zorza, 1998). Congress is considering rescheduling Rohypnol, GHB, Ketamine, and other rape-facilitating drugs as more dangerous, thereby enhancing the penalties for their use or distribution.

GHB: ANOTHER COMMON RAPE-FACILITATING DRUG

Although GHB has been tested in the United States, it has never been approved here for any medical use. It can promote the secretion of growth hormones from the pituitary glands of healthy people, but GHB has never been shown to promote muscle growth (Stone, 1997). Currently, GHB is being used or tested in Europe to treat alcohol withdrawal, cerebral edema, tachycardia, and narcolepsy. So, it does appear to have some legitimate medical uses (Krawczeniuk, 1993).

How GHB Is ADMINISTERED

Most GHB is sold as a clear or syrupy liquid, although it is sometimes produced as a white powder that looks like white laundry flakes. A rapist can carry GHB in liquid form in an eye-drop bottle and then administer a few squirts into the unwatched glass of an intended victim. Drinks laced with GHB can sometimes be detected because they may have an unpleasant, plastic, salty taste and even mild odor (Mitchell, 1998). However, it is not uncommon for rapists to mask the flavor and smell by adding the drug to a sweet liqueur or fruit juice.

EFFECTS OF GHB

GHB acts even faster than Rohypnol. Its effects typically begin 5 to 15 minutes after ingesting a dose, which is 1 to 2 teaspoons. GHB inhibits neurotransmitters from being released in the brain. For example, GHB decreases the levels of dopamine in the brain. Like Rohypnol, it can cause confusion, intense sleepiness, unconsciousness, dizziness, weakness, and memory loss. Most symptoms last 3 to 6 hours, but the drowsiness and weakness can continue for up to 3 days, the dizziness for 2 weeks, and confusion for several weeks (Mitchell, 1998). GHB can also cause nausea, agitation, euphoria, distorted perceptions, suppression of the gag reflex, seizures, heart and respiratory depression, and coma (Mitchell, 1998; Zorza, 1998). The dangerousness of GHB is underscored by the fact that the dose needed to obtain the "desired" rape-facilitating effect is only slightly less than the amount that can cause severe brain damage, even death.

Most available GHB is produced illegally by manufacturers outside the pharmaceutical industry. GHB is concocted from volatile solvents and caustic soda (lye). If its pH level is too high (and a pH of 12 is not that uncommon), GHB can cause caustic burns to the face, skin, and internal organs—even the vomit may be at unsafe pH levels (Nichols & Robshaw, 1999).

Alcohol and other drugs can enhance the effects of GHB, producing a possible fatal mix. Curiously, the body's melatonin levels potentiate GHB's effects, so that it is likely to have a greater impact when taken at night, especially in the winter, than when ingested during daylight (Zorza, 1998).

STREET NAMES

Other names for GHB include: bedtime scoop, cherry meth, easy lay, energy drink (referring to its saltiness), ever clear, G. gamma, Georgia home boy, G-juice, great hormones, grievous bodily harm (GHB), liquid E., liquid ecstasy, liquid sex, liquid soap, max (when dissolved in water and mixed with amphetamines), natural sleep 500, salt water, soap, sodium oxybate, scoop, somatomax PM, super-G, and water (Zorza, 1998).

GHB: Now a Controlled Substance

On February 18, 2000 President Clinton signed into law H. R. 2130, the "Hillory J. Farias and Samantha Reid Date-Rape Drug Prohibition Act of 2000." Among other things, this piece of legislation places GHB in Schedule I of the Controlled Substances Act. As a Schedule I controlled substance, possession and distribution of GHB is prohibited and may cause violators to be subject to stringent criminal sanctions. This act also directs the Secretary of Health and Human Services to develop and implement a national campaign to educate youths, educators, counselors, and law enforcement officials, among others, on the dangers of GHB and other such drugs. A special exemption of this law allows for ongoing research of GHB as a possible treatment for individuals diagnosed with narcolepsy.

The law is named after two prominent victims of GHB poisoning. Hillory Farias was a 17-year old from LaPorte, Texas who died in 1996 after ingesting a GHB-laced soda at a night club. Samantha Reid died on January 17, 1999 after she, too, had been given a soft drink spiked with GHB at a party (Sealey, 2000). A 16-year-old female friend of Samantha's also ingested the drug but survived despite slipping into a coma. Four men in the Reid case were subsequently convicted and sentenced to prison terms (Suhr, 2000).

HOW CAMPUSES SHOULD RESPOND TO DRUG-FACILITATED RAPE

One of the biggest problems for a college may be determining that a drug-facilitated rape even took place on the campus. Hence, the issues of reporting the assault and testing for the presence of the drug become crucial.

ENCOURAGING REPORTING

Campus administrators and personnel need to encourage students to report and assist in reporting any drug-facilitated rape (Sokolow & Koestner, 1999). Many victims may have known that they willingly consumed an alcoholic beverage but not realize that it was laced with a higher alcoholic concentration or with stronger drugs. That they "willingly" consumed the beverage will contribute to their guilt, shame, self-blame, embarrassment, and confusion.

Universities should have a policy, just as do most prosecutors' offices, that individuals will not be penalized for drinking when they were raped, even if their drinking violated university rules and policy (Sokolow & Koestner, 1999). It should be recognized that the rapist perpetrated a far worse crime, especially since he planned the crime by arranging to have the drink made stronger or knowingly added drugs to the drink.

To encourage students to help their peers, universities should also grant a similar limited immunity to those who report or cooperate in reporting and those who assist the victim (or a potential victim). Certainly, some students who come to a victim's assistance have been involved themselves in some type of wrong-doing (e.g., violating campus alcohol rules). A limited immunity would not excuse the most serious misbehaviors, but relatively minor ones might go unpunished with others treated with more lenience in recognition of the assistance provided.

TESTING FOR ROHYPNOL AND GHB

Because of the difficulty in testing for rape-facilitating drugs and the profound drowsiness that victims experience during the short period when testing might be positive, it is quite unlikely that there will be evidence that a drug was administered (Zorza, 1999). To preserve as much physical evidence as possible, the victim should not urinate, wipe, shower, bathe, douche, or launder or discard clothing worn during the assault. It is also unlikely that accurate testing can be done on campus or in the usual laboratories contracted by the campus health service. A urine sample must be obtained quickly from the victim or the opportunity to prove that a rape drug was administered will be lost permanently. Then there is the consideration that taking a sample must be balanced against the need to collect other evidence, as urinating will wash away semen.

Usually Rohypnol remains in the blood for only 2 to 4 hours after ingestion (Mitchell, 1998), but it can sometimes be detected in urine for up to 72 hours and Valium, with effects virtually indistinguishable from GHB, up to 96 hours. Therefore, urine is a more reliable medium for testing, and 96 hours is the recommended window for its collection (Zorza, 1999). GHB remains in the blood for at most 4 hours and in the urine for at most 12 hours.

Ideally for testing purposes 100 mL of urine should be collected from the victim or 30 mL of blood (in a "gray-top" tube that contains potassium oxalate and sodium fluoride as preservatives) as soon as possible (Zorza, 1999). Any vomit or remains of the drink should also be saved in a sealed container or plastic bag for later testing for the parent compound, rather than just the metabolites tested for in urine (B. Nichols, personal communication, April 30, 1999). In an emergency, the victim should be told to keep any samples in a clean, covered container and preserve them in her possession to establish custody until police or medical assistance can arrive. Any samples should be frozen, or at least refrigerated, and a chain of custody should be maintained (Zorza, 1999). It is unlikely that a college or university health clinic could do more than take samples, refrigerate them, and maintain a chain of custody (possibly involving campus security officials) until the samples can be turned over to police or medical authorities. Refrigerated or frozen samples can be tested even weeks or months later.

Hoffman-La Roche will test for Rohypnol and other drugs at no cost to law enforcement agencies, rape treatment centers, and health care providers. Testing is done at the El Sohly Laboratory in Oxford, Mississippi. They are reachable 24 hours a day at 1-800-608-6540 for testing information (Mitchell, 1998). It should be pointed out that the FBI's toxicology laboratory has found that Hoffman-La Roche's laboratory's immunoassay test uses a cutoff level that is too high to detect 43% of Rohypnol samples, and that other laboratories are performing considerably more accurate testing for that drug (Welner & Delfs, 1997; Zorza, 1999). Thus, in the event of a rape, campus police may want to speak to FBI toxicologist, Mark LeBeau (see phone number in Sources for Additional Information at end of chapter), or state and local prosecutors to establish where any testing should be done.

PROSECUTION CONSIDERATIONS

Campus police or the university health center medical staff may want to photograph any injuries that were inflicted on the victim. If she leaves campus, the campus police or health staff should make sure that they contact the rape crisis center, hospital, or law enforcement agency she seeks out for assistance. It is particularly important to photograph all of the injuries that are consistent with falling down (Mitchell, 1998). Those pictures will help establish for prosecution purposes just how incapacitated the victim was. Thus, if she was in such a drug-induced stupor that even a bad fall could not arouse her, it would explain why she could not have resisted the rapist's advances (Zorza, 1999). Photos of injuries have also proven valuable in helping women psychologically recover from the rape ordeal (Mitchell, 1998; Zorza, 1999).

To maintain an unbroken chain of custody, campus police should turn over any preserved evidence to the local police or prosecutor (Zorza, 1998). Campus police can also be credible witnesses for enabling local police to obtain warrants to search premises for evidence. It is not uncommon to find bubble packs, drug residue, and other evidence of drugs or their manufacture either at the scene of the crime or at the suspect's home. Bubble packs should be checked for suspect's fingerprints or for evidence of coconspirators. A check of the suspect's computer may reveal that he visited internet sites to obtain information about Rohypnol or GHB, including how to purchase low-cost GHB kits through the mail. The Federal Drug Administration, I should note, is currently trying to shut down these sites (B. Nichols, personal communication, April 30, 1999). Because it is not uncommon for drug-rapists to make a video of or to photograph their victims, evidence of film receipts may help implicate the suspect (Zorza, 1998).

Charging the Drug Rapist

Drug-facilitated rape crimes may be prosecuted at any of the following crime sites, some of which may coincide: (1) where the drug was illegally manufactured, (2) where the victim was drugged, or (3) where the victim was raped or assaulted (Zorza, 1998). When Rohypnol, GHB, or other rape-facilitating drugs were used in connection with a sexual assault, the alleged perpetrator could be charged with a variety of possible crimes, including: sexual assault or rape, sexual assault of a mentally or physically incapacitated person, sexual assault of a helpless person (which can apply to a person who voluntarily ingested a pill), possession and delivery of a controlled substance, aggravated battery, and kidnapping (B. Nichols, personal communication, April 30, 1999; Zorza, 1998). In the event of death, the perpetrator could be charged with manslaughter. Additional charges may be appropriate if the victim is a minor. Because the administering of illegal drugs indicates premeditation, conspiracy crimes could also be charged, even, possibly, if sexual assault does not occur (Zorza, 1998).

Use of Toxicologist Expert

If the case comes to trial, a qualified toxicologist is recommended to educate the jury about the effect of Rohypnol or GHB and to explain any apparent weaknesses in the case (Mitchell, 1998). Even though the victim may have "voluntarily" consumed the drug or "consented" to sexual acts while under its influence, unless the victim knew what was being administered and was aware of its effects and why it was being given to her, any apparent consent was not knowingly and freely given (Zorza, 1998).

TREATMENT CONSIDERATIONS FOR THE SURVIVOR

The road to recovery can be long and painful, even for rape survivors who were not drugged (e.g., Francisco, 1999; Raine, 1998). Although most rape survivors find the rape to be a devastating experience, those who have been drugged are far more vulnerable to serious psychological effects. Unlike rape survivors who recollect much of what happened to them, those surviving a drug-facilitated rape will never be certain; they may just have a nagging sense that they were drugged and raped. They may be profoundly ashamed by what little they do know, suspect, or learn; and they feel even more ashamed, guilty, and worthless if they think that somehow they willingly went along with any part of what transpired (Ledray, 1986). Drugged victims are unable to filter the traumatic events and work through them in their minds by mentally reliving and adjusting to them.

After being drugged and raped, survivors will need enormous amounts of reassurance that confusion and uncertainty are normal reactions. For this reason, it is important that they be given very supportive counseling assistance as soon as possible, preferably from a counseling center that provides rape crisis services (Ledray, 1986). Perhaps the only study of the effectiveness of rape crisis programs found that those who received counseling within the first 2 weeks of the assault were dramatically more improved than those receiving just medial and forensic assistance ("Study Finds Rape Crisis Programs Do Work," 1997). Richard Cleary, the psychology student who conducted this study, confirmed that the window of opportunity for this benefit may be as short as 2 weeks.

Survivors of date or acquaintance rape need to be believed and supported (Ledray, 1986). It is just as important that this belief in and support for the survivors come from campus police and other officials as from counselors, therapists, or medical personnel (Cooper, 1993). Victims should not be interrogated in a hostile manner or with judgmental "why" questions such as, "Why did you go to the party in the first place?" "Why were you out so late?" "Why didn't you leave earlier?" or "Why were you wearing that type of outfit?" (Cooper, 1993). Moreover, because victims of drug-facilitated rape desperately want to remember what happened to them, both for their own well-being and to assist in any subsequent prosecution or campus disciplinary efforts, they should not be subjected to leading questioning that may unwittingly cause them to adopt erroneous perspectives of the assault (B. Nichols, April 30, 1999, personal communication).

Because of the victim's confusion and profound feelings resulting from having been doubly victimized, the university's counseling, medical, and housing staffs should make efforts to accommodate her safety and confidentiality needs. It may be very helpful to offer her alternative housing (see chapter 4) or to provide her with a security alarm pendant to call for help if she feels rethreatened by the rapist or his friends. University staff should be fully cognizant of the fact that subsequent attempts to intimidate the victim are not uncommon. Twenty-two percent of stalking victims are sexually assaulted by the stalker, and sometimes the stalking only begins after the rape ("Stalking Often Linked to Sexual Assault," 1997). It may be easier and faster to take disciplinary action against the alleged rapist when illegal drugs are involved in a campus infraction. This may allow for the perpetrator to be quickly removed from campus. (See chapter 10 for information regarding the role of the university judicial affairs office in disciplinary actions.) Finally, college and university administrators should be aware that rape survivors are far less likely to sue institutions that have been protective, supportive, and caring.

CREATING A CAMPUS CLIMATE TO COMBAT DRUG-FACILITATED RAPE

Educational efforts may be the most effective way to prevent drug-facilitated rapes and to protect students. Many useful pamphlets and posters are available to raise students' consciousness about this type of assault. Placing literature in all campus restrooms might be the surest way to reach all men and women on campus.

The Rape Treatment Center, Santa Monica-UCLA Medical Center (310-319-4000) has released a series of well-designed, informative brochures, posters, and related materials to alert people to the dangers of Rohypnol, GHB, and other "rape drugs." These can be distributed by rape crisis services, the university counseling center, and through student affairs programming. The Santa Monica center can be contacted for a copy of their catalogue or a sample of their excellent brochure, "Rapists Are Using a New Weapon to Overpower Their Victims." This brochure includes an invaluable tear-off section that contains such useful information as how to tell if you have been drugged, what to do if you have been drugged, and how to protect your friends. The brochure wisely suggests not drinking beverages that have been passed around, left unattended, poured from a punch bowl, or taste or look unusual.

Hoffman-La Roche has also produced two fine pamphlets in conjunction with the D.C. Rape Crisis Center, "Substance Abuse & Sexual Assault" (may be photocopied without permission) and "When Drugs Are Used for Rape: What Counselors Need to Know." They can be obtained by calling 1-800-720-1076.

SUMMARY

The so-called date-rape drugs have added a terrifying dimension to sexual violence on college campuses. This chapter has focused on two distinct approaches for closing down the windows of opportunity available to rapists who premeditate their drug-induced assault. First, there is the importance of educating all members of the campus community about the effects and properties of the common rape-facilitating drugs. Second, predators who perpetrate these crimes must be held accountable. Hence, I have provided specific recommendations for collecting and preserving evidence.

Drug-facilitated rapes are devastating experiencing to the victims. When they have been drugged, victims find it much harder to seek help after the assault, thereby reducing the chance that they can ever document what happened. Because victims remember little, they are less likely to be believed and their assailant more likely to avoid any penalties. The victims are also less likely to feel understood and to have their experiences validated, with the result that they will require more time to heal—or never heal—compared to other rape victims.

As with efforts to put an end to all rapes, men *and* women must work together to stop drug-facilitated rapes and to come together to protect potential victims. Colleges and universities should have in place clear policies that hold perpetrators fully accountable. Likewise, campus policies should also be supportive of all survivors of these terrible rapes. In this regard, it is important that colleges and universities respond to victims in ways that (a) validate rather than censure their experiences, (b) provide for their physical safety, and (c) encourage their reporting the incident.

SOURCES FOR ADDITIONAL INFORMATION

American Prosecutors Research Institute, Violence Against Women Program. Phone: 703-549-4253. Webpage: **http://www/ mdaa-apri.org**

Date Rape Drugs Webpage: **http://www.shout.net/~res/drugs/ index/html**

Federal Bureau of Investigation, Narcotic and Dangerous Drug Section (for Rohypnol and other controlled substances). Contact Robert Lipman (202-514-0950) or Harry Natz (202-514-6112).

Federal Bureau of Investigation, Toxicology Laboratory. Contact Marc LeBeau (202-324-4329).

GHB and Ketamine contacts: Sharon Kurn, Office of Consumer Litigation, Department of Justice (202-307-0047), or William McConagha, United States Food and Drug Administration (301-827-1112).

REFERENCES

Allison, J. A., & Wrightsman, L. S. (1993). *Rape: The misunderstood crime.* Thousand Oaks, CA: Sage.

American Prosecutors Research Institute (Producer). *Rohypnol and GHB related assaults* [Video]. (Available from APRI, 99 Canal Center Plaza, Suite 510, Alexandria, VA 22314).

Boston Women's Health Book Collective (1998). *Our bodies, ourselves for the new century.* New York: Touchstone.

Brody, J. E. (1999, April 6). Coping with cold, hard facts on teen-age drinking. *New York Times,* p. F6.

Campagne, H. (1997, September 8). Measure targets "date-rape" drugs. *Massachusetts Lawyers Weekly,* 21.

Carpenter, J. (1999, January 9). Women warned about latest date rape drug. *Chicago Sun-Times,* p. 8.

Commonwealth v. Stilley, 689 A. 2d 242 (Pa. Super. 1997).

Cooper, D. (Producer). (1993). *Restoring dignity: Frontline response to rape* [Video]. (Available from Sage Publications, 2455 Teller Road, Thousand Oaks, CA 91320).

Croft, J. (1999, February 17). Brothers are convicted in "date rape" case. *Atlanta Journal-Constitution,* p. C3.

The date rape drug: The difficulty of obtaining convictions. (1997, March/April). *Prosecutor, Journal of the National District Attorneys Association, 31*(2), 28.

Foley, T. S., & Davies, M. A. (1983). *Rape: Nursing care of victims.* St. Louis, MO: C. V. Mosby.

Francisco, P. W. (1999). *Telling: A memoir of rape and recovery.* New York: Cliff Street Books.

Frank v. Superior Court and People, 770 P. 2d 1119 (Cal. 1989).

Gess, N., & Alberg, I. (1998). *Drug-facilitated rape* [Memo, Office of Intergovernmental Affairs]. Washington, DC: Department of Justice.

GHB designated schedule I drug. (1999). *Family Violence & Sexual Assault Bulletin, 15*(1), 28.

Gorman v. Grand Casino of Louisiana, 1 F. Supp. 2d 656, (1998).

Hall, F. C. N., Hirschman, R., Graham, J. R., & Zaragoza, M. S. (1993). *Sexual aggression: Issues in etiology, assessment, and treatment.* Washington, DC: Taylor & Francis.

Herring, D. (1996). Getting high from south of the border: Illicit smuggling of Rohypnol as an example of the need to modify U.S. response to international drug smuggling after NAFTA. *Loyola of Los Angeles International and Comparative Law Journal, 18*(4), 841–864.

Ingram, L. P. (1998, July 20). Date rape drug becomes law. *Michigan Lawyers Weekly, 27.*

Koss, M. P., Goodman, L. A., Browne, A., Fitzgerald, L. F., Kieta, G. P., & Russa, N. F. (1994). *No safe haven: Male violence against women at home, at work, and in the community.* Washington, DC: American Psychological Association.

Koss, M. P., & Harvey, M. R. (1991). *The rape victim: Clinical and community interventions* (2nd ed.). Thousand Oaks, CA: Sage.

Krawczeniuk, A. (1993). The occurrence of gamma hydroxybutyric acid (GHB) in a steroid seizure. *Microgram, 26,* 160–166.

Ledray, L. E. (1986). *Recovering from rape.* New York: Henry Holt.

Ledray, L. E., Simmelink, K., Pharris, M. D., & Valentine, S. (March 1, 1999). *The sane guide* [On-line] (Available: http://www.sane.sart.com).

Martin, P. Y., & Hummer, R. A. (1989). Fraternities and rape on campus. *Gender & Society, 3,* 457–473.

Men charged with on-line drug sales. (1999, August 16). USAToday [On-line] (Available: http://www.usatoday.com/life/cyber/tech/ctf851. htm).

Mitchell, K. (Producer). (1998). *Rohypnol and other drugs used to commit rape* [Video]. (Available from the University of Maine, Department of Marketing, 5761 Keyo Building, Orono, ME 04469).

Nichols, B., & Robshaw, D. (1999). *Date-rape drugs: Suggested techniques for investigating and prosecuting drug-facilitated rapes* [On-line] (Available: http://www.cavnet.org.).

Office of National Drug Control Policy (1998). *Drug Policy Information Clearinghouse Fact Sheet: Rohypnol* [Brochure]. Washington, DC: Author.

People v. Ing, 55 Cal. Rptr. 902 (1967).

Raine, N. V. (1998). *After silence: Rape and my journey back.* New York: Crown Publishers.

Rhine v. State, 336, P. 2d 913 (Okla. Crim. App. 1958).

Rhode, D. L. (1997). *Speaking of sex: The denial of gender inequality.* Cambridge, MA: Harvard University Press.

Rivinus, T. M., & Larimer, M. E. (1993). Violence, alcohol, other drugs, and the college student. In L. C. Whitaker & J. W. Pollard (Eds.),

Campus violence: Kinds, causes, and cures (pp. 71–119). Binghamton, NY: Haworth.

Schwartz, M. D., & DeKeseredy, W. S. (1997). *Sexual assault on the college campus: The role of male peer support.* Thousand Oaks, CA: Sage.

Schwartz, M. D., & Pitts, V. L. (1995). Exploring a feminist routine activities approach to explaining sexual assault. *Justice Quarterly, 12,* 9–31.

Sealey, G. (2000, February 7). "Date rape" drug trial begins. ABCNews. com [On-line]. Available: www.abcnews.go.com/sections/us/Daily News/daterape00207.html

Sokolow, B. A., & Koestner, K. H. (1998). *Total sexual assault risk management strategies for colleges.* Gulph Mills, PA: Campus Outreach Services, Inc.

Stalking often linked to sexual assault (1997). *Sexual Assault Report, 1*(1), 6.

State v. Lough, 889 P. 2d. 487 (Wash. 1995).

State v. Morowitz, 512, A 2d 175 (Conn. 1986).

Stone, B. (1997, February 18). FDA re-issues warning of GHB. *FDA Talk Paper,* T97–10.

Study finds rape crisis programs do work. (1993). *Sexual Assault Report, 1,* 17–31.

Suhr, J. (2000, March 30). 4 men sentenced to prison for date-rape drug death. ABCNews [On-line]. Available: abcnews.go.com/sections/us/ DailyNews/daterape000330.html

Valliere, V. M. (1997). Relationships between alcohol use, alcohol expectancies, and sexual offenses in convicted offenders. In B. K. Schwartz & H. R. Cellini (Eds.), *The sex offender: New insights, treatment innovations, and legal developments* (Vol. 2) (pp. 3–1 to 3–14). Kingston, NJ: Civic Research Institute.

Volavka, J. (1995). *Neurobiology of violence.* Washington, DC: American Psychiatric Press.

Welner, M., & Delfs, E. (1997). Rapists in a glass? The big picture of the Rohypnol wars. *The Forensic Echo, 1*(11), 4–10.

Zorza, J. (1998). Rohypnol and GHB: Terrifying date-rape drugs. *Sexual Assault Report, 2*(2), 17–30.

Zorza, J. (1999). Drug facilitated rape. *Sexual Assault Report, 2*(4), 49–60.

CHAPTER 4

Feminist Approaches to Addressing Violence Against Women

Jayne Schuiteman

This chapter explores the connection between women's studies/ feminist scholarship and various campus efforts to combat sexual violence. Its purpose is to provide a distinctly feminist understanding of sexual violence and the ways that feminist approaches to such violence can inform campus prevention and response efforts. The chapter begins with an introduction to the field of women's studies and feminist scholarship and provides the background necessary to examine feminist explanations for sexual violence. The chapter proceeds with an examination of antiviolence efforts typical of many college and university campuses as they respond to recent federal legislation designed to increase campus accountability in deterring and responding to sexual assault. As part of that examination, Michigan State University's approaches are highlighted as an example of the ways that institutions can combat campus violence that includes women's studies and service providers throughout the campus community. The chapter concludes with recommendations for other institutions interested in combining feminist scholarship with antiviolence efforts.

AN INTRODUCTION TO WOMEN'S STUDIES

Courses focusing on feminist issues appeared in college and university curriculums in the late 1960s, and by 1970 the terms "women's studies" or "feminist studies" were used to describe those courses (Ruth, 1995). What began as a scattering of a few courses across the curriculum is now recognized as a legitimate academic discipline with programs at all levels of study—ranging from an undergraduate minor to doctoral programs—at many institutions throughout the country. As a discipline, women's studies is relatively young, and its traditions and methods of inquiry are evolving. However, some basic information about the discipline follows that sheds light on feminist understandings of sexual violence and the role that women's studies plays in combating violence.

WOMEN'S STUDIES/FEMINIST SCHOLARSHIP AS THE ACADEMIC ARM OF FEMINISM

Women's studies is based in feminism. Some have referred to women's studies as the academic arm of the feminist movement. Likewise, women's studies is also linked with the feminist movement in its commitment to activism. Research and scholarship conducted from a feminist perspective seek to challenge relationships based on power and control (Kelly, 1988). Feminist theories attempt to understand and explain women's oppression in a hierarchical, patriarchal social structure. In her introduction to *The Politics of Reality: Essays in Feminist Theory*, Marilyn Frye (1983) stated:

> Trying to make sense of one's own feelings, motivations, desires, ambitions, actions and reactions without taking into account the forces which maintain the subordination of women to men is like trying to explain why a marble stops rolling without taking friction into account. What "feminist theory" is about, to a great extent, is just identifying those forces (or some range of them or kinds of them) and displaying the mechanics of their applications to women as a group (or caste) and to individual women. The measure of

the success of the theory is just how much sense it makes of what did not make sense before. (pp. xi–xii)

While women's studies is based in feminist theory, as a field of study it is inherently interdisciplinary. Analyses tend to supercede traditional academic boundaries. Women's studies scholars may be trained in a particular discipline, but their research and scholarship draw from fields such as history, philosophy, sociology, and psychology. Some feminists have even argued that the traditional division of knowledge into distinct disciplines is artificial at best and destructive at worst (Ruth, 1995). Rather, they believe human experience is incredibly complex and no one academic discipline can adequately explain those experiences.

Women's studies and feminist research are committed to understanding oppression based on gender as it intersects with age, class, race and ethnicity, ability, and sexual orientation. While there was an early emphasis on "sisterhood" and the mistaken assumption that all women were more alike than different, the movement now understands that women's experiences as women are diverse, and understanding that diversity is critical (Ruth, 1995). Additionally, the earlier assumption that all women were more alike than different reflected a White, privileged perspective. The early women's movement was criticized by feminists of color as being a privileged White women's movement. Even today, some question the extent to which women of color and White women have been able to work together to address the intersections of race, gender, class, and sexuality. However, inclusiveness remains a goal of the movement.

WOMEN'S STUDIES/FEMINIST SCHOLARSHIP'S ROLE IN ACTIVISM

Feminists seek to eradicate all of the "isms," not just sexism, and the following quotation illustrates that commitment:

The reason racism is a feminist issue is easily explained by the inherent definition of feminism. Feminism is the political theory and practice that struggles to free all women: women of color, working-class women, poor women, disabled women, lesbians, old women—as well as White, economically privileged, heterosexual women. Anything less than this vision of total freedom is not feminism, but merely female self-aggrandizement. (Smith, 1982, p. 49)

The link between women's studies and the feminist movement also implies a role in activism, particularly on college and university campuses. Any effort to eradicate the various "isms" confronted by society will, of necessity, motivate people to action. Much of the research and scholarship produced by feminist academics dealing with sexual violence, for instance, has been used by activists as they do their work in the battered women's shelters, rape crisis centers, and child abuse prevention programs. Likewise, women's studies programs have always encouraged and promoted activism on campuses as students, faculty, and staff work to improve the conditions and climate for all members of their communities.

Feminist theory has always informed feminist activism; likewise, feminist activism has also informed feminist theory. The two are intricately linked. However, feminist scholarship has been criticized as being shielded in an academic ivory tower, sometimes with little connection to the real work of feminist practice occurring in the community. By way of example, a recent seminar brought together members of the academic community with practitioners in the battered women's movement that included shelter directors and representatives of state-wide coalitions dealing with domestic and sexual violence. The intent of the seminar was to give practitioners an opportunity to tell the researchers what they would like to see researched. However, as conversation between the two communities unfolded, it was clear that the practitioners were at times frustrated and even suspicious of some of the research efforts that were clearly well intentioned. Researchers were told that much of their work had little meaning to the day-to-day operations and concerns of many shelter employees. Additionally, the practitioners pointed to multiple research efforts that had questionable motives, such as more recent variations on the theme of "why does she stay?" which often resulted in further blaming the victims of domestic violence.

While those kinds of criticisms are certainly justified, there are other examples of a more positive relationship between scholarship and practice. Many colleges and universities provide some form of self-defense training for women. At Michigan State University, self-defense training for women dates back to the early 1970s. Semester-long classes that are part of the curriculum as well as 2- to 3-hour informal seminars are available to students. The university has made a commitment to ensure that the classes and seminars are taught by women who understand sexual violence from a feminist perspective. That perspective informs how sexual violence is explained and the resulting strategies designed to prevent or deter assault. Students in the classes and seminars are empowered to take action instead of restricting their behaviors. Those responsible for developing the seminar and class curriculums have explicitly used feminist explanations for sexual violence as the foundation for instruction, thereby making a very direct and positive connection between theory and practice.

In the first section of this chapter, an introduction to the discipline of women's studies was presented in the context of feminism: first as the academic arm of the feminist movement and second as playing a significant role in feminist activism. The following section of this chapter will examine the role of women's studies/feminist scholarship in campus-response efforts regarding sexual violence. Various experts in the area of sexual assault prevention and response have discussed the importance of women's studies in educating the campus community about sexual violence, notably Mary Harvey (in Sweet, 1985). Her work as well as others' will be discussed in this section.

WOMEN'S STUDIES/FEMINIST SCHOLARSHIP AND ITS RESPONSE TO CAMPUS SEXUAL VIOLENCE

Because of its prevalence on campuses, sexual assault, and more specifically, date and acquaintance rape, has received a significant amount of attention from the academic community in recent years. A number of studies in the last decade have indicated that rape and attempted rape occur with greater frequency than once believed (Koss, Gidycz, & Wisniewski, 1987; Warshaw, 1988). Statistics regarding reported cases of sexual assault are considered misleading at best when attempting to understand the frequency of sexual violence. When comparing national statistics from the

Federal Bureau of Investigation Uniform Crime Reports regarding actual reported assaults and The Bureau of Justice National Crime Victimization Survey, which includes anonymous reports of sexual assault not necessarily reported to law enforcement agencies, it is estimated that no more than one in five sexual assaults is reported to authorities (Bachman & Saltzman, 1995; FBI Uniform Crime Reports, 1995). Additionally, many consider that estimate to be conservative because of the ways that sexual assault and forcible rape are defined when compiling national statistics. Moreover, stranger assaults are more likely to be reported than date/acquaintance assaults. In the most recent National Crime Victimization Survey, it was reported that fully three quarters of the rapes and attempted rapes experienced by respondents were perpetrated by assailants known to the victims (Bachman & Saltzman, 1995). According to the National Violence Against Women Survey sponsored jointly by the Centers for Disease Control and Prevention and the National Institute of Justice, one in six women and girls experience some form of sexual violence during their life-times (Tjaden & Thoennes, 1998).

There are many reasons why assaults tend to go unreported and as a result, researchers have attempted to obtain more accurate information about the frequency of assault through anonymous surveys. To date, one of the most comprehensive studies looking at date and acquaintance rape on college and university campuses was commissioned by the *Ms.* Foundation. In that study, over 3000 college-age women and men were surveyed at more than 30 colleges and universities across the country (Warshaw, 1988). The researchers found that 20% of the women had experienced rape or attempted rape. Koss et al. (1987) found that 27.5% of college women reported being victims of rape or attempted rape. Additionally, 53.7% of women, including those who had reported being raped, indicated that they had experienced some sort of unwanted sexual contact. The research seems to support the feminist notion that coercive sexual practices are a "normal" aspect of heterosexual dating relations in this particular culture and our culture is one that supports rather than abhors rape (Donat & D'Emilio, 1997).

Given the frequency of violence against women in this culture, feminist scholars have examined all forms of sexual violence, including rape, domestic violence, sexual harassment, and sexual abuse. Feminist researchers were among the first to critically examine sexual violence in an effort to understand its role in the oppression of women. A feminist analysis of sexual violence is critical as a starting point for all efforts that seek to end violence throughout campuses and larger communities. In this section of the chapter, a feminist explanation for sexual violence will be provided. That explanation, in turn, will be used to discuss the role of women's studies/feminist scholarship in campus prevention/response efforts. Finally, the section will conclude with a discussion of the efforts at Michigan State University as a case study of practices that combine feminist scholarship and activism in combating sexual violence on campus.

WOMEN'S STUDIES: FEMINIST THEORETICAL PERSPECTIVES OF SEXUAL VIOLENCE

Date and acquaintance rape can be understood within the context of a feminist analysis of sexual violence. Two works, both published in the 1970s were pivotal in providing a feminist understanding of sexual violence and its role in maintaining a gendered social order. Susan Griffin (1971) argued that rape is not a crime of sex, but rather a crime of violence that serves to maintain social control over women. Griffin also articulated an argument regarding "the male protection racket," whereby women seek the protection of men from other men. Additionally, Griffin raised comparisons between heterosexual sex and rape, explored the myths associated with rape that place the blame for victimization on the victims themselves, and questioned the very constructions of masculinity and femininity that allow women to be perceived as "good" victims.

Susan Brownmiller's (1975) *Against Our Will: Men, Women, and Rape* was the second classic work that provided a feminist analysis of sexual violence. While criticized for a sweeping analysis that at times ignored history and cross-cultural differences in sexual assault, Brownmiller put forth a thesis that remains foundational for thinking of rape as a means of social control. In the introduction she wrote:

From prehistoric times to the present, I believe, rape has played a critical function. It is nothing more or less than a conscious process of intimidation by which *all men* keep *all women* in a state of fear. (Brownmiller, 1975, p. 5)

Brownmiller (1975) argued that while not all women are raped, the fact that some women are assaulted keeps all women in fear, thereby limiting their freedom. Likewise, while not all men commit rape, all men benefit from the socially prescribed roles and limitations that women experience as a result of their fear.

More recently, theorists such as Suzanne Pharr (1997) and Carole Sheffield (1997) have discussed sexual violence as a cornerstone of patriarchy. In discussing the notion of "sexual terrorism," Sheffield (1997) notes that male efforts to control the female body in a variety of ways, including the threat of sexual violence, is the mainstay of patriarchy. Violence against women serves the purpose of reminding women that their bodies are not their own and that access to the female body can be demanded at any time, regardless of the issue of consent. In this regard, Sheffield (1997) noted that, "Violence and its corollary, fear, serve to terrorize females and to maintain the patriarchal definition of woman's place" (p. 110). Pharr discussed violence and the threat of violence against women as but one means of control. She argued that, "Sexism, that system by which women are kept subordinate to men, is kept in place by three powerful weapons designed to cause or threaten women with pain and loss. As stated before, the three are economics, violence, and homophobia" (p. 9). In specifically addressing the issue of violence, Pharr discussed battering, rape, and incest as measures to keep women in their place. Violence is "used to wreak punishment and to demand compliance or obedience" (Pharr, 1997, p. 13).

A new generation of feminists has recently begun to criticize analyses of power and gender oppression that were generated in the 1970s and 1980s. Representative of those new voices is Naomi Wolf (1993). Wolf has been critical of what she has termed "victim feminism," defined as "when a woman seeks power through an identity of powerlessness" (Wolf, 1993, p. 135). She argued that many feminist analyses of power, springing from the second wave of feminism of the early 1970s, cast all institutions and corresponding forms of institutional power as *man*-made and therefore, problematic. Rather than seeing power as something morally neutral, capable of being used for good or evil, power itself was cast as evil (Wolf, 1993). Furthermore, Wolf argued that some feminists have gone so far as to not only distance themselves from any forms of power, but have also attempted to define victim status itself as a form of strength and identity. The result has been a backlash against legitimate efforts to protest and eradicate sexual violence.

More recently, debate has arisen regarding the use of the terms "victim" and "survivor." Victims are often portrayed as passive, vulnerable, and weak whereas survivors are often thought of as active, courageous, and empowered (Kelly, Burton, & Regan, 1996). These authors argue that neither aspect of the dichotomy is particularly useful in that such definitions unnecessarily link people to a regrettable past. Instead, sexual victimization should be viewed as a one-time occurrence rather than a life-long characteristic. Power analyses such as Wolf's (1993) in which women are not seen as completely powerless or totally controlled by a gendered hierarchy as well as the questioning of just how much and how long one is effected by sexual violence, point to new trends in how sexual violence is being defined and discussed by feminist theorists.

The preceding discussion points to power, dominance, control, and fear as core elements for understanding sexual violence as a means of maintaining patriarchy. Those same elements can also be examined in the context of campus culture. Young women arrive on campus, often excited about their opportunities to experience new freedom and responsibility. However well intended, efforts to increase awareness and promote safety on campus often reflect the very concepts of patriarchal control that sexual violence and the threat of violence perpetuate. The messages that new women students hear regarding sexual assault often increase fear and cause women to restrict their behaviors in an effort to avoid assault. For instance, women are warned about the dangers of walking alone on campus after dark. They are told to attend parties or other social events only when accompanied by other friends. Women are warned about the dangers of alcohol consumption and its role in sexual assault. While none of these "warnings" are problematic in and of themselves and may in fact be considered by many to reflect "common sense," the cumulative effect of such warnings can lead women to restrict their behavior and increases their level of fear. Women who dare deviate from such behavioral prescriptions and act independently are often chastised and worse, blamed for their victimization, should it occur.

WOMEN'S STUDIES: CONTRIBUTIONS TO CAMPUS ANTIVIOLENCE EFFORTS

Bohmer and Parrot (1993) conducted extensive interviews with college and university administrators, campus sexual assault victims, parents of some victims, and victims' attorneys. Additionally, the researchers examined campus codes for approximately 50 colleges of all types in all regions of the country. In their discussion of institutions' responses to sexual violence, the authors state:

> All colleges deal with campus sexual assault—whether they think they do or not, and whether they do it well or badly. College responses to sexual assault range from being proactive and attempting to create a fair and safe environment for their students to ignoring the problem and blaming the victims for being raped. (Bohmer & Parrot, 1993, p. 123)

Because of the wide range of institutional response to sexual violence, recent federal legislation holds colleges and universities more accountable for proactive efforts to decrease the prevalence of assault and measures to meet the needs of victims. The Campus Sexual Assault Victim's Bill of Rights Action of 1991 (H.R. 2363), sponsored by Congressman James Ramstad of Minnesota, was revised and signed into law as a part of the Higher Education Amendments of 1992. The Ramstad Amendment requires institutions of higher education to formulate and distribute a sexual assault policy. Additionally, in their policy the institution must include efforts designed to increase the campus community's awareness of rape, programs geared toward prevention, as well as procedures that should be followed after an assault occurs (Bohmer & Parrot, 1993).

Beginning in 1991, the federal Student Right to Know and Campus Security Act stipulated that colleges and universities collect data and publish reports on campus crime on an annual basis. Additionally, some states have passed legislation that would hold their colleges and universities more accountable for campus sexual violence. As a result of this legislation, most colleges and universities have developed more specific means of addressing sexual assault. Prevention and deterrence programs are more common and take on a variety of forms. Campus police or security officials have become more responsive to sexual assault victims and efforts are underway to encourage more victims of assault to report to campus authorities. Additionally, campus police and security officials are trying to be more visible to members of campus communities as responsive resources regarding sexual assault. Finally, counseling options, either on or off campus, are being made more available and more visible to students. Those responsible for providing such counseling opportunities have historically relied on accurate information about the nature of assault and victimization, much of it gathered from feminist analyses of sexual violence. Thus, students are receiving more accurate information through a variety of channels.

The link between women's studies/feminist scholarship and response efforts to sexual violence on college campuses is critical. Women's studies programmatic efforts contribute significantly to the ability of colleges and universities to comply with the requirements of state and federal mandates. As part of a discussion regarding a survey of exemplary rape programs done for the National Center for the Prevention and Control of Rape, survey and study author Mary Harvey had this to say about campus efforts:

> (T)he real measure of a school's commitment to dealing with this problem is the range of services it provides. It should have preventive services, crisis intervention, possibilities for long-term treatment, advocacy, and women's studies programs that educate about violence. The quality of a university's services to rape victims can be measured by the degrees to which these things are in place. (in Sweet, 1985, p. 59)

The role of women's studies in assault prevention and response is important for several different reasons. First, as has been discussed throughout this chapter, the research generated by women's studies scholars serves to inform service providers in their day-to-day dealings with students in their campus communities. Second, most women's studies courses include content that explicitly examines sexual violence. Those classes range from introductory courses that survey a wide range of issues central to women's lives, courses that examine topics related to specific aspects of violence such as "women and the law," as well as entire courses devoted to feminist analyses of sexual violence in its various forms. Such content provides in-depth educational opportunities for students to learn more about these issues but also indicates to the entire campus community the seriousness of sexual violence. Finally, faculty members who conduct research on rape, domestic violence, and sexual harassment serve as important resources on campus as well as positive role models of those who are trying to make a difference to improve the quality of life on campus and throughout the broader community.

In the following section, Michigan State University will be examined as an example of the various ways that women's studies and feminist scholarship interface with violence prevention and response efforts on campus.

WOMEN'S STUDIES: PREVENTIVE ROLE AT MICHIGAN STATE UNIVERSITY AS A CASE STUDY OF APPLIED ACTIVISM

Michigan State University (MSU) has a long history of providing quality services related to sexual violence. Beginning in 1980, the MSU Sexual Assault Crisis and Safety Education Program was founded within the student counseling center. The program makes use of student volunteers who do peer counseling as they staff a 24-hour crisis line. Student volunteers also advocate for assault victims, often accompanying them to police agencies, assisting them in pursuit of medical care, and providing support as cases proceed through the criminal justice system. The program also makes use of full- and part-time professional staff who provide individual and group counseling. Finally, both volunteers and professional staff participate in a wide range of educational efforts throughout the campus community related to sexual violence.

In the early 1970s assault prevention services were first provided on campus, on a very informal basis, in the student union by an organization called the Feminist Self-Defense and Karate Association (FSDKA). FSDKA offered self-defense workshops and martial arts classes to women students both on campus and throughout the greater Lansing community. Eventually FSDKA's offerings were institutionalized by MSU. Currently, the Kinesiology Department offers a semester-long self-defense class, and the Intramural Sports Women's Self-Defense Program offers 2- to 3-hour workshops on assault prevention.

Michigan State University is also the only campus in the country that has a shelter for victims of domestic violence. MSU Safe Place opened its doors in June 1994. In addition to a full-time director, Safe Place employs graduate assistants and relies extensively on student volunteers. Besides sheltering victims and children of domestic violence, Safe Place provides educational outreach to the campus community and beyond. The primary focus of campus-based educational programs is relationship violence. Safe Place educates the campus community, particularly students, about violence between heterosexual or same-sex dating partners. Outdated beliefs about domestic violence (e.g., that domestic violence only occurs in the context of heterosexual married relationships) are still held by many students. Beyond the campus community, Safe Place has developed an educational program for businesses and corporations throughout Michigan. The program examines workplace violence, generally, as well as the more specific role of domestic disputes as part of the backdrop for many instances of workplace violence.

The Department of Police and Public Safety at MSU developed the MSU Police Sexual Assault Response Guarantee. The guarantee begins with the following statement: "Sexual assaults, including date/acquaintance rape, are a very serious concern of the University. If you feel you are the victim of a sexual assault on campus, your MSU Police Department will guarantee you the following:" Ten responses are then outlined including: willingness to meet privately in a place of the victim's choice; treating the individual and his or her case with courtesy, sensitivity, dignity, understanding and professionalism; and the promise of a full investigation of an individual's case, assisting the victim to achieve the best possible outcome. The tenth point stipulates that a case will be taken seriously, regardless of the gender or sexual orientation of the victim or suspect. The Sexual Assault Response Guarantee has served as a model for police departments across the nation who, in turn, have developed their own similar guarantees.

There are other units across campus that participate in MSU's sexual assault prevention and response effort. They include the Women's Resource Center, the Olin Health Center, Residence Life, and assorted student groups. Perhaps what makes the University's efforts unique is not so much what is offered to the campus community, but the ways in which individual units have formed a strong coalition around sexual assault prevention and response. Representatives of all of the units and programs that deal with safety and response meet monthly. This group serves as a channel of communication for service providers, functions as a forum for discussion of pertinent issues, and allows for the coordination of efforts that is critical for a successful and comprehensive campuswide response to sexual violence. The group's facilitator is a faculty member from the Women's Studies Program. She works extensively with various service providers across campus, teaches a course for the women's studies program called "Sexual Violence: Theory and Response," and conducts research related to sexual assault and sexual harassment. Thus, a strong link between the academic and service aspects of the University has been institutionalized through the coalition.

Links between women's studies scholars and violence prevention efforts are evidenced in other ways at MSU. There are a number of women's studies courses that have content related to sexual violence. Introductory women's studies courses are very popular at the University and tend to have high enrollments each semester. Those classes survey a number of critical issues related to women's lives, including sexual violence. Students read a number of selections that provide a feminist analysis of the various forms of sexual violence. Additionally, other women's studies courses also address aspects of sexual violence from varied perspectives. One particular course, "Women and the Law," includes a volunteer component as part of the grading system. Students can volunteer at one of several different agencies, including MSU Safe Place. Courses in lesbian studies specifically examine aspects of relationship violence as they play out in same-sex couples. A two-semester course taught in the Psychology Department provides students with the opportunity to spend one semester learning about domestic violence from a feminist perspective as well as advocacy skills on behalf of the victims of domestic violence. Students then spend the following semester assigned to a small "case load" of battered women who they advocate for as the women pursue alternative housing, job opportunities, public assistance when necessary, and other avenues that would allow them independence from their batterers.

Perhaps one of the most popular women's studies courses offered is "Sexual Violence: Theory and Response." The course draws not only women's studies majors, but students from across the university who are majoring in degree programs where their professions will likely bring them into contact with issues related to sexual violence. Students majoring in psychology, criminal justice, social work, nursing, and so forth are typically represented in the class. The course provides an in-depth feminist analysis of rape in its various forms, domestic violence, the sexual abuse of children, and sexual harassment. Students also have the opportunity to listen to guest speakers from within the campus community talk about their service programs as they relate to sexual violence as well as volunteer at those programs for course credit. Thus, a link is established between a theoretic understanding of sexual violence and the agency involved in "doing something" about the issue.

While the above focused specifically on the example of one institution, generalizations can be drawn that would be beneficial to other institutions interested in establishing alliances between women's studies and programs designed to deal with sexual violence. Such colleges or universities may already have women's studies programs or departments in place. Others may be considering establishing such programs. The recommendations discussed below are most pertinent to institutions with already established women's studies programs or departments. Colleges or universities interested in establishing women's studies as a discipline on their campuses will face a different set of challenges that exist far beyond the scope of these recommendations.

RECOMMENDATIONS FOR ESTABLISHING WOMEN'S STUDIES/VIOLENCE PREVENTION LINKS

This section of the chapter will be divided into three subsections. The first focuses on necessary policies that must be in place if campuses are to effectively deal with sexual violence. Because aspects of these policies are based in law, they are necessary regardless of possible links to women's studies/feminist scholarship. However, even policies based in law will benefit from a feminist foundation for understanding sexual violence. The second subsection will look at a campus sexual assault program development and the need for inclusivity with regard to gender. Finally, this section of the chapter will conclude with a discussion of the complementary nature of feminist scholarship and service, including the possibility of a consultation role between faculty members and service providers.

Policies Grounded in Feminist Perspectives

First and foremost, institutions must be in compliance with federal and state legislation intended to protect students with regards to sexual violence. The Ramstad Amendment to the Higher Education Act stipulates that institutions of higher education provide a statement of policy regarding campus sexual assault programs and the procedures followed once a sex offense has occurred. According to Bohmer and Parrot (1993), "Some administrators think sexual assault is not a problem on their campus. As a result, many institutions do not have appropriate policies against such behaviors. Students are given the implicit message that acquaintance rape and sexual assault are tolerated on campuses, and that working with the criminal justice system will usually not result in a conviction" (p. 183).

Ideally, an institution's policy regarding sexual assault should be based on a feminist understanding of such violence. As indicated previously in this chapter, a feminist understanding would include an analysis of power, dominance, and control as a means of maintaining patriarchy as core elements in explaining sexual assault. Policies and procedures must adequately reflect the realities of sexual violence and not perpetuate the myths that feminist researchers have sought to expose. Historically, the victims of sexual assault have been reluctant to report their experiences to law enforcement agencies, medical personnel, and campus administrators precisely because of the myths surrounding rape and other forms of assault. Policies that place responsibility for assault with the perpetrator rather the victim are crucial if assault is to be dealt with successfully.

Inclusivity

Educational programs geared toward both women and men should also reflect a feminist understanding of sexual assault. If programs are directed only to women and what they can do to prevent or avoid assault, an implicit message accompanies such efforts: that women are responsible for assault. As Bohmer and Parrot (1993) explain, "educational programs should be addressed to men as well as women, because rape will not stop until men stop raping" (p. 200). Clearly, the solution is fairly simple: Men must take responsibility for their behaviors and stop raping. However, in reality, the societal complexities associated with sexual violence render such a straightforward solution somewhat meaningless. Until men can better understand their roles in the scenario and learn to change their behaviors, a need to teach women avoidance strategies will be maintained. However, the fine line associated with personal responsibility and victim blaming is a difficult line to walk. When women are told what they can and cannot do to avoid rape, the underlying message places full responsibility on women and allows men "off the hook." Additionally, women may develop a false sense of security, assuming that if they follow all of the suggestions offered to them around avoidance, they will not be raped. Such a belief is misguided and potentially dangerous. Only a concerted effort to educate both women and men on college and university campuses will allow that fine line of personal responsibility to be walked successfully.

At MSU, two programs involve men in prevention efforts. Both Safe Place and the MSU Sexual Assault Crisis and Safety Education Program have positions for Male Outreach Coordinators. These individuals work both individually and collaboratively to bring information about sexual assault and relationship violence to male students throughout the campus community, including members of varsity athletic teams as well as members of the fraternities. Their goal is help men understand that they are accountable for their behaviors and that they can work to end sexual violence.

The Complimentary Nature of Feminist Scholarship and Service

Adherence to state and federal legislation regarding sexual violence is primarily the responsibility of campus administrators. Services associated with sexual assault are primarily the responsibility of program service providers. Hence, it is entirely possible that the important link with the academic side of the college or university through women's studies and feminist scholarship could be overlooked as an important component of the entire assault prevention effort. However, women's studies faculty members must also do their part to establish a working relationship with administrators and service providers. On large and small campuses alike, there is typically a clear distinction between the academic and nonacademic sides of the institution. It is very easy for college and university faculty members to spend all of their time involved with their teaching, research, and departmental responsibilities, giving little or no thought to the service aspects of the campus. Yet, given the historic link between feminist academic pursuits and activism, it is critical that feminist scholars extend themselves to campus efforts that promote women's interests, particularly assault response/prevention programs. The formation of alliances or coalitions involving both faculty and service providers is but one way for that to happen. It may be possible for faculty who are doing work in the area of sexual violence to make the latest research available to service providers on a regular basis. Faculty with expertise in particular areas could serve as consultants to various programs. It could also be very beneficial for service providers and faculty to work together on joint research projects.

Women's studies departments should be very visible in their support of response/prevention efforts on campus. For instance, when sexual violence is discussed in the classroom, not only should theoretic discussions occur about the nature of assault, but practical information regarding the institution's response to assault should also be included. Women's studies classes can operate as a forum for letting students know about policy, procedures, prevention and response efforts. Inevitably, when conversations about sexual violence occur in college classrooms, some students decide to talk with their instructor about their own experiences of assault. There are times when a faculty member is the first person these students have ever confided in about their situations. In such cases, instructors must be well informed about how to advise the student for support and services within the campus community.

Michigan State University serves as an example for how such a consulting relationship can be established. Each year, all undergraduate academic advisors are informed of university resources regarding sexual assault. Emphasis is placed on the need for student support services should they disclose to an instructor or advisor that they have been victims of rape or other forms of sexual violence. In this case, the director of the Sexual Assault Crisis and Safety Education Program is in direct consultation with advisors and faculty about the resources available to students through that particular program. Additionally, because the consultation relationship is established early each academic year, it is fairly common for the director to receive phone calls from concerned faculty and advisors for advice regarding their work with students who have experienced some form of assault. A strong working relationship between women's studies/feminist scholars and assault prevention/response efforts enhances the entire university or college approach to sexual violence. The entire campus community can see concern expressed from different aspects of the institution ranging from the administration, to service providers in various programs, to entire fields of discipline such as women's studies. Such a wide range of interest in these issues sends a powerful message to students, faculty, and staff, indicating the school's commitment to effectively dealing with sexual violence.

SUMMARY AND CONCLUSIONS

This chapter has introduced readers to the field of women's studies and a feminist analysis of sexual violence. As a discipline, women's studies seeks to understand gender as it contributes to the unequal distribution of power within contemporary cultures. However, it goes beyond an analysis of gender alone and attempts to explain the crosssection of gender, race, ethnicity, age, ability, and sexual orientation in power distributions. For most feminist scholars, sexual violence and the threat of violence are central aspects of any theory that explains gender dominance. Thus, feminist scholars have given sexual violence significant attention.

Women's studies/feminist scholarship has traditionally been viewed as the academic arm of the women's movement. The women's movement has explicitly worked to improve the lives of all women and is committed to activist efforts to bring about that goal. The presence of women's studies departments on campus has often resulted in an increase in activism regarding gender issues. Feminist students and faculty can work together to draw attention to the issues that impact women's lives on campus, and sexual violence is certainly no exception.

Women's studies classes often include material about sexual violence as part of the curriculum. Introductory survey courses as well as whole courses devoted to sexual violence in its various forms draw attention to the issue and serve as but one more way to indicate to the campus community that the institution takes the issue of sexual assault seriously. Feminist scholars doing research in the area of sexual violence can work with service providers throughout the campus community. Those efforts might include the formation of coalitions, alliances, providing consultation, and making current research available.

Feminist analyses of sexual violence have produced response efforts based on the notion of empowerment. Traditionally, women seeking to prevent assault have been taught to limit their behaviors, and as a result, limit their freedom. Women were taught not to go out alone after dark, women students were told not to take night classes, and many learned to avoid certain areas of campus considered too remote and potentially dangerous. A feminist understanding of assault that considers the roles of power, dominance, and control as motivating factors teaches women to be strong and assertive. Rather than restricting behavior, women are learning how to assertively defend themselves and unabashedly define their boundaries with respect to others. Survivors of assault learn not to blame themselves for their victimization. Rather, professionals informed by a feminist perspective assist survivors in moving through a healing process that encourages dignity and self-respect, whether they are seeking medical attention, working with mental health experts, reporting to police agencies, or pursuing cases through the criminal justice system or campus judiciary system.

Women's studies/feminist scholars are critical elements in an effective effort to combat sexual violence on college and university campuses. Such programs and individuals serve as a critical link between the academic, administrative, and service arenas on campus. A strong liaison among those areas will only strengthen the entire campus antiviolence effort.

REFERENCES

Bachman, R., & Saltzman, L. (1995). Bureau of Justice Statistics, Special Report. Violence against women: Estimates from the redesigned survey. U.S. Department of Justice. Washington, DC.

Bohmer, C., & Parrot, A. (1993). *Sexual assault on campus.* New York: Lexington Books.

Brownmiller, S. (1975). *Against our will: Men, women, and rape.* New York: Simon and Schuster.

Donat, P., & D'Emilio, J. (1997). A feminist redefinition of rape and sexual assault: Historical foundations and change. In L. O'Toole & J. Schiffman (Eds.), *Gender violence: Interdisciplinary perspectives* (pp. 184–193). New York: New York University Press.

Federal Bureau of Investigation Uniform Crime Reports. (1995). U.S. Department of Justice. Washington, DC.

Frye, M. (1983). *The politics of reality: Essays in feminist theory.* Freedom, CA: The Crossing Press.

Griffin, S. (1971). Rape: The all-American crime. *Ramparts, 10,* 26–35.

Higher Education Amendments of 1992, Pub. L. No. 102-325, Section 486(c) (1992).

Kelly, L. (1988). *Surviving sexual violence.* Minneapolis, MN: University of Minnesota Press.

Kelly, L., Burton, S., & Regan, L. (1996). Beyond victim or survivor: Sexual violence, identity, and feminist theory and practice. In L. Adkins & V. Merchant (Eds.), *Sexualizing the social: Power and the organization of sexuality* (pp. 77–101). New York: St. Martin's Press.

Koss, M., Gidycz, C., & Wisniewski, N. (1987). The scope of rape: Incidence and prevalence of sexual aggression and victimization in a national sample of higher education students. *Journal of Consulting and Clinical Psychology, 55,* 162–170.

Pharr, S. (1997). *Homophobia: A weapon of sexism* (2nd ed.). Berkeley, CA: Chardon Press.

Ruth, S. (1995). An introduction to women's studies. In S. Ruth (Ed.), *Issues in feminism* (3rd ed.) (pp. 1–19). Mountain View, CA: Mayfield Publishing.

Sheffield, C. (1997). Sexual terrorism. In L. O'Toole & J. Schiffman (Eds.), *Gender violence: Interdisciplinary perspectives* (pp. 110–127). New York: New York University Press.

Smith, B. (1982). Racism and women's studies. In G. Hull, P. Scott, & B. Smith (Eds.), *All the women are white, all the blacks are men, but some of us are brave* (pp. 48–51). Old Westbury, NY: The Feminist Press.

Student Right to Know and Campus Security Act of 1990, Pub. L. No. 101-542, 20 U. S. C., Section 1092(f) (1990).

Sweet, E. (1985). Date rape: The story of an epidemic and those who deny it. *Ms., 14,* 56–59.

Tjaden, P., & Thoennes, N. (1998). Prevalence, incidence, and consequences of violence against women: Findings from the National Violence Against Women Survey. Research in Brief. National Institute of Justice/Centers for Disease Control and Prevention. Washington, DC: U.S. Department of Justice.

Warshaw, R. (1988). *I never called it rape: The Ms. Report on recognizing, fighting, and surviving date and acquaintance rape.* New York: Harper and Row.

Wolf, N. (1993). *Fire with fire.* New York: Random House.

CHAPTER 5

A Sexual Assault Education and Risk Reduction Workshop for College Freshmen

Barbara Fouts and Jenny Knapp

To proactively address the issue of campus sexual assault, prevention and education programs are becoming fairly common on university campuses. The content, philosophy, and implementation of these programs vary tremendously and often reflect the perceived needs of each university community. This chapter is about how a mandatory sexual assault education program for incoming freshmen was developed and implemented to address the needs at one university. That university is Northern Illinois University (NIU), student population approximately 22,000, located in the rural community of DeKalb. This chapter is also about what the program developers learned along the way.

THE NIU INITIATIVE: AN HISTORICAL BACKDROP

When the issue of campus sexual assault received national attention in the early 1980s, NIU established a Sexual Assault Response Team (SART) to serve victims of sexual assault. SART was a coalition of campus offices (Counseling & Student Development,

University Health Service, University Police, University Judicial Office, and Sexual Assault/Abuse Services) with a designated representative in each office to streamline the process of help-seeking for victims and to collect data on reported assaults. The SART representatives, as a "sideline" to their regular duties, provided educational workshops for the campus community, but a coordinator of SART was needed to handle the volume of requests and to develop a consistent program that incorporated media materials and workshops. In response to this need, the first author in September of 1991 established Students Organized Against Rape (SOAR), a peer facilitated sexual assault education program that in time was to offer 25 to 30 educational workshops per year. Two years later, in 1993, the first author established a curriculum for a 3-credit, semester-long course to train the peer facilitators.

The SART representatives discussed on several occasions the possibility of providing mandatory sexual assault programming, but this idea was not fully developed until the spring of 1998, when a series of events occurred in the DeKalb community, on campus, and across the state. The chain of events started when the DeKalb community was the site of a drug bust by the Illinois Attorney General's Office. Three men not affiliated with the University were arrested for the distribution of the illegal drug gamma hydroxybutyrate (GHB) as a part of an operation to target GHB trafficking. GHB, along with Rohypnol, had been linked to a number of reports of drug-facilitated sexual assault across the country. Shortly thereafter, a NIU student came forward charging that she was sexually assaulted at a fraternity house while under the influence of GHB. The story of this assault was picked up by a Chicago television station and introduced on the evening news as "the sex scandal at NIU."

A number of similar incidents reported by victims across the state led the Illinois Attorney General to sponsor an Emergency Campus Summit on Date Rape Drugs. The Summit served as a conference and clearinghouse of information about sexual assault. Following the Summit, the Attorney General's Office issued a report outlining a number of policies and procedures that colleges and universities could implement to proactively address sexual assault and date-rape drugs within their communities. Mandatory sexual assault education that incorporated information about date rape drugs was strongly recommended for all new students attending Illinois colleges and universities. Thus, in response to the Summit's recommendation regarding education, NIU expanded its SOAR program to include mandatory sexual assault education workshops for the 3000 incoming freshmen at the beginning of the fall 1998 and spring 1999 semesters. The president of the university supported the initiative and earmarked monies to pay for additional graduate assistants, peer educators, and supplies. The SOAR sexual assault education program coordinator, this chapter's first author, spearheaded the initiative.

BEGINNING CONSIDERATIONS

When faced with the daunting task of implementing sexual assault education on a large-scale basis for incoming freshmen, we were fortunate to have a wealth of data and experience to guide us. Data gleaned over the years from SART's involvement with sexual assault victims provided us with some crucial information about the NIU campus:

- The majority of assaults took place in residence halls and off campus apartments.
- The most likely victims of sexual assault were freshmen women.
- The first 2 months of each semester had the highest incidence of assault.
- Over 65% of assaults involved alcohol and took place between acquaintances.

Furthermore, since its inception in 1991, SOAR's student facilitators have led scores of educational workshops on residence hall floors, sorority houses, and classrooms. Participants, for the most part, were females, with only about 10% of the workshops requested by male groups such as fraternities. The SART data and the programming experiences of the SOAR coordinator provided a foundation for topics that would be focal points within the mandatory workshop such as the role of bystanders, verbal and nonverbal communication, and alcohol and drug use.

FOUNDATIONAL PRINCIPLES: COMMUNITY AND RISK REDUCTION

A concept fundamental to both the SOAR program and the educational workshops is that sexual assault is a community issue, not just a woman's issue. We believe that sexual assault, and violence against women generally, impacts the lives of everyone. Thus, prevention and education efforts require a collaborative community of men and women, students and administrators, to speak out and to educate the campus constituents about rape.

At NIU (and most college campuses), the students at greatest risk for sexual assault are freshman women. With the freshman community concentrated in the residence halls, it was natural to establish a linkage between NIU's Student Housing and Dining Services and SOAR to implement mandatory sexual assault education. The central role that residence hall directors and resident assistants play in the lives of students is frequently overlooked. They have almost daily contact with students and are responsible for fostering a sense of community within the residence halls. Also, the hall staffs are often the first individuals whom rape victims approach for assistance. Thus, it was decided to hold the sexual assault education workshops on each residence hall floor to target the group most at risk for assault (freshmen), in one of the riskiest locations (residence halls), and where the critical issue of community could be simultaneously addressed. The focus on residence hall as community resulted in the incorporation within the workshops of a bystander behavior theme (see chapter 7), which focuses on empowering students to speak out and serve as leaders.

The other foundational principle, risk reduction of sexual assault, is often misunderstood and needs to be clarified. Some regard the term to mean that women are taught how to avoid rape by changing their behavior and by monitoring the behavior of the men they date. That conception of risk reduction is ill conceived because it implies that women are responsible for men's behavior, too. Our educational approach is to make a distinction between personal avoidability versus responsibility (cf. Abbey, 1987): women may be able to identify high-risk situations and environmental factors that can put them at risk of assault, but they are never responsible for another person's actions. Nor are they expected to stop rape by themselves. This concept of risk reduction allows participants to understand that the victim is not to be blamed.

SINGLE- OR MIXED-GENDER WORKSHOPS

Over the years, it was the experience of the SOAR coordinator and peer facilitators that participants' defensiveness was decreased and gender-based polarization minimized in single gender workshops or when the genders were together for only portions of the program. Too often we had witnessed male participants responding defensively to criticism by trying to convince the females that they were the rule-abiding exceptions as compared to the real "bad guys" out there. Thus, for the mandatory education workshops, we attempted to have separate groups with same gender facilitators. This decision was supported by a study comparing mixed- and single-sex formats, which found that the all-male program produced the only reduction in rape-related attitudes and myths among men (Berkowitz, 1994).

However, we soon learned that implementing single-gender workshops on a large scale would become a logistical nightmare, given that the majority of the 85 residence hall floors at NIU are coed. To address the floor gender compositions and to take into account the unique needs of men and women, we developed a 2-hour workshop in which men and women are combined during the first hour but segregated during the second hour. The topics presented in the mixed gender section are information about resources on the NIU campus, community issues, and definitions of terms. The men's section of the workshop addresses the issues of consent, peer pressure, and bystander behavior, with the women's concentrating on risk reduction and bystander behavior. At the University of Illinois, Champaign, mandatory sexual assault education has been in place for several years, and their staff assisted in the development of our workshop outline (M. Best, personal communication, April 13, 1998). With their permission, we made revisions to their workshop material and incorporated it into our treatment of bystander behavior and consent.

Selection and Training of Peer Educators

During the previous 6 years, the first author had been involved in the training of SOAR peer facilitators, some 100 in number, through a 3-credit, semester-long course. The course content covers the complex dynamics of sexual assault, forms and expressions of campus violence, and group leadership skills. Students in this SOAR training course are typically recruited from the ranks of student leaders and resident assistants. We also encourage former workshop participants with exceptional communication and leadership skills to enroll in the SOAR class and train as peer educators. Some of our most outstanding peer educators were themselves workshop participants.

In late spring of 1998 when SOAR was given the funds to implement the sexual assault education initiative, 12 students were enrolled in the course; 10 women and 2 men. Additional peer facilitators were urgently needed in anticipation of the incoming freshmen class of 3000, but there was no time to teach another semester-length course. Instead, an abbreviated training was held for a diverse cadre of 20 student leaders who were nominated by faculty members and student services administrators. Many of the 20 had not even been aware that this 3-credit course even existed. All were excited to be a part of the new educational initiative.

Although the students were not put through a formal screening process, we paid careful attention to their attitudes and perceptions throughout the training. Our previous experience taught us that sometimes students seek SOAR training for inappropriate reasons, such as to gain status, to make an organization "look better" (in the case of a fraternity on probation), or to work through their own issues as a victim or friend of a victim. During this abbreviated training, we recommended three participants leave the facilitation team due to some of these reasons. Removing trainees is never easy, but it is necessary to ensure we have leaders who are emotionally ready for the rigors of the facilitation role.

Training for the remaining 17 trainees occurred during an intensive weekend that included role-played practice sessions followed by feedback. At the weekend, each trainee received a manual containing a workshop outline, relevant readings, tables of NIU SART data, campus resources and phone numbers, and a sample of handouts that would later be given to the freshmen. For the second leg of their training, they were required to observe the more experienced facilitators who had responsibility for leading the workshops during the first week of mandatory sexual assault education for the freshman. Continuing through the semester, periodic trouble-shooting and discussion sessions are scheduled for both neophyte and experienced facilitators as part of their on-going training. These components of training are described in more detail below.

The Weekend Training

We began the weekend training session by developing rapport and trust between the peer facilitators. This was accomplished through exercises in which the trainees shared reasons for their becoming involved in sexual assault education, as well as disclosing some personal details about themselves. These disclosures naturally led to discussion about NIU's campus climate and participants' personal stories related to alcohol, drugs, college dating relationships, and sexuality. The more didactic portion of training progressed through (a) a review of literature on sexual assault, the dynamics of rape, and an overview of rape trauma and services for victims; (b) a how-to presentation of group leadership and discussion skills; and (c) a step-by-step survey of the workshop, including rationale for the contents. We concluded the weekend training by placing the peer facilitators into small groups to role play sections of the workshop, with a graduate assistant (GA) or senior peer educator serving as observer. The role-playing in small groups allowed everyone to learn from each other and obtain individualized feedback.

Observation of Experienced Facilitators and Ongoing Training

Following the weekend training, the peer educators are assigned several nights to observe the more experienced facilitators presenting the first week of workshops. Afterward, they volunteer to assist on specific workshop nights. Each workshop requires three or four peer educators, depending on the gender make-up of the floor, and one GA. Initially, the GAs play larger instructional roles, but as the peer educators grow in confidence and presentation skills, the GAs shift to a supervisory role, stepping in if the facilitators need assistance. Prior to each workshop, the assigned peer facilitators meet with the supervising GA to discuss process issues and to divide up the leadership responsibilities. Afterward, all members of the team meet to discuss any problems or concerns. Every 2 weeks, all of the facilitators convene to discuss how things are going, share concerns, and prepare for upcoming workshops. This meeting is essential for fostering group cohesiveness and for continuity in training because it involves necessary trouble shooting and the imparting of information about changes in the program and upcoming workshops.

PROGRAM DESCRIPTION AND FACILITATION

The SOAR workshop is specifically designed to address the unique needs of freshman mixed-gender audiences. Beyond conveying information to the freshmen, our aim is to empower them to make wise choices and to provide them with tools to reduce the risk, and therefore the incidence, of sexual assault.

The NIU sexual assault education program, offered to all first-year students, spans a period of 2 months, during which approximately 90 workshops are presented. The workshops are held Monday through Thursday, 7:00 p.m. to 9:00 p.m., with two or three taking place concurrently in several residence halls. Currently, the workshop consists of five sections:

- Introduction (10 minutes)
- Video and discussion (25 minutes)
- Definitions and terms (15 minutes)
- Issues pertaining to single gender (50 minutes)
- Closing (15–20 minutes)

We should mention that the workshop content, as distributed to the peer facilitators at the start of the program, has undergone continual revision and fine tuning. This has been part of our learning and discovery process. After the first couple weeks of presenting and observing the flow, we realized that there needed to be changes in the sequencing and content of workshop topics. For example, we felt it more beneficial to switch discussion about campus resources to the introduction from its original place in the closing. We discovered that some participants left the workshop early because they became emotionally overwhelmed when some of the content impinged on a past personal experience. Also, by the time of the closing, other students were fidgety and not listening carefully. Hence, it made sense to inform students up front about the important campus resources so those students who needed them most would have them.

Also, during the first month the GAs were constantly reviewing, observing, and analyzing the presentations to convey the information in as interesting and genuine fashion as possible. Presenters discovered their own style of delivery rather than relying on rote recitation. As a result of our open-mindedness, flexibility, and self-critiquing, by the end of the 2 months the written format was easier to follow and the presentation of the workshop went significantly more smoothly than on the first day.

THE WORKSHOP FORMAT

When we present to a mixed-gender group of freshmen, our format requires two rooms. One must be large enough to fit the entire group of men and women. In this room all students are gathered for the first three sections of the workshop. Together they (1) hear the workshop introduction and receive information about campus resources, (2) view and discuss a specially prepared video, and (3) learn about definitions and terms. We believe that by combining the men and women for this portion of the workshop an environment is created in which everyone can comfortably express her or his concerns about the issue of sexual assault. After completing the first three sections, men and women are separated for 50 minutes to discuss issues relevant to their gender. The groups reconvene in the large room for the workshop conclusion.

What follows are more detailed descriptions of each of the workshop's sections: introduction, video and discussion, definitions and terms, single gender issues, and closing.

Introduction

The workshop begins with the facilitators introducing themselves and describing the SOAR program at NIU. From the first instant, the facilitators endeavor to create a welcoming, empathic, and sincere atmosphere. They acknowledge that sexual assault is not an easy topic to discuss, and they share analogies and examples with which the audience is likely to be familiar. A warm-up activity follows that pulls for opinion and personal experiences. For example, the participants are asked, "Why do you think first year students are most at risk?" and if they remember when they first learned about sex. This latter question relates to the topic of sexual assault in that there may be shared stories and, for some, uncomfortable feelings. Opinions may be delicately challenged by the dissemination of data that reveal the actual incidence of sexual assaults at NIU and on campuses nationwide.

Facilitators cover the agenda and explain the ground rules for expected audience behavior, such as displaying sensitivity toward the topic. The facilitators strike a balance between their gatekeeping functions and the need to maintain a nonthreatening environment by injecting tension-relieving humor into the workshop where appropriate. Besides establishing at the outset a conducive learning atmosphere, the facilitators immediately strike up an interactive dialog that is maintained from introduction to closing. Audience involvement is crucial because it helps keep attention focused and increases retention of information. Although the same material is covered in every workshop, the interactive style imbues each with its own distinctive character.

Video

The summer before the workshops began, we scripted and assisted in producing a 9-minute video that serves as a stimulus for discussion of some sensitive issues pertaining to campus sexual assault: verbal and nonverbal communication, the role of bystanders, alcohol and drug use, risk reduction, and scope of personal responsibility. We chose these focal points based on our study of the SART data and from our previous workshop experiences. During our years of leading SOAR workshops, we found that these themes emerged repeatedly; thus, our plan was to introduce the themes in the mandatory workshop and weave them into the activities.

The theme of verbal and nonverbal communication addresses the misinterpretations and assumptions students can make about each other in social, dating, and sexual situations (e.g., when someone invites you into their room, he or she is interested in sex; "no" only means "no" if it is said emphatically). We raise questions about how students choose to drink and how alcohol and other drugs impact judgment or leave one vulnerable to assault. The topic of alcohol and other drug use is treated in a manner that encourages participants to consider how they choose to drink and how alcohol and other drugs impact one's judgment and ability to fend off an attack. Bystander behavior addresses the role that peers can play in intervening with friends during high-risk situations. In the video we use, bystander behavior comes into play with regard to such questions as: what responsibility, if any, do you have for an intoxicated friend? Should you let an intoxicated friend walk back to her room with her only escort being a man she has just met?

In casting the video, four actors were carefully selected to reflect cultural diversity. An African American female and Hispanic male portray a couple (Jill and Chris) who are friends of Elaine and David, two Caucasian students. The Caucasian actors were intentionally chosen to portray victim and perpetrator so as to avoid any invidious stereotyping of minorities. The video is plotted so that there is a common scenario with three different outcomes. After each of the three video segments, the workshop facilitators stop the video and engage participants in discussion. Although the video engages participants so that they can follow the sequence of events to gauge risk, we constructed the video to show how men and women can change their behavior to prevent sexual assault.

In the first segment, the four student-actors are drinking together in a residence hall room. Elaine and David eventually pair off to walk across campus to her own residence hall room. Before leaving, Jill extracts a promise from Elaine that she will call when she reaches her room. Elaine is slightly inebriated; David, we learn from Chris, might not have a trustworthy reputation. Back at Elaine's room, David continues drinking. Her communication toward him is equivocal: she changes into more comfortable "sweats," reclines on her bed, and nonverbally displays both discomfort with and tacit acquiescence toward David's gradual sexual advances. This first segment culminates with David forcing himself on Elaine despite her eventual verbal command for him to stop.

At this point, the facilitators encourage discussion of each character's behavior and what they might have done differently. For example, could Jill have done more for Elaine's safety? What were Chris's concerns and how might he have intervened? What were David's and Elaine's expectations, and how could they have been more explicitly communicated? What was Elaine communicating nonverbally? Does David have a responsibility to be more forthright with his intentions?

The second segment employs an ending where no assault occurs. Instead, David picks up on Elaine's inebriation and ambivalence, inquires about it ("What's going on here? I thought you wanted this?"), and stops his physical advances. One of the key discussion points triggered by this segment focuses on what participants would think and feel if the man were to abruptly back off as David did when confronted by "mixed" messages from Elaine. Interestingly, a large majority of the women participants express positive comments about David's forthright inquiry. Many women reveal that in their experiences men almost never clarify consent issues with them. This point proves extremely illuminating to the male participants.

The third segment depicts a situation in which assault is again prevented. This is due to Elaine's assertiveness ("we've had too much to drink, and we're going too fast"), and to more direct communication between Elaine and David about their feelings and intentions. Participants are invited to comment on critical differences in the characters' behaviors and reactions during this segment. Female participants, we have found, are about evenly split as to whether they believe they could envision themselves acting in such an assertive manner under similar circumstances.

Definitions and Terms

Following the video, the facilitators lead a 15-minute discussion of the definition of sexual assault according to Illinois law, as well as terms pertaining to sexual assault. To begin, participants are asked for their definition of sexual assault. After ideas are shared, one of the facilitators recites a summary of the definition according to Illinois law (Illinois Compiled Statues, 1998). Four important terms are extracted from this definition for closer examination: *penetration*, *force*, *threat of force*, and *knowing consent*. Participants give their opinions as to the meaning of these terms, and then facilitators guide them through the statute's definitions.

At times, some participants question the validity of these legal definitions. Facilitators, trained to avoid wrangling, are quick to point out that their job is to help participants understand the law, not necessarily accept it. Facilitators also note that laws may vary from state to state, but that students are bound by Illinois law if they commit a sexual assault in state.

At this point in the workshop, participants are likely to raise questions about false reports and consent. The most frequent questions from male participants are: (a) "What if she said yes the night before and changes her mind in the morning? Is that sexual assault?" (b) "What if a woman claims she was assaulted to get even with a man?" and (c) "If both parties are drunk, is it still sexual assault?" In response, facilitators point out that false reports of rape are rare and no more common (about 8%) than false reports of other crimes (FBI Uniform Crime Reports, 1995); moreover, it is far more likely that a woman will not report a rape. Facilitators also add that consenting to sex and then regretting a sexual act does not meet the definition of sexual assault. With respect to the question about alcohol and impairment, it should be kept in mind that consent from someone under the influence does not automatically constitute rape because there are varying levels of intoxication and capacities to consent. The facilitators explain that legally an individual who is intoxicated to the point of being passed out or asleep is regarded as unable to give consent to sex. However, if two drunken people engage in sex, the person who performs the penetration may be vulnerable to criminal or judicial charges. Many participants argue that it is "unfair" to blame the male if the woman has been drinking or if both parties are intoxicated. The facilitators are trained to acknowledge that although this may not seem "fair," this is how the law views such matters. To prevent drawn-out debate, facilitators will nudge the discussion forward, encouraging participants to examine how they can reduce their risk of engaging in the dangers of drunken sex and thereby reduce the risk of assault, sexually transmitted disease, pregnancy, and regretful sex.

After discussing these dangers, the guidelines for consent are introduced as a framework for positive behavior and a model that reduces the likelihood of misunderstandings that a man will be accused of a sexual assault. These guidelines (see Berkowitz, 1994) help take the legalistic discussion out of the workshop and focus on positive, healthy behavior. Consent is present when both parties are fully conscious, are equally free to act (e.g., the woman is not coerced or constrained), and have clearly communicated their intent.

This third section concludes with a brief discussion of NIU's sexual assault policy, which is contained in the student judicial handbook. We emphasize that NIU seeks to have a safe environment for all students and that the adoption of the sexual assault policy is to set forth definitions, outline reporting procedures and adjudication, identify the range of penalties, and provide resources for education and support. An important point of policy is that NIU will not bring charges of underage drinking against victims who report alcohol-related sexual assaults. Participants are encouraged to review the policy and to pursue any questions with the SOAR staff or NIU's Judicial Office.

Women's Section

At this point, participants are divided into single gender groups that convene in separate rooms. Students are assured that this division by gender is only to allow groups to discuss issues that are of specific concern to men and women.

Commensurate with the workshop's programming goals, the women's section targets the issues of risk reduction (i.e., identifying characteristics of sexually aggressive men), bystander behavior, verbal and nonverbal communication, and the role played by alcohol. The activities utilized to generate dialogue are *sentence completions* and *social/sexual scenarios*.

Not only does the sentence completion activity help the women identify beliefs and attitudes about sexual assault, it also allows for some of those beliefs and attitudes to be challenged without individuals being attacked. It also serves as an ice-breaker whereby facilitators can gauge the soundness of the beliefs and attitudes about sexual assault. Sometimes an audience will respond with all the appropriate answers, and the facilitators will quickly assess that these participants will need extra challenging. The activity begins with the women responding to three statements:

- I do not think I will be sexually assaulted because . . .
- During interactions with men, it bothers me when . . .
- List the precautions you to take to reduce your risk of sexual assault by a stranger . . . an acquaintance . . .

The purpose of each of the statements is to generate discussion from which specific topics can be elicited. For example, the first statement is designed to bring to the fore the women's belief that they are immune to sexual assault risk, because sexual assault happens to women who are "bad" (e.g., dress provocatively, drink, use drugs, tease men). Such a belief contributes to victim blaming, leads women to ignore risk situations, and obscures the real cause of sexual assault, which is men's illegitimate attempts to exert power and control over women. Facilitators counter with questions (e.g., "Does anyone want to respond to that?" "Does anyone think or feel differently?") that lend themselves to peers challenging peers. Regarding the belief that abstaining from alcohol prevents sexual assault, facilitators point out that one's intoxicated peers still represent environmental risks and that any nonalcoholic drink can be spiked with rape-facilitating drugs.

Following sentence completion, women are divided into groups of four or five to discuss bystander behavior scenarios. This activity is intended to equip women with ideas and strategies for extricating themselves from uncomfortable situations. In their "mini-groups," participants are given a few minutes to read the scenario and brainstorm realistic ways to cope with the risky situation. In the meantime, facilitators circulate among the mini-groups, either verbally reinforcing some of the strategies or challenging participants to consider the consequences of the strategies they have chosen.

After the sentence completion activity, the participants respond to two "real-life" social and sexual situations. Our goal is to equip participants with ideas and strategies to reduce the risk of an assault or to be effective interveners. The scenarios, based on actual experiences, target the themes of verbal and nonverbal communication and bystander behaviors. In the first scenario, a man and a woman, close friend since high school, spend an evening visiting and drinking with old high school peers. The man, who is visiting from another university, asks to spend the night in the woman's room, claiming that he is intoxicated and unable to drive. Later that evening, the woman awakens in shock to find her friend on top of her, kissing her and removing her clothes. In the second scenario, two female friends are at a party, drinking. One of the friends, clearly intoxicated, is being "hit on" by a man who invites her to join him in his room. Listening to all of this, the more sober friend feels uncertain about what to do next.

With participants again in mini-groups, the following questions are used to generate discussion to the first scenario: (a) what would you do in this situation? (b) what would prevent you from asserting yourself? (c) what could you do that might stop his behavior? Discussion questions for the second scenario are: (a) what responsibility do you have, if any, for intervening in this situation? (b) what do you do if your friend insists she is "okay," even though she is evidently intoxicated? (c) if you intervene, and the man pressures you to "mind your own business" or insists he can get her home safely, what do you do?

After a few minutes for discussion, the groups are asked to share their ideas with all the women participants. Using the first scenario as an example, aggressive responses (e.g., "Kick him between the legs," "Punch or scratch him") to the first question predominate, and these usually evoke a lot of laughter. The workshop facilitators must support such responses but also challenge the participants to consider whether all women could react in a similarly aggressive or assertive manner (note discussion question b pertaining to the first scenario). This challenge allows participants to share that they are not as assertive with someone they know or care about for fear of embarrassing the other person and helps to generate some alternative (and creative) ways to escape from a potential sexual assault: "What are you doing? Get off me! I have to go to the bathroom!" "I'm having my period and I think I'm going to throw up!").

Once the scenario discussion is completed, the facilitators conclude this section of the workshop by stressing that these activities do not imply that it is the sole responsibility of women to prevent sexual assault or that reducing risk requires women to be accountable for men's actions. Lastly, any remaining questions are answered prior to the men and women regrouping for the workshop's conclusion.

Men's Section

To accomplish the overall programming goals, the men's section addresses the role of alcohol and other drugs in sexual assault, bystander behavior, and verbal and nonverbal communication. As with the women, the activities used to engender discussion are sentence completions and social/sexual scenarios. Before getting to these activities, the men usually have some carry-over questions about the sexual assault law and consent. At this point, a typical question is: "Can you tell me again how I know if I have consent?" There are also more complaints about how the law is unfair.

The facilitators are prepared for some rowdiness, graphic language, crude or sexist remarks, and laughter due to the men's nervousness and discomfort. Some participants use sexist or crude comments as *tests*, to see if facilitators can play along with some of the fun (which is important to do, within limits, to ease anxiety within this group) or if the facilitators can maintain their composure (and hence, credibility).

The sentence completion activity begins with men generating responses to five statements that are posted around the room:

- A woman is consenting to sex when she . . .
- A man is owed or should expect sex when . . .

- I feel manipulated by women when . . .
- When a woman sends me conflicting messages where her behavior says yes and her words say no, I believe . . .
- I feel a woman wants sex when . . .

Each incomplete statement is crafted to evoke specific salient issues or topics. For example, the purpose of the first sentence stem is to bring to the fore men's stereotypes about consent and to set the stage for deeper discussion of the guidelines for consent (see Berkowitz, 1994). Responses to the statements are facilitated in a manner similar to that used in the women's section. After the men have completed the activity in their small group, a facilitator reviews responses and reads aloud those that are thoughtful, responsible, or humorous, as well as some that reflect rape-supportive beliefs and misunderstandings of consent. Typical responses to the first incomplete sentence are: "When she comes back to my place," "after we've made out for a while," "if she does not stop me," and "when she says 'yes'." Clearly, some of these responses are examples of rape-supportive attitudes that require challenging. Our facilitation strategy is to invite the participants to challenge each other, using questions such as, "Does anyone have a different opinion? Does anyone want to respond to that?"

Next, sexual scenarios are introduced to equip the men with ideas and strategies to reduce the risk of perpetrating an assault or to be an effective intervener. The two scenarios pull for themes concerning consent, the use of alcohol, peer pressure, and bystander behavior. The first scenario places the workshop participants at a party with peers who have been drinking. Participants are to envisage an intoxicated male friend who is interested in inviting a woman back to his room. In the second scenario, participants are confronted with a situation in which a male friend is considering having sex with a female friend who has passed out in his room. The male friend is also being encouraged by some members of the residence hall floor to have sex.

In small groups of four or five, the men are given 5 to 7 minutes to construct responses that are later shared with the entire complement of men. Using scenario one to illustrate the process, we find that the majority of male participants recognize that the alcohol has impaired the friend's judgment; however, they are conflicted about their responsibility to intervene. Most are clueless about the concept of bystander behavior or what to expect if they did intervene. Although some men believe they need to stop the friend, more typical responses are: "I should mind my own business. If he wants to go back with her, why should I stop him?" or "He's old enough to make his own decisions." The facilitators challenge these choices by asking, "What if the man in the scenario is you and your friend stood by and did nothing? How would you feel?" or, "What if the woman in the scenario is someone you care about?" These challenges usually lead to a heated discussion concerning bystander behavior and the circumstances in which peers hold back from intervening with each other. We find that participants commonly share incidents, and remorse, when they should have intervened with a friend, but did not (e.g., with an intoxicated friend who insists on driving). These disclosures have a powerful impact on the participants, but facilitators, we have learned, need to handle them carefully to ensure that they do not shut down the thread of discussion.

The Closing

When both genders are reconstituted, facilitators allow the men and women to share some points from their small groups. Following a summarization of the workshop's major points, the facilitators close the workshop with comments on three important topics: (a) the impact of victim blame, (b) reviewing campus resources for sexual assault victims and survivors, and (c) campus opportunities for proactive involvement against sexual assault. Briefly, facilitators explain society's tendency to blame victims for the assault; highlight victims' feelings of shock, disbelief, fear, and grief; and describe the impact of these emotions on victims' help-seeking. Because assault victims are likely first to approach a friend, we distribute a handout that contains suggestions for how to offer support and comfort as well as information about helping resources on campus. Finally, facilitators introduce the idea of participants becoming active agents within the campus community to reduce the incidence of sexual assault at NIU, an idea commensurate with the bystander intervention philosophy. A variety of options are offered that include: enrolling in the SOAR course, serving as a peer facilitator, attending other related educational events, challenging sexist jokes or crude comments about sexual assault, and performing community volunteer work.

WORKSHOP EVALUATION

Our one-session educational workshop was designed to address the following goals:

- Inform participants about campus resources and the issue of sexual assault as it pertains to the NIU community
- Loosen and challenge myths about sexual assault
- Raise consciousness levels
- Make explicit various risk factors such as date rape drugs and alcohol
- Introduce the concepts of bystander behavior and community responsibility

It was not our goal to target males who are at risk of raping or to change the proclivity of men who might rape since these individuals have been shown to possess certain personality characteristics (e.g., hostility towards women, impulsivity, hypermasculinity, and antisocial orientation) that are resistant to change (see chapter 1). The literature suggests that participants who attend single session workshops do not change their attitudes or behaviors (Borden, Karr, & Caldwell-Colbert, 1988) but report being more informed about sexual assault prevention and rape counseling services (Holcomb, Sondag, & Hatton-Holcomb, 1993). Our goal is to enlist the support of the nonraping men to thwart and challenge the behavior of the sexually aggressive men by focusing on the issues of risk reduction, bystander behavior, and consent for sexual activity.

To obtain a preliminary understanding of the impact of the workshops, participants were asked to complete a 10-item survey that was designed to assess their knowledge of the workshop content in the target areas. Separate surveys were used for men and women. Survey items for women included questions about forced sexual experiences, ability to identify sexually aggressive behaviors and characteristics of men, and appropriate actions for reducing the risk of assault and intervening with peers. Items for men included questions about the use of physical force, coercion, or alcohol to obtain sex; definitions of consent; and appropriate actions for intervening with a peer.

We found that for the women there were significant increases, preworkshop to postworkshop, in their endorsing appropriate responses with respect to:

- identifying characteristics of sexually aggressive men (e.g., men who ignore personal space, abuse alcohol or other drugs, sexualize conversations)
- identifying behaviors that reduce the risk of sexual assault (e.g., trusting one's judgment, taking precautions when drinking)
- identifying resources for victims
- intervening with peers in high-risk situations (e.g., notifying a Resident Assistant or locating others to help a peer who drank too much in a party situation).

For the men, there were significant increases from the preworkshop to the postworkshop assessment in respondents endorsing appropriate responses in:

- acknowledging that sex with an intoxicated or drugged partner can be considered sexual assault
- identifying the criteria for consent in sexual activity
- identifying alternatives to using force in equivocal sexual situations (e.g., pausing to inquire of partner)
- intervening with peers in high-risk situations (e.g., notifying a Resident Assistant or locating others to help a peer who drank too much in a party situation)

CHAPTER SUMMARY

Sexual assault is an issue that many college campuses are addressing through educational programming. When faced with implementing a mandatory sexual assault education program, we found that not only are there many different philosophies and methods for programming but that the research to gauge the effectiveness of such programs is still in its infancy. We attempted to incorporate the philosophies and workshop goals that were reasonable to implement in a short period of time (approximately 2 hours) and that would transfer well to our institution. We hope that by sharing our process we can assist other institutions that may be considering initiating such a program.

REFERENCES

Abbey, A. (1987). Perceptions of personal avoidability versus responsibility: How do they differ? *Basic and Applied Social Psychology, 8,* 3–20.

Berkowitz, A. D. (1994). A model acquaintance rape prevention program for men. In A.D. Berkowitz (Ed.), *Men and rape: Theory, research, and prevention programs in higher education* (pp. 35–42). New Directions for Student Services, No. 65. San Francisco: Jossey-Bass.

Borden, L. A., Karr, S. K., & Caldwell-Colbert, A. T. (1988). Effects of a university rape prevention program on attitudes and empathy toward rape. *Journal of College Student Development, 29,* 132–136.

Federal Bureau of Investigation Uniform Crime Reports (1995). Washington, DC: U.S. Department of Justice.

Holcomb, D. R., Sondag, K. A., & Hatton-Holcomb, L. C. (1993). Healthy dating: A mixed-gender date rape workshop. *Journal of American College Health, 41,* 155–158.

Illinois Compiled Statues. Chapter 720, 5/12-12(f) (1998).

CHAPTER 6

Changing a Culture: Sexual Assault Prevention in the Fraternity and Sorority Community

Ron Binder*

The prevalence of sexual assault among college students is well documented (Koss, 1988; Parrot & Bechhofer, 1991). Studies indicate that 25% of undergraduate college women are the victims of sexual assault or sexual coercion (Koss, 1988). A similar percentage of undergraduate men either admit to sexual assault or sexual coercion, or demonstrate behavior that fits the definition of sexual assault (Elliot & Brantley, 1997). Campus administrators know that during the college years many students will be the victims of sexual assault or will be close friends with someone who is a victim of sexual assault. Although the fact of sexual assault is well substantiated, prevention is less certain. After presenting some issues that characterize campus sexual assault and place it within the context of the fraternity and sorority community, this chapter will deal primarily with what can be done to change the culture surrounding sexual assault in that community.

---

*The author is indebted to Loretta Bohn for her editorial assistance and to Don Apparius for the reference to *Davis v. Monroe County Board of Education.*

120

When examining the issue of sexual assault, it is helpful to note how sexual assault perception and prevention have evolved. A number of years ago, it was thought that sexual assault occurred primarily between two individuals who did not know each other (i.e., stranger rape). The prevailing prevention strategy focused exclusively on the potential victims, primarily women, and included avoiding unlit areas on campus, walking in pairs, and learning self-defense techniques. Campus committees examined poorly lit areas to make recommendations on improved lighting, particularly after an assault. Some of these strategies, like emergency call boxes on campuses, are still in use and work well when trying to prevent sexual assault between strangers.

The profile of sexual assault on the college campus has changed over the past decades. Studies reveal that stranger rape accounts for a small percentage of sexual assaults on campus. A recent college survey by Elliot and Brantley (1997) showed that sexual assault by strangers is as low as 2% (3% for women and 1% for men). The reality is that most instances of sexual assault occur between individuals who know each other. Under these circumstances, the strategies for dealing with sexual assault are vastly different. Gary (1994) believes that the campus response to sexual assault has changed for four reasons. First, the roles of men and women in society are changing. Second, the terms "date rape" and "acquaintance rape" are now attached to behavior and are in the lexicon of students and administrators. Third, society is reframing its perceptions of the responsibility and blame for rape. Finally, the Campus Awareness and Security Act (1992) mandates that colleges and universities provide educational programs on sexual assault. A fifth reason, not cited by Gary, might be that universities and administrators are required to report crime statistics, both on and off campus, to the public and to prospective students and parents (Student Right to Know and Campus Security Act, 1990). These reports become public documents. As a result, the public holds institutions accountable for their prevention of, and response to, assault incidents.

CHARACTERISTICS OF SEXUAL ASSAULT

Understanding the characteristics of date and acquaintance rape on the college campus allows for greater opportunities for prevention. Burkhart and Stanton (1988) and Parrot (1989) noted that victims tend to be female, have low self-esteem, follow the traditional feminine sex roles, have had previous encounters involving sexual coercion or sexual assault, and have high status within their peer groups. Perpetrators tend to be male, do not realize their behavior constitutes sexual assault, have low self-esteem, follow the traditional masculine sex role, and want to improve their status among peers.

Muehlenhard, Friedman, and Thomas (1985) found that men with traditional views of sex roles justified sexual assault under three conditions: if the date ended up in the man's apartment, if the woman asked the man out, or if the man paid the expenses. Ward, Chapman, Cohn, White, and Williams (1991) found that most experiences happen in residences, are party-related, and usually involve alcohol use. Finally, Aizenman, Andrews, Witt, and Burns (1994) stated that date rape occurs on the second or third date, at the residence of the offender or victim, and in situations where the offender and victim are not emotionally involved with each other. Taken together, these studies create a portrait of sexual assault on the college campus that allows educators to fine-tune their prevention programs.

THE ROLE OF ALCOHOL

The issues of alcohol abuse and sexual assault go hand in hand. The majority of the victims and perpetrators consumed alcohol prior to or during the incident (Perkins, 1992). In addition, 68% of college students who have had intercourse have done so while under the influence of alcohol (Elliot & Brantley, 1997). Abbey (1991) contends that alcohol is indirectly responsible for assault; she postulates that men misperceive women's sexual intent and that the use of alcohol by either party worsens these misperceptions. The result is a situation ripe for sexual assault. The perpetrator's use of alcohol lessens the sense of accountability ("I did not know what I was doing"); the victim's use of it increases self-blame ("I shouldn't have been drinking"). These findings, combined with a recent study concerning the prevalence of alcohol abuse in the fraternity and sorority (Greek) community (Wechsler, Austin, & DeJong, 1996), indicate an explosive situation.

PROFILE OF THE FRATERNITY AND SORORITY COMMUNITY

The fraternity and sorority community on most college campuses comprises a significant proportion of the undergraduate student population. Second only to the number of students living in residence halls, and more than the number of students involved in intercollegiate athletics, Greeks tend to be highly organized and highly visible. At state-assisted schools, between 10% and 15% of students belong to such groups. At some major universities over 25% of the undergraduate population belongs to a fraternity or sorority. At a few small schools the figure is above 50%. The percentage of campus leaders who are members of the Greek community is disproportionately high. Women in sororities make up the largest undergraduate women's group on most campuses.

Some administrators and faculty have advocated removing fraternities and sororities from the campus as a solution to sexual assault, but this view is misguided. Under the First Amendment guarantee of freedom of association, fraternities and sororities have a legal right to exist at state universities. There is recent speculation that this right may be conferred at private schools also (Burke, 1999). Therefore, for the foreseeable future these student groups will remain an integral part of the campus environment. The challenge for administrators is to work with these organizations, their alumni, and their national headquarters to change the culture of sexual assault by making the most of characteristics unique to the Greek community. Those who ignore this population may miss an opportunity to bring about campus culture change.

SEXUAL ASSAULT AND THE FRATERNITY AND SORORITY COMMUNITY

Sexual assault in the fraternity and sorority community is well documented (Boeringer, Shehan, & Akers, 1991; Ehrhart & Sandler, 1985; Schwartz, 1991; Warshaw, 1988). Boeringer et al. (1991) found that in all-male groups, such as athletic teams and fraternities, the traditional feminine and masculine roles are reinforced, and rape myths tend to be more widely accepted. These characteristics have been shown to lead to a higher prevalence of sexual assault perpetrated by men. Fraternities may be particularly vulnerable because they attract some members whose personal characteristics place them at higher risk for perpetrating sexual assault.

Garrett-Gooding and Senter (1987) found a moderate relationship between fraternity membership and attitudes toward sexual coercion. In a shocking study concerning gang rape, Sanday (1990) found that athletic teams or fraternities committed 20 of the 24 gang rapes reported on college campuses since 1980. O'Sullivan (1993) postulated that such rapes involve a "male bonding," with the focus on gaining the acceptance of other men within the group rather than on the actual sex act. In group-think mentality, individuals commit acts they would not normally consider. For example, typical perpetrators, aged 20 to 24, attend a social event where alcohol and drugs are being used and join in what begins as an acquaintance rape. The commonality of these elements is perhaps one of the greatest concerns for campus administrators who work with cohesive groups like athletic teams and fraternities. Given such findings, directing resources especially toward educating these student groups—as part of an overall prevention program—is a wise use of funds.

Studies of risk of sexual assault among sorority women have produced equivocal results. Ogletree (1993) found that sorority women were not necessarily more susceptible to sexual assault; Schwartz (1991) showed that, due to their acceptance of the traditional gender roles, they were more susceptible. Bohmer and Parrot (1993) suggested that sorority women might be at increased risk due to their likelihood of socializing with fraternity men. Administrators at large campuses and at private schools should note Koss's (1988) finding that women on such campuses actually have a much higher rate of sexual assault. These studies suggest that the fraternity and sorority environment and the athletic environments are where prevention efforts should be directed if the culture of sexual assault is to be challenged.

OPPORTUNITIES TO PREVENT SEXUAL ASSAULT

Many opportunities to prevent sexual assault exist in the fraternity and sorority community. Increasingly, national fraternities and sororities expect chapters to provide members with annual educational programming on sexual assault. They make available excellent information and programming resources such as workshops, national and regional conferences, videotapes, and articles in national publications. For example, Phi Kappa Tau fraternity and Delta Zeta sorority for a number of years have produced a program at their joint regional educational conference that examines sexual assault from a student's perspective. Often, these programs are held in conjunction with local rape crisis centers, whose staff may make presentations. At other times national organizations may sponsor expert alumni or professional guest speakers whom colleges might not otherwise afford. These programs and events, which can be opened to the entire campus, highlight the issue of sexual assault.

National headquarters can also enact policies to combat sexual assault. An excellent example is the prohibition of "little sister" programs, whereby women become affiliated with a fraternity in a surrogate relationship. Members of these programs, which functioned as auxiliaries, were not full members of the sponsoring organization and had no voice in its governance. Problems associated with little sister groups were common. Aizenman et al. (1994) related the exploitation of little sisters for gang rape. Often, to gain membership as a little sister, a woman was expected to have sex with a high percentage of the brothers, or at the very least, she had to be dating a member of the fraternity. In addition to the sexual assault ramifications, lawsuits from little sisters suing for full membership under Title IX caused most national fraternities and sororities to abandon these groups in the early 1990s to preserve their single-sex status. Many sorority national organizations also prohibited their members from taking membership in such groups. The policy implications for colleges and universities are clear: these types of groups should not be allowed to exist on the college campus. University recognition and other privileges should be withheld from big and little sister groups. National organizations should be informed if such groups exist on the campus.

Besides the nationals' efforts at programming and policy making, colleges and universities can play a preventive role by offering programming on issues of risk management, alcohol and substance abuse, and sexual assault. Presented as Greek 101 or new member programs, these seminars are frequently aimed at new members of fraternities and sororities, although other high-risk groups, such as athletic teams and students new to residence halls, can also benefit. The new environment and the myriad adjustment issues that male and female students must face are not to be taken lightly. Since sexual assaults tend to take place in the first few weeks of school (Finely & Corty, 1993), offering these programs at this time is a way to target resources when they are most needed. In addition to programming aimed at new members, colleges and universities also provide programming for entire chapters. Having chapters use the expertise available on the campus creates a win–win proposition, as chapters often use campus programs to satisfy national requirements that they provide this type of education to their members. We will discuss later how such programs are designed and implemented.

Finally, many colleges and universities now require fraternities and sororities to document annual programming in areas such as alcohol prevention, risk management, and sexual assault to retain institutional recognition. The University of Maryland, Ohio State University, Emory University, Louisiana State University, and University of North Carolina–Chapel Hill are examples. Although these requirements are relatively new, they are a helpful tool when universities work with fraternities and sororities. Similar opportunities, to be discussed later, present themselves when an individual or a chapter faces disciplinary action.

THE NEED FOR A COMPREHENSIVE APPROACH

If sexual assault is to be prevented in the Greek community, it must be addressed in a comprehensive manner. Although education programs are important, they should be part of a complete plan rather than a single strategy. Such a plan involves at least four elements: presenting educational programs, stating clear policies and sanctions, monitoring the types of social events, and anticipating problem situations for students.

Presenting Educational Programs

A comprehensive sexual assault education program in the fraternity and sorority community is directed at new members and entire chapters and consists of several educational programs: risk management, alcohol and substance abuse, and sexual assault. In this way, students not only learn about sexual assault, but also about issues that are closely linked to its occurrence. Providing educational programming on a comprehensive level increases the chance of a substantive change in sexual assault within the campus culture.

Risk Management Programs

A risk management program sets the stage by showing the prevalence of risk on a college campus, particularly for individuals in the Greek community. This program: (a) details the number of incidents involving fraternities and sororities, (b) presents the types of legal cases generated nationally and locally through such risk, (c) discusses the types of lawsuits arising from such acts, and (d) educates students on the school's and nationals' risk management policies. Risk management strategies are taught in the hope that students will make informed decisions about how much risk they and their organizations are willing to assume. Additionally, this program is important in helping students realize that they take on an added level of responsibility when they join fraternities and sororities and that they should act accordingly. Finally, this program should highlight the promise every member takes when joining a Greek organization to uphold policies and to show care and concern for fellow members. The campus Greek advisor, university legal counsel, representatives of the national organizations, or an outside speaker specializing in risk management can provide this type of program. It is vital that students receive copies of all relevant policies, including the campus sexual assault policy, if they are to be expected to abide by those policies. National fraternities and sororities have been educating their members on risk management for a number of years. Campuses should also be providing this education to ground students in the expectations of their campus, including the expectations for sexual conduct.

Alcohol and Substance Abuse Programs

The alcohol and substance abuse program is relevant because of the connection between alcohol and sexual assault. Finley and

Corty (1993) estimate that 95% of sexual assaults involve the use of alcohol—in some cases to physiologically toxic levels. This study also documented that 25% of students (evenly split among men and women) had unwanted sex due to the use of alcohol and that 15% of the men and 10% of the women had more than one such incident of regret involving alcohol. As noted earlier, this phenomenon is interesting in that alcohol is not necessarily a direct cause of sexual assault; rather, alcohol interferes with how men and women perceive each other's intentions. Given the recent data on the level of alcohol abuse and binge drinking in the Greek community (Wechsler et al., 1996), this group is primed for education on this subject.

Most student health centers have staff who are fully qualified to provide such education. Topics that need attention in an alcohol and substance abuse seminar include:

- the prevalence of problems associated with alcohol (using local campus data to increase the impact)
- signs of abuse and addiction
- how to get help for oneself or friends
- secondhand effects of alcohol abuse on friends and roommates
- specific substances that affect sexual conduct

One substance is Rohypnol. Known as the "date-rape drug," this colorless and odorless drug, when added to drinks, causes a victim to black out. People under its influence are highly susceptible to sexual assault, with the added problem that they cannot identify their attacker(s). Students need to know about such drugs—drugs that were unknown as recently as 5 years ago—and what to do if they suspect that they are victims. (The reader is directed to chapter 3 for more information on Rohypnol and other rape-facilitating drugs.) Staff in the student health center should know how to detect such a drug and what to do on first contact with a victim. When substance issues arise, it is likely that the student health services staff is proficient in the delivery of information; administrators should rely on this group of professionals to deliver this program. A good alcohol and substance abuse program offers another opportunity to discuss the issue of sexual assault and increases the chances of a meaningful change in the campus culture.

Sexual Assault Programs

There is considerable debate as to the delivery and content of sexual assault programs. There are four basic issues: (1) whether the program should be single or mixed gender, (2) whether it should involve peer educators or staff, (3) when to offer it, (4) and if it should be required. Research on these issues has yielded mixed results. Some studies have shown that single-gender workshops produce significant change (Lenihan, Rawlins, Eberly, Buckley, & Masters, 1992), while others show change in coed groups (Harrison, Downes, & Williams, 1991). Although education on sexual assault can affect men's perceptions (e.g., Johnson & Russ, 1989), the literature is inconclusive about the educational methods that are most effective. Practitioners may find that other considerations, such as logistics and opportunities, will more greatly influence their decisions about program content and delivery. For example, some Greek professionals advise fraternities only. This creates an opportunity for a program for men only. Other Greek advisors work with both fraternities and sororities and thus have an opportunity for mixed-gender programs (although they may opt to have single-gender programs). As an advisor under both systems at different schools, I have used both methods, with little difference in outcome. I do not imply that future studies will not find differences in outcomes, but that the current literature does not offer a compelling case to offer programs either way.

Many educators believe that a peer-led program is preferable; others believe that staff- or faculty-led programs work better, and arguments can be made for a combination. Berkowitz, Burkhart, and Bourg (1994), at Hobart College, select and train highly motivated undergraduate peers to deliver a single-gender program on sexual assault for new male students in a small group setting, usually in the residence halls or Greek houses. This program is predicated on the idea that new male students look to their peer leaders to set the tone for the campus.

The University of Georgia has offered two types of programs over the years. Originally, Georgia used a single-gender (men's) program presented jointly by staff and students. Personnel in the Police Department, Student Affairs, and Greek Life delivered content, with student discussion leaders assuring participants that they were allowed to speak freely on the issue in that setting. This engendered frank discussions among the students as to the confusing issue of sexual assault, society's mixed messages on the subject, dating expectations in a new environment, and the expectations of new members. The present approach utilizes professional speakers who address both new members and, in an in-service training session, chapter presidents (Atkinson, personal communication, July 6, 1999).

The University of North Carolina–Chapel Hill, which follows the National Interfraternity Conference's (NIC; 1999) model for sexual assault education, is a staff-delivered program that makes use of campus and community resources. Students attending the program rotate through a number of stations where experts address different topics concerning sexual assault. Staff from Student Health Services deal with the health aspects of sexual assault, including such drugs as Rohypnol. Student Legal Services staff talk about North Carolina's laws and the legal ramifications of a sexual assault charge. Representatives from the Dean of Students Office discuss the campus policy regarding sexual assault and the process involved in either pressing charges or defending oneself. The Orange County Rape Crisis Center personnel detail how to work with survivors of sexual assault—both the immediate attention they need and the long-term care they may require. Finally, invitees from women's groups address the sexual stereotypes that pervade the college campus. This format has built-in flexibility because students are rotated through the stations and the number of stations can vary depending on the issues that need to be addressed.

Prior to the current program at UNC–Chapel Hill, students and staff worked together to present the issues of sexual assault, relying on small groups to foster discussion and cover some of the above topics. Although this program was viewed as a success, students and staff, liking the NIC model, wanted to try a different approach. This experience teaches that no one idea may be correct for a campus and that the key is to explore the many facets involved in such programs and choose the one that best meets the campus's needs. Administrators should also realize that programs can change over time.

STATING CLEAR POLICIES AND SANCTIONS

Clear policies are essential to preventing sexual assault (Hughes & Sandler, 1987). Bachman, Paternoster, and Ward (1992) have documented the deterrent effect of sexual assault policies. Spelling out what constitutes sexual assault for a particular campus—and widely disseminating that definition—is important, as the topic is fraught with misunderstandings.

The Student Right to Know and Campus Security Act of 1990 mandates that colleges and universities receiving federal funds must certify that they have policies and programs in place to deal with campus crime, including sexual assault. (In fact, the Supreme Court noted in *Davis v. Monroe County Board of Education* [1999] that administrators who are apprised of sexual assault allegations but do not act create federal funding liability for the university, regardless of what policies may or may not exist.) Most universities include such policies in their student handbooks, which are generally distributed to new students at orientation or when they matriculate. Merely including the policy in the student handbook is not enough. It is imperative that sexual assault policies, which have been shown to affect a large portion of the campus community, are highlighted as often as possible. Students need to know what constitutes sexual assault on their campus and where they can go for help and guidance. Students also need to know the consequences for violating policies. Whenever a program about sexual assault is given, staff should endeavor to distribute the campus sexual assault policy.

In addition to highlighting and disseminating sexual assault policies, institutions should also address the issue of campus reach. That is, how far does the campus policy extend? Studies show that most sexual assaults occur off-campus (Koss, 1988), generally in student residences. The Higher Education Amendments of 1998 mandate that colleges' and universities' annual security reports include student behavior that occurs off-campus. Thus, campus policies should cover not just the geographically defined campus, but should reach to the areas that students actually inhabit. For many campuses this will include private residence halls, the student organizations (mostly, but not exclusively, Greek housing), and apartment complexes.

Finally, policies need to include student organizations and athletic teams, not just the behavior of individual students. Student organizations, whether housed on campus or off, have responsibility for their actions, particularly if an assault occurred on their property or at their event. It is wise not to state a geographic limit because student-group and athletic-team behavior can occur anywhere, including in neighboring states. The University of Georgia, for example, has jurisdiction over student-group behavior without geographic limit. However, the organizations have due-process rights, just like individuals (*Alpha Tau Omega Fraternity, Tau Chapter, Undergraduate Students v. University of Pennsylvania and George S. Koval*, 1984).

MONITORING THE TYPES OF SOCIAL EVENTS

One of the unique characteristics of the fraternity and sorority community is the many types of theme events held throughout the year. Historically White fraternities and sororities host mixers between a fraternity and a sorority, band parties for invited guests, date parties, formal events, out-of-town events, and trips to the beach (for chapters near a coast). Historically Black fraternities and sororities sponsor late-night dances on campus, sometimes followed by an even later off-campus party. Although not all events necessarily lend themselves to sexual assaults, some, particularly those involving overnight stays, tend to generate more problems than others.

Fraternity and sorority formals, held annually by each chapter, involve dates and very dressy attire. As a precaution, most sororities require their chapters to choose a location within 30 miles of campus, thus not necessitating an overnight stay. Administrators who work with sororities should ensure that these policies are enforced by the students. Fraternities, however, generally do not make these stipulations, with the result that overnight stays—sometimes in exotic locations far from campus—are common. Overnight stays and the presence of alcohol can create a situation that may encourage sexual assault, particularly for new members attending for the first time. Students should be encouraged to discuss sleeping arrangements ahead of time.

Though lacking dressy attire, beach trips are similar to formals in that the chapter will go away for the weekend, with dates. Again, if sleeping arrangements are not talked about ahead of time, new members especially are put in a volatile situation. A discussion with student leaders at an all-Greek retreat can identify some of the pitfalls of such events.

Theme parties can present problems if the theme is not appropriate. Themes involving the excessive use of alcohol, set-up dates, and those condoning unusual behavior can create situations that might encourage sexual assault. Proposed themes should be discussed in advance with student leaders, alumni advisors, and the national headquarters if there is potential for problems.

Another identifying characteristic of fraternity and sorority activities is the printing of T-shirts to commemorate certain events. Schools should not try to censor these items, but can and should confront student leaders about inappropriate themes and symbols. Administrators should not be shy about challenging inappropriate themes as a way to set a positive tone about preventing sexual assault and alcohol abuse.

Finally, due to the prevalence of alcohol in sexual assault cases, the monitoring of alcohol use is important. Nearly all national fraternities and sororities prohibit common-source containers (kegs, bars, and alcoholic punch), on or off campus. Many campuses prohibit alcohol at fraternity and sorority houses on campus. This prohibition extends to properties that are off-campus but that any reasonable person would determine to be Greek houses, including off-campus properties that members may rent to form unofficial houses. Colleges and universities would be wise to reasonably inquire into such residences and to discuss alcohol policies with chapter leaders, alumni advisors, and the national headquarters. Since, as the literature has pointed out, sexual assault occurs at social events, at student residences, and off-campus, administrators, alumni advisors, and national headquarters need to be diligent about educating students about the risk associated with the use of such facilities.

ANTICIPATING PROBLEM SITUATIONS FOR STUDENTS

As students matriculate, the issue of sexual assault may be more prominent at some times than at others. Anticipating these moments and directing resources toward them may reduce sexual assault risk. As noted earlier, the first few weeks of school is a time when new students adjust to college and its myriad expectations. It is also a time that is fraught with risk for sexual assault. Many campuses require new students to live in a residence hall their first year, and given new surroundings, with new levels of freedom, students may need extra guidance. Programs on sexual assault directed specifically at these new students are a good use of resources.

For the fraternity and sorority community, the first few weeks of school bring new members, a majority of whom are first-term freshmen adjusting to both the school and the fraternity or sorority. The fraternity or sorority that provides a high-quality environment can aid the adjustment for its new members; the chapter that neglects to do so can actually be detrimental. Requiring all new members of fraternities and sororities to attend programs on sexual assault and other issues is a worthwhile policy. At this early point in their fraternal experience, students are easily motivated to attend such programs and can find them stimulating. And, as mentioned earlier, many national fraternities and sororities require such programs.

Another problem time for students occurs during large out-of-town athletic events. For some schools, these are regular events, such as football games in the fall or basketball games in the spring. The combination of going to an unfamiliar territory, having unclear expectations, allowing haphazard sleeping arrangements, and using alcohol can lend themselves to sexual assault. Such events may be more inviting to new students and thus create a situation that is fraught with problems. Administrators would be wise to work closely with student health professionals and with the athletic department to disseminate information on how to prepare for and handle out-of-town events. This approach of prevention and follow-up is more likely to be used by most universities than close monitoring of each event.

The fraternity and sorority new-member education program at UNC–Chapel Hill is one example of a comprehensive approach to sexual assault prevention that incorporates education, clearly stated policies, and discussion of potential problem situations. New members are expected to attend a series of four educational seminars during the pledge period (or the next time the series is offered, if their recruitment was not at the beginning of a semester). Topics include risk management, alcohol and substance abuse, health issues, and sexual assault. Conducted over a 4-week period after recruitment has concluded, programs rely heavily on campus resources. Student Health Services staff present on alcohol and substance abuse as well as health issues. A consortium of staff from Student Health, Dean of Students, Student Legal Services, and the local Rape Crisis Center presents the sexual assault program, with all the staff and community facilitators pooling their unique expertise. As a motivational tool, we take attendance after each session and send the results to presidents and advisors by electronic mail, and post overall attendance on the Greek Affairs web site. At the conclusion of the series, we compute an overall attendance figure for each chapter and publicize it on the overall Greek Report at the end of each semester. Finally, each semester these new-member programs are timed to end before Fall or Spring Break, as these can be times when opportunities for sexual assault are heightened. By taking timing into account this way, we hope to arm students with the knowledge and education they need to make good decisions at critical times.

DISCIPLINE

Discipline for sexual assault in the fraternity and sorority community takes place on two levels, individual and chapter. Individuals involved with sexual assault generally are under the purview of the Dean of Students Office, which handles individuals who violate the code of student conduct. However, it is often difficult to determine whether a sexual assault has taken place due to alcohol use and other factors. Greek advisors can be helpful by using their influence to bring both parties into the Dean of Students Office to talk frankly about the episode.

Additionally, administrators should seek the cooperation of chapter leaders. Whether by using their influence to bring students into the office or by confirming that students have been talking among themselves about an alleged incident, most chapter presidents will cooperate fully and want to distance themselves from the offending individual, even providing a chapter composite to identify their individual members. Reluctant leaders can be shown that it is in the interest of the chapter to act forthrightly, and this approach generally secures cooperation, particularly when media scrutiny threatens. Alumni advisors and national headquarters staff, who generally have experience handling discipline cases, should be contacted at the beginning of administrative involvement, with or without the cooperation of student leaders.

The next step in this process requires the chapter to make use of its internal judicial board to discipline the offending member. As private organizations, fraternities and sororities are not bound by the same due-process rights as colleges and universities, although they must follow their promulgated procedures. Although it is not a substitute for the campus judicial process, internal discipline can be a powerful tool because it is both a peer-driven process and because it usually occurs more quickly; this allows for corrective behavior to be required soon after the act. The central tenet of such organizations is to follow the teachings and principles of the founding members, thus giving chapters tremendous leeway in disciplining their own members, with the ultimate penalty being removal from the chapter. The literature regarding the characteristics of a perpetrator of sexual assault shows that separation from the peer group is a powerful penalty. Campus administrators should work with chapters and their alumni advisors during this process.

In addition to individual discipline, there are situations in which chapters disseminate literature (flyers, handbills) with sexist remarks or have strippers at events. Administrators must understand that these forms of speech, no matter how reprehensible, are covered under the First Amendment. Universities that discipline students and groups for this behavior will find an unsympathetic court system. Instead, campus officials should make use of their relationships with alumni advisors and national headquarters to bring about change. Often an agreement can be reached to educate the members on sexual assault and sexism. Chapters can often be convinced that it is in their best interest to cooperate with the campus to correct problems.

Finally, the Family Educational Rights Protection Act (1974) prohibits the disclosure of individual discipline cases, but it does not proscribe disclosure in group cases. Colleges and universities may disclose cases involving student groups at any time. Organizations see this as a powerful deterrent. For this reason, group cases should be noted on any summary reports about the fraternity and sorority community and disseminated to the public. Prospective students and parents, particularly, should be accorded their full rights to this information.

SUMMARY

Fraternities and sororities are an integral part of nearly a thousand campuses in North America. Although sexual assaults occur in the Greek community, the unique characteristics of that community also offer opportunities to educate students and to positively affect a college culture at risk for sexual assault. Using a comprehensive approach—including programming, policy development, and administrative involvement—can change this culture. Wise college and university administrators will work with the fraternity and sorority student community, chapter leaders, alumni advisors, and national headquarters to bring about these changes. Abandoning the fraternity and sorority community solves little and may create more risk for students and the larger campus community.

REFERENCES

Abbey, A. (1991). Acquaintance rape and alcohol consumption on college campuses: How are they linked? *Journal of American College Health, 39,* 165–169.

Aizenman, M., Andrews, C., Witt, P. H., & Burns, W. D. (1994). Date rape awareness programming. In J. M. Gary (Ed.), *Campus community confronts sexual assault* (pp. 69–80). Holmes Beach, FL: Learning Publications.

Alpha Tau Omega Fraternity, Tau Chapter, Undergraduate Students, v. University of Pennsylvania and George S. Koval, 10 Phila. 149 (1983).

Bachman, R., Paternoster, R., & Ward, S. (1992). The rationality of sexual offending: Testing a deterrence/rational choice conception of sexual assault. *Law and Society Review, 26,* 343–372.

Berkowitz, A. D., Burkhart, B. R., & Bourg, S. E. (1994). Research on college men and rape. In A. D. Berkowitz (Vol. Ed.), *New directions for student services: Men and rape: Theory, research, and prevention programs in higher education* (pp. 3–15). San Francisco: Jossey-Bass.

Boeringer, S. B., Shehan, C. L., & Akers, R. L. (1991). Social contexts and social learning in sexual coercion and aggression: Assessing the contribution of fraternity membership. *Family Relations, 40,* 58–64.

Bohmer, C., & Parrot, A. (1993). *Sexual assault on campus: The problem and the solution.* New York: Lexington Books.

Burke, T. M. (1999). The Dartmouth decision: The end of another Greek system? *Fraternal Law* (no. 68), 1–4.

Burkhart, B. R., & Stanton, A. L. (1988). Sexual aggression in acquaintance relationships. In G. W. Russell (Ed.), *Violence in intimate relationships* (pp. 43–45). New York: PMA.

Campus Awareness and Security Act of 1992, Pub. L. No. 102-325, 106 Stat. 448 (1992).

Davis v. Monroe County Board of Education, 119 S. Ct. 1661 (1999).

Ehrhart, J. K., & Sandler, B. R. (1985). *Campus gang rape: Party games?* Washington, DC: Association of American Colleges.

Elliot, L., & Brantley, C. (1997). *Sex on campus: The naked truth about the real sex lives of college students.* New York: Random House.

Family Educational Rights Protection Act of 1974, Pub. L. No. 93-380, 88 Stat. 571 (1974).

Finley, C., & Corty, E. (1993). Rape on campus: The prevalence of sexual assault while enrolled in college. *NASPA Journal, 34,* 113–117.

Garrett-Gooding, J., & Senter, R., Jr. (1987). Attitudes and acts of sexual aggression on a university campus. *Sociological Inquiry, 57,* 349–371.

Gary, J. M. (Ed.). (1994). *Campus community confronts sexual assault.* Holmes Beach, FL: Learning Publications.

Harrison, P. J., Downes, J. D., & Williams, M. D. (1991). Date and acquaintance rape: Perceptions and attitude change strategies. *Journal of College Student Development, 32,* 131–139.

Higher Education Amendments, Pub. L. No. 105-244, 112 Stat. 1837 (1998).

Hughes, J. O., & Sandler, B. R. (1987). *"Friends" raping friends: Could it happen to you?* Washington, DC: Association of American Colleges.

Johnson, J. D., & Russ, I. (1989). Effects of salience of consciousness-raising information on perceptions of acquaintance versus stranger rape. *Journal of Applied Psychology, 19,* 1182–1197.

Koss, M. (1988). Hidden rape: Sexual aggression and victimization in a national sample of students in higher education. In A. W. Burgess (Ed.), *Rape and sexual assault II* (pp. 3–26). New York: Garland.

Lenihan, G. O., Rawlins, M. E., Eberly, C. G., Buckley, B., & Masters, B. (1992). Gender differences in rape supportive attitudes before and after a date rape education intervention. *Journal of College Student Development, 33,* 331–338.

Muehlenhard, C. L., Friedman, D. E., & Thomas, C. M. (1985). Is date rape justifiable? The effects of dating activity, who initiated, who paid, and men's attitude towards women. *Psychology of Women Quarterly, 9,* 297–310.

National Interfraternity Conference. (1999). *Intersections: Exploring health and safety issues.* Indianapolis, IN: Author.

Ogletree, R. J. (1993). Sexual coercion experience and help seeking behavior of college women. *Journal of American College Health, 41,* 149–153.

O'Sullivan, C. S. (1993). Gang rape on campus. In A. Parrot & L. Bechhofer (Eds.), *Acquaintance rape: The hidden crime* (pp. 140–156). New York: Wiley.

Parrot, A. (1989). Acquaintance rape among adolescents: Identifying risk groups and intervention strategies. *Journal of Social Work and Human Sexuality, 8*(1), 47–61.

Parrot, A., & Bechhofer, L. (Eds.) (1991). *Acquaintance rape: The hidden crime.* New York: Wiley.

Perkins, H. W. (1992). Gender patterns in consequences of collegiate alcohol abuse: A ten-year study of trends in an undergraduate population. *Journal of Studies of Alcohol, 53,* 458–462.

Sanday, P. R. (1990). *Fraternity gang rape: Sex, brotherhood, and privilege on campus.* New York: New York University Press.

Schwartz, M. (1991). Humanist sociology and date rape on the college campus. *Humanity and Society, 15,* 304–316.

Student Right to Know and Campus Security Act of 1990, Pub. L. No. 101-542, 104 Stat. 2381, (20 U.S.C.A. § 1092(f)(7)) (1990).

Ward, S., Chapman, K., Cohn, E., White, S., & Williams, K. (1991). Acquaintance rape and the college social scene. *Family Relations, 40,* 65–71.

Warshaw, R. (1988). *I never called it rape: The Ms. report on recognizing, fighting and surviving date and acquaintance rape.* New York: Harper and Row.

Wechsler, H., Austin, B., & DeJong, W. (1996). *Secondary effects of binge drinking on college campuses.* Newton, MA: Higher Education Center for Alcohol and Other Drug Prevention.

CHAPTER 7

The MVP Program: Focus on Student-Athletes

Jeffrey O'Brien

"Is this realistic?" is the question posed to workshop participants following the introduction of one of the MVP Playbook (Mentors in Violence Prevention Project, 1994a) scenarios into a young men's or women's discussion group. The scenario, which may depict battering, sexual harassment, or a potential rape involving alcohol, does not change our reason for asking the question.

In a time when young people so often follow the lead of pop culture as champions of the phrase, "keepin' it real," the Mentors in Violence Prevention (MVP) Program seeks to accomplish that goal with each team or leadership group participating in a training program. We believe it is imperative to gain agreement from each team or leadership group, in their own words, that the scenario they will discuss is realistic and therefore relevant to their personal experience. The acknowledgment by the group that abuse is perpetrated by men in their respective social circles brings an often abstract issue right into the midst of the discussants. It becomes real and personal. It also preempts some of the predictable minimizing and deflection tactics employed by participants who otherwise may proclaim, when the conversation has gotten too "real" for them, "Yeah, but this kind of thing doesn't happen on our campus."

I certainly hold no illusions that our program is a save-all or end-all initiative, and furthermore, I am not trying to mislead the reader into believing that every participant in an MVP training program is receptive to our ideas. I do believe that we offer a unique service, however, to an at-risk population, in a way that can benefit an entire college community. I have yet to facilitate a training session that failed to produce several students who sincerely thanked me for "speaking the truth," or for being "the first man to say it was OK to show emotion and define my own masculinity." Or who simply shook my hand. They are grateful for the opportunity to discuss these issues and for the safe space our format provided for them.

In this chapter, I reveal my experiences, and those of my colleagues, with student-athletes, student leaders, U.S. Marines, and professional athletes throughout the country. I will share the guiding principles behind the MVP Program, paying particular attention to our bystander approach to gender violence prevention. I will also give the reader several examples of discussions from MVP training sessions that are generated from the key teaching tool of the MVP Program, the MVP Playbook, as well as other program exercises.

WHAT IS MVP?

Jackson Katz, the Founder and Executive Director of MVP Strategies, Inc., has been a social activist for almost two decades. He is also the cocreator of the MVP Program at Northeastern University. Although they are often confused, MVP Strategies and the MVP Program are separate entities. The MVP Program began as a burning issue in Katz's mind regarding how to get men involved in women's almost single-handed effort to combat men's violence against women—women had been alone in this struggle long enough. He learned of the progressive efforts initiated through Northeastern University's Center for the Study of Sport in Society (CSSS). In 1992, Katz approached CSSS administrators with an idea for utilizing male athletes with their unique cultural status to serve as role models and mentors in preventing men's violence against women. CSSS administrators, recognizing how this idea would complement their existing outreach programs that utilized male and female athletes speaking out on issues of race, conflict resolution, and academic values, embraced Katz's idea and helped develop it. Initially funded through the U.S. Department of Education's Fund for the Improvement of Post-Secondary Education (FIPSE), MVP began its inaugural year, 1993, by providing training for male college sport teams.

What MVP does is to bring to the forefront the inescapable fact of *men's violence against women*. Because more than 90% of violent crimes in this country are perpetrated by males (FBI, 1993), the issue of gender must be a main ingredient in violence prevention programs. MVP is a prevention and education program that gives men an opportunity to talk about masculinity and how it is entwined with violence against women. Male student-athletes, as Katz surmised, are in a unique position to help change the traditional hegemonic masculine role model and to redefine masculinity. The key to prevention, from the MVP perspective, is to tap into the leadership potential within these athletes, thereby empowering them to engage in proactive bystander behavior, the "backbone" of the MVP philosophy, when they are privy to abusive situations.

WHY FOCUS ON COLLEGE STUDENT-ATHLETES?

We live in a sports culture, and the sports world was, and in most ways remains, dominated by males. In the United States, we place a disproportionate emphasis on sports, often at the public expense of education and the arts. As a result, athletes are granted an elevated status in our society. One needs only observe the stadium deals being offered to sports teams by cities that are mortgaging their future to keep their home team happy— and rich. Many Americans are obsessed with athletes and hang on their every exploit. This is especially so with athletes from the traditional masculine sports such as football, basketball, and baseball. The good news is that athletes can be utilized to affect cultural change in ways that other people cannot. For proof, look at what Dick Butkus and Bubba Smith were able to do for the Miller Brewing Company.

In the early 1970s, the Miller Brewing Company bought the rights to a small Chicago brewery that had failed miserably in marketing Meister Bräu Light to women. Prior to putting the new Miller Lite on the market, Miller conducted market research to determine what men and women wanted in a beer. At this time, it was not considered acceptable for "real" men to be calorie conscious, but men responding to their market research indicated that they wanted a beer that did not fill them up and had a good flavor ("tastes great/less filling"). Most women responded that they were not interested in drinking beer.

Executives at Miller faced a dilemma. They knew from the research that men wanted to drink their beer, but they also knew that it was socially unacceptable or "unmanly" to drink a light beer. They had to find a way to grant men "permission" to drink a light beer. So, they hired two of the toughest men of all time, according to traditional societal standards, from the icon of masculinity, the National Football League (NFL). Smith and Butkus became spokesmen for Miller Lite, starring in an ad campaign that won advertising awards nearly every year for the next decade. Because of their status as tough athletes, and therefore "real" men, no one could question the masculinity of these large football players. What Miller did was grant millions of men permission to drink a light beer and maintain their masculinity. In the early 1980s, Miller Lite became the official beer of the NFL, representing an incredible sociocultural shift in male attitude and behavior.

MVP was, and still is, striving to achieve the same type of cultural shift in men's thinking about men's violence against women, to make it socially unacceptable for a man to abuse a woman. Katz's idea was to have student-athletes model a new form of masculinity that did not equate men's strength with dominance over women. This shift also meant focusing on men, not as potential perpetrators of violence against women, but as potential bystanders who speak up or take action in the event of other men's abusive behavior against women (Katz, 1995).

THE MVP PROGRAM: A DESCRIPTION

The most common training models for athletic departments consist of 90-minute awareness raising sessions for mixed- or single-gender groups of student athletes or a follow-up train-the-trainers program for selected leaders. A key component of any training is the MVP Playbook.

This Playbook is the essential teaching tool of the MVP Program. There are both male and female versions. The Playbook contains scenarios that challenge the student-athletes' thinking and actions regarding a wide spectrum of abusive behaviors, from battering to gang rape to harassment of lesbians and gay men. The scenarios are intended to depict realistic situations to evoke highly interactive discussions. In fact, student-athletes are encouraged to share their experiences pertaining to each and every scenario.

After the participants are introduced to the scenario, one of the athletes reads a brief "train of thought" script that simulates the kind of "internal dialogue" one might say to oneself to arrive at a good decision. The train of thought concept is adapted from a model developed by Ronald Slaby (1997), an early adviser to MVP, that provides a basis for understanding the behaviors of victims, perpetrators, and bystanders. The reading of the train of thought is followed by a list of options from which the student-athlete participants can select the intervention of their choice. Examples of scenario, train of thought, and options list are set forth later in the chapter.

MVP's second phase involved inspiring female leadership. In the spring of 1995, a female component, similar to the men's, was introduced that addressed women as bystanders and sought to empower them to interrupt and confront sexist behaviors and abuse. Currently, MVP trainers, male and female former professional and college athletes, work together to model respectful behavior between men and women, in both mixed- and single-gender workshop sessions. For many participants, it is the first time they have observed a male and a female interact in a cooperative and respectful manner. During these sessions, the facilitators share responsibilities and eliminate any form of gendered hierarchy in presentation style.

Lately, we have experimented with several variations of our program in Massachusetts. One of these variations utilizes a 10-hour training format that takes place in 90 to 120 minute sessions over a span of 3 to 5 months. We have seen tremendous results in young people who have undergone this extended training, likely due to the added time for participants to develop a trust in the facilitators and to digest new information. Through our MVP Training Institute, we are in the process of scheduling regional trainings for higher education professionals or selected student leaders so that they can be facilitators in gender violence prevention and education on their respective campuses.

MVP GOALS

We believe that each team or leadership group we train has the unique opportunity, as leaders, to influence their peers in a positive way. Each training brings a new opportunity to inspire someone with the will and ability to act. The goals of the MVP Program are to: (a) raise awareness; (b) challenge thinking; (c) open dialogue; (d) motivate leadership; and (e) inspire proactive bystander behavior.

The goals are neither achieved independently nor forced into a predetermined timeline. The goals are interconnected and, therefore, they are achieved concurrently. Each group brings to the respective training the personal experiences and "baggage" of the individual participants, which determines the amount of time spent on each exercise or issue. Progression through the MVP curriculum is an educational process, with each session building on the issues discussed in the previous session. What follows are examples of activities and ideas that are utilized to achieve these goals.

RAISING AWARENESS

There are many MVP techniques designed to personalize the tragedy of men's violence against women. A key component of raising awareness is to engage participants in what we term "remedial empathy" exercises.

Empathy Exercise

Undoubtedly our key empathy exercise takes place at the outset of the training, immediately following the opening remarks. It involves a visualization in which we ask the team or leadership group to:

Take a few deep breaths. . . . Close your eyes and imagine the woman closest to you—your daughter, sister, mother, or girlfriend. . . . She may be at a party, in a room or walking down the street when she is approached and assaulted by a man. . . . Now imagine that there is a third person at the scene, a bystander who sees what's happening to the woman you love and is in a perfect position to help, but chooses to do nothing. . . . The bystander either watches or walks away.

My female cofacilitator and I direct a brief discussion by asking a series of questions, beginning with, "How did it feel to imagine the woman you care about the most being assaulted by a man?" Following a few moments of understandable silence, the replies usually include, "helpless," or "vengeful, furious," as well as "confused." When asked to talk about the bystander, the typical responses are, "gutless," "just as guilty as the attacker," "punk," "coward," and "scared."

With this exercise, we set the stage for a discussion on bystander behavior by asking the team members to raise their hands if they felt the bystander should have done something, anything, to help their loved one in that situation. By making the issue of men's violence against women a personal one, each of the participants quickly comes to believe the bystander should have intervened. The issue is no longer abstract, and the personal nature of the exercise changes the dynamic of the discussion.

This exercise serves another valuable purpose later in the training session when we discuss nonviolent options for interventions using scenarios from the MVP Playbook (Mentors in Violence Prevention Project, 1994a). In these scenarios, participants visualize themselves as bystanders who witness depictions of some forms of abusive behavior taking place. In this circumstance when the scenario places them in the bystander role, some participants will opt for noninvolvement, claiming, "It's none of my business" or "It depends on whether I know her." We then ask them to recall their feelings about the bystander who stood idly by as their loved one was being abused, and we pose the question,

"Did it matter if the bystander knew your loved one when you imagined her being assaulted?" In this way, we attempt another "empathy reframe" regarding the issue of men's violence against women.

Taking Precautions

In a mixed-gender session, we facilitate an exercise, using a black-board or flipchart, that we begin by asking the men to list all of the precautions they take, on a daily basis, to prevent themselves from being sexually assaulted or raped. Aside from the usual comic responses such as, "stay out of prison" or "put on underwear," the men have nothing to list. We then ask the women the same question, and, without exception, they fill their side of the board with prevention strategies they are forced to practice daily. When the women have finished, the resulting visual effect is a saddening eye-opener for all in the room:

Men   **Women**

Lock doors   Check backseat   No eye contact
Check under car   Be aware of surroundings
Dress conservatively   Park in well-lit areas
Carry pepper spray   Monitor drinks while out
No high heels when walking alone
Carry keys as weapon   Change jogging route
Cross street when a male is approaching
Lock car doors when driving   Leave lights on
Notify friend of your whereabouts
And on and on . . .

We then stimulate a discussion by asking the group a series of questions. Here is an example from a recent training:

Male Facilitator:	I have a couple of questions for the men. First, were you aware that your female counterparts take all of these precautions on a daily basis?
Dave:	No.
Miles:	I was. I grew up with my mom and two sisters and they used to do all that stuff.

Antonio:	I do most of those things, too. It's not only females who have to protect themselves.
Male Facilitator:	As a man, who and what are you protecting yourself from?
Antonio:	From getting beat down.
Male Facilitator:	Beat down by who?
Antonio:	Dudes. Roughnecks.
Male Facilitator:	Remember, the question pertains to sexual assault. Do you feel there's a difference between the fear of sexual violation for a woman and the fear of getting beat down for a man?
Participants (several females):	Yes! (Following a brief debate, most participants agree).
Male Facilitator:	How does it make you feel to know your female counterparts do all of these things to protect themselves from men? [Silence]
Dave:	It sucks!
Miles:	It makes me angry that my mom and sisters have to do all that shit.
Antonio:	I'm ashamed to be a man.
Jeff:	That's just the way it is, man. You can't change that.
Male Facilitator:	We'll come back to that, because that's an important comment.
Female Facilitator:	How about the women? Were any of you surprised by your list?
Marissa:	No. I'm conscious of the things I do every day.
Lisa:	Yeah, kind of. It's just that those things are so habitual that I just do them. I don't even think about it.
Female Facilitator:	How does seeing this list and thinking about it make you feel?
Vicki:	It makes me mad. Things are so unequal.
Lisa:	Sad.
Vicki:	I want to show this to every guy I know!
Female Facilitator:	Do you think this [pointing to flipchart] affects relationships between men and women?
All:	Yeah! No doubt!
Female Facilitator:	How?
Miles:	Trust! How can you expect a girl to trust you if she has

Marissa: to do all that stuff every day?
A guy has to pass a lot of "tests" to see what type of person he is. I know some girls who give quizzes to guys.
Participants: [Laughter].

My female cofacilitator and I then shifted the focus in this session by sharing personal stories that included ideas for the group on how to recognize and respond to situations where a woman may feel threatened or uncomfortable. For example, I talked about some proactive steps I have taken, as a man, in attempts to make women more comfortable, such as crossing the street or "giving space" and distance to an unfamiliar woman whom I am walking toward. My female cofacilitator asked the men what goes through their minds when two or three women approach them on the street. After some laughter and comments like, "I'm trying to figure which one I'm going to talk to," she replied, "You mean your heart wasn't racing? You weren't thinking about what kind of shoes you had on in case you had to run? You weren't mapping out an escape route, or preparing yourself for some excessive crude staring or crude gestures?" The young men responded with surprise and frustration; they have never considered that they pose an inherent threat to women simply because they are men living in a rape-supportive culture.

Following a few examples and lively discussion, we wrapped up the exercise by reminding the participants that we live in a culture that condones sexual assault, but as leaders, they can help change that culture by sharing their awareness with their peers. They can affect change by recognizing potential situations of discomfort and fear and by responding appropriately—if they are up to the challenge. It is important to recognize that it is a challenge.

What Constitutes Abuse?

Before anyone can be expected to confront abusive behavior, one must be aware of what it is that needs to be confronted. As part of our introductory sessions, we engage participants in a discussion to identify and understand what is abusive. We ask them if they can list for us the different types of abuse subsumed under the "umbrella term" *men's violence against women* as well as examples of each. Once again, the resulting visual image is compelling. For example, here is a list from a recent training:

Verbal	Physical	Emotional	Sexual
swearing	hitting	lying	rape
put-downs	throwing	manipulation	harassment
yelling	things	cheating	sexual assault
spreading	dragging	controlling	withholding
rumors	kicking	possess-	sex
tone/content	shaking	iveness	pornography
lies	punching	isolation	
threats	walls	withholding	
	hair-pulling	love	
	murder		
	stabbing		

For many participants, this is the first time that they have heard these acts described as abusive. Many of these behaviors have been normalized in our culture, with the result that, except for the more obvious physical and sexual forms of abuse, the other versions tend to be minimized. Such a simple exercise helps both male and female participants define abuse.

CHALLENGING THINKING

One of our ways to challenge thinking is to focus on the powerful influence of the media on mainstream culture. Many harmful beliefs and actions become "normalized" or "mainstream" as they are filtered through music videos, song lyrics, and movie depictions. In fact, these beliefs and actions are all too rarely challenged or critically analyzed. MVP, by consistently reframing issues and allowing for open dialogue, encourages participants to make their own judgments, as opposed to passively accepting excuses such as, "boys will be boys" or engaging in the kind of victim-blaming we sometimes see in the media in response to claims of sexual harassment, assault, or rape.

We may ask members of a team to recount the first questions posed by the media when a woman claims that she has been raped. The ensuing discussion invariably focuses on the woman and her role in the rape. The team members, conditioned by a rape-supportive culture, ask about what she had been wearing, if she had been drinking, whether she "led the guy on," why she decided to go back to his room, and if she had a promiscuous history. Males are usually perceived in a positive light. The discussion then turns to questions such as: why do we "line up" behind men when they are accused of violating a woman? why are women portrayed as villains?

Another issue MVP addresses is homophobia. We ask our student-athlete participants to consider the many subtle and overt ways homophobia is used in their peer culture. Of course, the use of derogatory terms for gay and lesbian people is commonplace on college campuses. Most of our participants have an extreme fear of being tagged with such labels. Of all the sensitive issues we discuss, maintaining a lengthy discussion on homophobia is generally the most difficult. The 1998 murder of Matthew Shepherd, a first year student at the University of Wyoming, prompted us to use proactive dialogue on this issue. MVP challenges participants to confront homophobic attitudes as masks for insecurity and discriminatory hate. Human dignity and respect are key themes in these discussions.

We often use examples from popular culture to highlight an MVP scenario or supplemental exercise discussion. By using examples from the television shows the student-athletes watch, the music they listen to and watch (music videos), and the magazines they read we are helped to empower them to dissect and understand the messages they receive regarding gender roles, violence, sexuality, and alcohol. The *Sports Illustrated* swimsuit issue, mysoginistic song lyrics, *Ally McBeal*, and movies like "Varsity Blues," "American Pie," and "Swingers" act as springboards in our discussion about the reinforcement of traditional gender roles and their connection to men's objectification of and violence against women. It is imperative to provide an understanding, by way of facilitating discussion, of how individuals learn to be men and women in our society.

As an optimistic postscript to this section, I should mention that I am constantly receiving communications from former workshop participants who ask me, for example, if I watched the latest episode of "Party of Five" or what I thought about the sympathetic portrayal of Denzel Washington's character, an abusive father and husband who kills his wife in the film, "He Got Game." What these former participants are demonstrating is that they have been empowered, that they are becoming critical and aware, no longer passively receiving messages from the media, challenging their peers, and engaging them in dialogue.

OPEN DIALOGUE

As educators, one of our main objectives is to maximize participant involvement while also disseminating information. One technique we use is simply to ask questions. Here is an excerpt from a recent MVP training with a mixed-gender group of Division I college student-athletes that illustrates how we use questions:

Male Facilitator:	We use the phrase men's violence against women instead of domestic violence or dating violence because we want our language to reflect reality. For example, if you took, on average, 100 cases of violent crime committed in the U. S., how many out of 100 would you think would be perpetrated by men?
Participants (several):	95 . . . 88 . . . 75 . . . 90.
Male Facilitator:	Regardless of whether the victims are male or female, more than 90% of violent crimes are committed by men.
Joe:	It's only that high because guys don't report it.
Male Facilitator:	Why do you think guys fail to report being victims of female abuse?
Darryl:	They're embarrassed. No guy is going to admit he's being beat up by his girlfriend.
Tim:	Yeah. The cops won't take him seriously either!
Male Facilitator:	Good point. Let me ask you this: Do you think a woman who is being beaten on by a man puts on her Sunday best dress and skips down to the courthouse, proud to report that she is being abused by her partner?
Participants (several):	No.
Male Facilitator:	Do you think she may also be embarrassed and possibly humiliated, as well?

Participants (several):	Yeah.
Male Facilitator:	We appreciate that there is a lot of underreporting, but honestly, who do think is being threatened into silence more often, men or women?
Participants (several):	Women.
Tim:	I hear what you're saying, but . . . man, you don't know the girls around here. They're smacking us around!
Participants:	(Laughter).
Male Facilitator:	No one deserves to be hit. Let's be clear: violence and abuse are wrong, regardless of the perpetrator, and I would advise anyone, male or female, to end any relationship that is not healthy for you. But let's also be serious: we are here because a woman is beaten by a man every 12 to 16 seconds, because battered women's shelters are sprouting up in every community and there are still not enough to house half of the women and children fleeing abusive men, because the leading cause of injury to women, ages 15 to 44, is battering. We acknowledge that women can be violent as well, but the overwhelming majority of the violence is male-perpetrated. Let me ask you this: Has anyone ever been to a battered men's shelter?
Participants:	(Silence).

Not only do questions tend to open up dialogue, but we ask questions to address the traditional views of many participants, particularly the views of male participants. We recognize that many people have beliefs steeped in patriarchy and, therefore, we believe it is necessary to refute those traditional misconceptions surrounding gender-based violence, while being sensitive to the manner in which we do so. Obviously, we would not be encouraging honest participation or creating a safe environment if we responded judgmentally to our participants' predictable comments. We very clearly communicate that our discussion will focus on the overwhelming majority of the violence, which happens to be perpetrated by males.

One aspect that has remained constant in the MVP program is the focus on bystander behavior for eliminating men's violence against women. By focusing on the participants' roles as bystanders in preventing abuse, young men and women feel more comfortable in discussing our scenarios and the underlying issues such as the construction of masculinity and femininity as they relate to men's violence against women. This comfort level enhances the exchange of dialogue between participants.

LEADERSHIP MOTIVATION

All of our activities and discussions have an overarching focus, and that is on *leadership*. We constantly seek to motivate the student-athlete leaders in the room to take action in their peer culture. This is not easy. We realize that what we ask can be very difficult, because speaking out requires the courage and strength to move against the strong currents of social influence that teach us to be passive or physical in the face of abuse.

MVP trainings are facilitated with the understanding that not everyone will be ready or willing to play an active role in preventing abusive behavior. For example, if we took a representative sample of 10 people from any group, we estimate that two or three will not respond favorably to our program, regardless of what we say. Conversely, two or three people will be motivated to act; they have been waiting for permission or reassurance that these issues are their issues, and that they do have a role in confronting abusive peers. With these ends of the spectrum entrenched in their beliefs, four to six are on the fence, not really sure which way to go. We believe that these participants have probably witnessed several acts of sexist abuse ranging from "locker room" jokes objectifying women, braggart talk about who "scored" with whom, various degrees of sexual harassment, to several forms of physical abuse by male peers against women. We also believe that, although they may disagree with and even be repulsed by such talk or actions, they do not feel empowered to interrupt or prevent this behavior. The social consequences may be too severe for them, or they may simply believe that it is none of their business. These are the student-athletes that we try to reach. Empowering them with concrete options for intervention, we seek to inspire the leadership potential in each one of them.

Throughout each of our training sessions we empower participants to believe in their abilities as leaders to effect change in their peer cultures and beyond. We also challenge them to speak up for what they believe is right. To that end, we begin each training by asking the student-athletes to define leadership in their own words. They may be asked to refer to these definitions during aspects of the training when difficult decisions need to be made on sensitive issues.

It would be impossible to motivate our student-athlete participants if we regarded them suspiciously as potential perpetrators. Quite the contrary, MVP " . . . addresses them as brothers, friends, teammates, popular students, and, very importantly, as potential mentors for younger kids" (Katz, 1995, p. 164). Moreover, many student-athletes have rarely been asked to be leaders outside of the athletic realm. The opposite is typically the case: *many of them receive overt messages simply to stay out of trouble.* MVP challenges them to be leaders in all aspects of their lives. Teammates, friends, and other students are looking to them for cues on behavior and for modeling what is or is not "cool" and acceptable. MVP, as it actualizes Jackson Katz's (1995) vision, makes them aware of this.

BYSTANDER BEHAVIOR

Our education and prevention training is predicated on an innovative bystander approach, a key element of which is empowerment. MVP empowers student-athletes by providing "real" options for them to use (as leaders) in the face of abusive behavior. Participants can be in complete support of our ideas, but without options for intervention, they will be powerless to act. Traditionally, men, and some women, have been taught that men's violence against women, in all its forms, is such an extreme behavior that the appropriate response to it is to do nothing or intervene physically. Discussions generated from the MVP Playbook (Mentors in Violence Prevention, 1994a) challenge this traditional mode of thought. Both the male and female versions of the Playbook consist of a series of social scenarios that the MVP trainers use to develop concrete options for interrupting, confronting, and preventing abuse by friends, peers, or teammates.

It is important to note that MVP Playbook discussions are facilitated by single-gender teams (male facilitators with male participants, female facilitators with female participants), while the MVP exercises are facilitated by mixed-gender teams with mixed-gender participants. The decision to segregate genders during the Playbook discussions was predicated on our wanting open rather than polarized conversations that pit men against women. Research has borne out the effectiveness of such a strategy (see Berkowitz, 1994).

To illustrate the power bystanders have to control a situation, we often ask student-athlete participants to consider what happens, at a high school or social gathering, when two young men square off in preparation for a fight. How do their peers respond? Do they plead with the "scrappers" to reconsider? The answer is an overwhelming "no." Bystanders usually cluster around, as the excitement builds, urging on the two youngsters who are stuck in the middle. I say "stuck" because anyone who has been in that situation knows that one, if not both, of the potential combatants are afraid and hope someone steps in to break it up. Unfortunately, once the crowd has gathered, there are few good ways for a young male to retain his "manhood" if he fails to fight. Imagine, however, that the bystanders reacted negatively to the idea of a fight or pulled their friend out of the middle of an escalating situation. Now, it becomes socially unacceptable or "uncool" to fight. If the social pressure were removed from fighting, the desire to fight would become insignificant because fighting would no longer inflate male status, and the incidents of violence perpetrated by males could decrease dramatically. If bystanders were empowered with realistic prevention strategies, they would be able to defuse most incipient conflicts.

To give the reader a clearer understanding of an MVP Playbook discussion, I'll use the scenario called, "Illegal Motion," from the male version of the MVP Trainer's Guide (Mentors in Violence Prevention Program, 1994b). This scenario evokes discussion about alcohol and consent and is a situation that many of the student-athletes have either witnessed or participated in. We start off by asking one of the participants to read the scenario aloud:

At a party, you see a teammate trying to get an obviously drunk woman to have sex with him. She's not just buzzed; she's stumbling over her own feet. You know the woman and she seems reluctant. (p. 16)

After the scenario is read, another participant reads aloud the accompanying "train of thought" of the bystander. The train of thought concept is adapted from the Habits of Thought model developed by Ronald Slaby (1997) of the Harvard Graduate School of Education, who was an early advisor to MVP. Slaby's model provides a basis for understanding the behavior of victims, perpetrators, and bystanders. The model suggests that a person's behavior is the outcome of social experiences, including personal experiences with violence, interacting with habits of thought (i.e., beliefs, impulsive and reflective tendencies, and problem-solving skills). Practically speaking, the train of thought is a kind of "mental checklist" for the men to engage in when they happen to be in these situations; it realistically captures the "internal dialogue" of a bystander. The train of thought accompanying the Illegal Motion scenario reads as follows:

> They're both adults. But she can't be fully consenting if she's drunk, can she? . . . I've heard about too many cases of sexual assault that start out like this. . . . Could this be one in the making? . . . What about my relationship to my teammate? . . . Is he older than me? . . . Does he have more status? . . . Will he even listen to me? . . . Is it part of my responsibility as a teammate and/ or friend to provide him with some guidance? . . . What, if anything, am I supposed to do in a situation like this? (Mentors in Violence Prevention Program, 1994b, p. 16)

After both the scenario and train of thought have been read, the cofacilitators work to get the student-athletes talking. We ask the participants if this scenario is realistic, does it happen in the participants' worlds? After establishing that the scenario, indeed, is realistic, we ask if anyone has a personal story or experience they could share with the group. To contribute to the growing trust and to model open dialogue, the cofacilitators also share personal anecdotes during scenario discussions.

As the group begins discussing potential options for intervention, the cofacilitators use the scenario as a springboard into a larger discussion about masculinity (femininity in the female scenario), alcohol, consent, and rape. Throughout the ensuing exchange, we direct participants to the MVP Playbook's working definitions of rape and consent involving alcohol. We also examine male socialization in the sports culture and beyond by asking, "What are the goals of many men on weekends?" Predictably, and regardless of age, the responses include "get drunk" and "get laid." We dig deeper. We ask why most young men feel the need to accomplish these "goals" every weekend. For most, this is the first time they have been asked to consider why men engage in potentially harmful and emotionally disconnecting behaviors. We ask other questions (e.g., "Where do men receive the messages that this is what men do?" "What does it mean to be a man?"), keeping them general in nature so that participants do not feel personally attacked.

We use the Illegal Motion scenario to talk not only about coercive behaviors but also the role of alcohol and other drugs in the lives of the participants. Some participants will talk about how they plan on getting a few drinks into the targeted woman to "loosen her up." I may attempt to animate discussion on this topic by first asking them how they would feel if their sister or girl friend were treated the same way, as an object to be conquered. Then, when discussing options for intervention I usually ask participants why would bystanders *not* intervene in this scenario? That question also sparks discussion that usually comes around to the topic of premeditated schemes that were hatched with companions earlier in the evening. What we uncover by asking the difficult questions within an atmosphere of trust and openness is the bitter truth about how these schemes lead to collusion: "If you were sitting with a group of friends earlier in the day talking about getting drunk with women and having sex and if this was the 'collective mission,' to disrespect women, then why would any of you intervene if one of your pals was fulfilling his 'mission'?" We put this scheme out on the table to allow the student-athletes to critically analyze their peer culture and to be informed about the tremendous responsibility of a proactive bystander.

My cofacilitator and I often play a devil's advocate role during scenario discussions, pressing participants to think on their feet to develop several intervention strategies for each situation. It can be challenging to move male athletes past the most popular option, physical intervention, but without exception, male groups are able to list a wide range of creative, nonviolent ideas by the conclusion of the scenario. For example, we encourage participants to brainstorm possible distraction techniques that interrupt potentially combative behavior.

After the participants have compiled a substantial list of real options that they would actually use, we ask for a volunteer to read the options in the Playbook. For the Illegal Motion scenario, the six options are:

- Nothing. It's none of my business.
- Talk to my teammate. Remind him that he has to be real careful in dealing sexually with a drunk woman, but back off if he won't listen.
- Gather some of my teammates to get him to leave her alone.
- Find one or more or her friends and urge them to take her home.
- Tell the host or hostess of the party that I'm worried about the situation, and warn them that they might have some legal responsibility to act.
- Personal option _____. (Mentors in Violence Prevention, 1994b, p. 16)

MVP: A LOOK TO THE FUTURE

A growing service area within higher education is in student affairs. Greek organizations, Residence Life Departments, and orientation programs provide ideal forums for MVP training. We have begun training-the-trainers programs for students affairs staff, and the program enables trained members of the college community to replicate MVP on their respective campuses. The train-the-trainers model has also proved successful with health-care professionals, coaches, youth workers, high school students, and the U.S. Marine Corps. In the past 2 years noncommissioned Marine staff officers, trained in the MVP curriculum at bases around the globe, have performed their own training with new recruits and military personnel, and high school leaders have led training sessions with 8th-grade students. Additionally, the National Football League and the National Basketball Association have been recipients of awareness-raising training from MVP.

Our goal is to train as many qualified facilitators as possible so that they can transplant their MVP Training Institute experiences onto their respective campuses or organizations. At each such Institute, participants will have brainstormed possible intervention strategies with colleagues from other universities, creating a network for sharing successes and obstacles in MVP implementation. This is an exciting time for MVP as we look forward to improving the lives and cultures of many students on many campuses.

REFERENCES

Berkowitz, A. D. (1994). A model acquaintance rape prevention program for men. In A. D. Berkowitz (Ed.), *Men and rape: Theory, research, and prevention programs in higher education* (pp. 35–42). New Directions for Student Services, No. 65. San Francisco, CA: Jossey-Bass.

Federal Bureau of Investigation (1993). *Uniform crime reports.* Washington, DC: Author.

Katz, J. (1995). Reconstructing masculinity in the locker room: The Mentors in Violence Project. *Harvard Educational Review, 65,* 163–174.

Mentors in Violence Prevention Project (1994a). *The MVP Playbook.* (Available from the Center for the Study of Sport in Society, Northeastern University, 360 Huntington Avenue, Suite 161CP, Boston, MA 02115).

Mentors in Violence Prevention Project (1994b). Trainer's Guide (College). (Available from the Center for the Study of Sport in Society, Northeastern University, 360 Huntington Avenue, Suite 161CP, Boston, MA 02115).

Slaby, R. (1997). Psychological mediators of violence in urban youth. In J. McCord (Ed.), *Violence and childhood in the inner city* (pp. 171–206). New York: Cambridge University Press.

CHAPTER 8

Helping Co-Habiting College Students Manage Angry Feelings to Prevent Relationship Violence

Francesca Giordano

Developmental theorists have suggested that the college years require balancing needs for autonomy and attachment (Chickering & Reisser, 1993; Josselson, 1996). Hence, this is a time devoted to the development of the individual self as well as relationship and intimacy skills. Striking this balance is not easy because the conflicts attendant to self and relationship development make these anxiety-ridden years as well. With regard to self-development, traditional-age college students face such challenges as achieving intellectual and vocational competence, coping independently with life's exigencies, and managing one's complex emotions (Chickering & Reisser, 1993). For many students, this is also the time when they experience the interpersonal dynamics associated with significant love relationships: romantic and sexual relationships merge into more adult-like unions, and students practice premarital experiences, like living together. Fear, frustration, worry, and anger join excitement, joy, surprise, and love in the ever-changing landscape of the college student's world.

Unfortunately, when college students begin living together, aggression and violence may become factors in the relationships.

Verbal aggression (e.g., yelling, belittling, threats, sarcasm), physically threatening behavior, and physically abusive behavior (e.g., shoving, slapping) are not uncommon. It is understandable that some relationships will erupt into anger and violence, given the pressures of college demands, the anxiety of establishing independence from parents, and the couples' underdeveloped relationship skills. Not only do these couples fail to display appropriate relationship skills, but they are practicing ineffective and damaging coping behaviors that may become the way each member of the couple reacts to relationship stress and frustration in the future. Breaking what could be an emerging cycle of aggression can be accomplished by helping partners effectively manage feelings of anger and relational conflict. Moreover, when counseling targets anger management *and* conflict resolution, that treatment facilitates *both* self and relationship development. Counseling services and student development programming devoted to the issue of anger management are also likely to find a wide audience in couples who are at risk for a first episode of relationship violence.

This chapter examines anger intervention strategies for college students who are currently experiencing or are at risk for interpersonal violence. Although interpersonal aggression occurs in gay and lesbian relationships, I focus this chapter on interpersonal aggression in heterosexual college student relationships. I address the topic from four perspectives. First, the emotional nature of angry, violent-prone relationships in college students is explored. Next, I examine the developmental relationship needs of college students for the dynamic interplay of angry emotions as precursors to interpersonal violence. Third, I discuss gender differences in how anger is experienced and manifested. Finally, I suggest intervention strategies for student affairs staff and college counselors.

Before I begin a discussion about college student couples experiencing relationship violence, I must speak to aggression and violence toward women in relationships. The link between domestic violence treatment and anger management is clear: often abusing partners are unable to manage their angry feelings and the resulting conflicts escalate into violence. The domestic violence literature makes a strong statement about the importance of anger and aggression management (Cullen & Freeman-Longo, 1996). The literature suggests that the first step in intervention is to separate the couple to protect the woman. To many college counselors it may be tempting to take a "nondevelopmental" approach by working individually with each student and encouraging them to break up—especially if the couple has not yet formed a "permanent" relationship bond. However, there are several compelling reasons to work on the anger-based, developmentally focused issues *within* the relationship without encouraging its break up. For instance, students may not continue with any counseling that threatens the integrity of the relationship. Counseling that affects the power dynamics within the relationship to the extent that the abuser feels threatened may inadvertently put the woman in danger. Additionally, it is important to understand that both members of couples are in psychological distress. Even when the relationship ends, the students' untreated issues may affect their next relationship. When working with the couple, the college counselor has the opportunity to build a bond with both partners. This increases the likelihood that separately or together they will both continue in treatment. The preceding recommendations are *not* meant to suggest that women should stay in unhealthy and dangerous relationships; rather, counselors should implement a "no violence" contract and a safety plan as a first step in any intervention plan.

CHARACTERISTICS OF INTERPERSONAL VIOLENCE IN COLLEGE STUDENT RELATIONSHIPS

Roloff (1996) suggested that interpersonal violence in relationships has two basic continua of characteristics. The first, emotional abuse, is composed of negative affect, psychological abuse, verbal aggressiveness, and coercive communication. The second, physical aggression, includes all other types of violent behaviors, including sexual violence. Although a positive correlation exists between the frequency of emotional abuse and the use of physical aggression (Stets, 1991), there is only equivocal evidence of a causal cycle in which verbal aggression provokes physical aggression. Yet, for all types of interpersonally violent relationships, angry feelings are a component of the conditions under which aggression occurs (Roloff, 1996). As a consequence, all college student relationships that have characteristics of physical, sexual, or emotional aggression potentially need anger treatment.

Violent relationships are common on college campuses. Premarital violence affects more than 30% of dating college students (Sugarman & Hotaling, 1989) and nearly 40% of victims continue their relationships despite suffering abuse (Lloyd, Cate, & Henton, 1984). Courtship violence and psychological abuse seem to be characteristic of negative emotional relationships for African American as well as White college students (Clark, Beckett, Wells, & Dungee-Anderson, 1991). Brodbelt (1983) suggested that significant degrees of aggression pervade the college dating scene with violence centering around threats, pushing, slapping, and punching.

Several researchers have examined the nature of college students' cohabiting relationships in which violence is present. Rosen (1996) indicated that studying the characteristics of abusive premarital partnerships offers "an opportunity to study the entrapment processes that are free of some of the encumbrances of marriage" (p. 153). There is substantial evidence that these relationships, even in the early stages of courtship, are characterized by emotional immaturity and enmeshment compared to other college student relationships. Violent couples are more insecure, fearful, and angry with each other. For example, Hanley and O'Neill (1997) found that violent college student couples reported greater commitment to their relationships than nonviolent couples, but were also more likely to disagree with their partner's level of emotional commitment, suggesting higher level of jealousy. Obsessive love for one's partner (Bookwala, Frieze, & Grote, 1994) and feelings of romantic jealousy (Bookwala, Frieze, Smith, & Ryan, 1992) were found to be strong predictors of courtship violence. In some college women a correlation has been found between low self-esteem, a desire to forgive violence, and little intention to exit a relationship (Katz, Street, & Arias, 1997).

Rosen (1996) offered an extensive description of violent premarital relationships, which clearly suggests couples' limitations in intimacy and relationship skills. Early in the life of these relationships, individuals are drawn to each other through the romantic fantasy that the relationship can meet all needs and erase all problems. The relationships can evolve into romantic fusion, where the absence of intimacy and individuation is replaced with a kind of enmeshed attachment and bonding. Once violence occurs, the women develop a variety of dysfunctional coping strategies, which include avoidance, placation, and illusions of control.

Interpersonally, violent couples are characterized by the role angry feelings play as triggers for conflict and aggression. Anger by itself is not necessarily destructive, but prolonged and uncontrollable anger is dysfunctional. It is the escalating nature of couples' anger and the dysfunctional beliefs from which the anger arises that cause damage. For example, aggressive couples may not be able to curb their anger expression from escalating into violence, and they may also use more verbally aggressive displays of anger such as yelling, disdain, and sarcasm (Roloff, 1996). Both men and women experience elevated levels of anger and bitterness as consequences of these relationships (Rosen, 1996).

Additionally, several negative belief and attributional systems have been found to be associated with angry reactions in college men. Beliefs about assignment of blame is one striking example. Men who struggle with anger control are more likely than women to place blame and responsibility onto their partner for relationship difficulties (Felson, 1997; LeJeune & Follette, 1994). These men also evidenced distorted perceptions around the consequences of violence and a need to control the relationship. For example, violent men were more likely to expect that their violence will result in winning an argument, while nonviolent men believed violence would end a relationship (Riggs & Caulfield, 1997). Violent men perceived their partner's behavior as threatening and in need of control (Stets, 1991). Distorted perceptions of partner behavior is more important than any other factor in determining whether violence will be used to resolve conflict (Clark, Beckett, Wells, & Dungee-Anderson, 1994).

Finally, the role of dysfunctional anger expression and its potential for violence have been linked to the fused, immature relationship system described by Rosen (1996). In fused, immature relationships, the presence of aggression appears to suppress the expression of complaints about partners' behavior; that is, the anticipation of aggressive repercussions has been found to be associated with withholding complaints about partners' controlling behavior and with higher relational dependence (Cloven & Roloff, 1993).

In summary, research has identified some distinctive characteristics of college students' violence-prone romantic relationships. For example, partners display emotional immaturity, dependency, and jealous feelings, as well as a dogged commitment to the relationship. Partners resort to threats or placation to control the others' behavior, and these efforts often escalate into verbal and physical aggression. Furthermore, one partner's behavior may be viewed through distorting interpersonal schemas, which lead the other to perceive threat or assign blame.

THE DEVELOPMENTAL RELATIONSHIPS NEEDS OF COLLEGE STUDENTS

Before I can begin to examine treatment interventions, I must also look at healthy, normal, developmental and emotional relationship processes in college students. This understanding of normal emotional and relational college student development offers a foundation on which treatment of violence-prone couples can be built. First, I discuss the nature of anger, and I follow with an exploration of the developmental issues pertaining to emotional and relationship growth.

THE NATURE OF ANGER

Anger is an emotion that ranges in intensity from annoyance to rage. Theories of emotional response suggest that (a) all emotions have unique characteristics, (b) are used as information on how an internal or external event is experienced, and (c) play a role in interactions with others. Malatesta and Izard (1984) pointed out that like other emotions, anger has physiologic characteristics (increased muscular tension, heart rate, and blood pressure), behavioral characteristics (including facial expressions such as a flushing, clenched jaw, and pursed lips; and changes in vocal tone and body movements), and subjective characteristics. The exact manifestation of behavioral and subjective characteristics seems to vary greatly from individual to individual. Both men and women can increase their awareness of how and when they are angry by examining subtle changes in thought and behavior.

The theoretic understanding of the nature of anger has been dominated by a cognitive-behavioral perspective. This orientation suggests that people experience angry feelings within a cognitive context. Both angry feelings and their associated cognitions offer information about the impact of internal or external events. For example, people *feel* anger because they *think* their rights and boundaries have been violated by an individual or event.

Cognitive theory contends that this informational aspect of anger centers on cognitive appraisal. In this sense, thoughts about an individual or an event lead to recognition of a slight or wrong. For example, when an event is appraised as a slight, anger is felt. Angry feelings have been linked to specific cognitive appraisals, such as the thoughts that a situation is unwanted and caused by someone else and beliefs that a more positive outcome was deserved (Thomas, 1993). Beck (1976) has argued that although angry appraisals are linked to intentional, malicious, or unjustified actions, they can be based on faulty or distorted cognitions. Cognitive-behavioral treatment emphasizes teaching clients to recognize distorted cognitions as a first step in reducing angry feelings.

The treatment of anger from this perspective has often been called the management of anger, which implies that anger is a negative or undesirable emotion linked to difficulties in controlling impulses. When negative behavior results from these difficulties, the angry feelings are treated with behavior-based strategies designed to identify triggers and modify the negative (often aggressive) responses. Clients are taught to counter their anger-engendering cognitions with more appropriate "self-talk" and to replace negative behaviors with incompatible, nonaggressive behavioral responses (McKay, Rogers, & McKay, 1989).

Although the cognitive-behavioral perspective on anger has dominated the research and treatment literature, there are two other major theoretic schools of thought that appear to have particular relevance for college students. Humanistic views of anger emphasize its "orienting" properties, in which the impact of an individual or an event is conveyed through emotions

(Greenberg & Safran, 1989; Rogers, 1961). This perspective emphasizes the informational aspect of anger. The information that angry feelings convey suggests an emotional reaction. For example, the amount of anger one member of a couple feels for another may be a gauge of the overall strength of the relationship. Another advantage is that the humanistic view affords a developmental perspective from which anger can be seen to resonate with students' needs to individuate from parents. In this sense, angry college students might be understood as attempting to prove they are separate individuals from their parents. A counselor who works with college students from a humanistic orientation may view intense, pervasive anger, not only as a reaction to the emotional intensity of a relationship, but also as the absence of a higher level developmental skill—the ability to soothe the anxiety caused by intimate relationships.

Another school of thought emphasizes the clear role anger plays in interpersonal transactions and how anger often occurs in a social context (Averill, 1982; DeRivera, 1984). Anger helps people to interpret relationships and may serve as a catalyst to change them. For example, individuals become angry because social interactions do not result in positive outcomes for them, or angry feelings disrupt relationships because the feelings are not effectively communicated. Considering anger from an interactional perspective illuminates the need for skill development in the management of anger. The aggressive couple is understood as lacking communication or problem-solving skills that could be used to prevent angry feelings from escalating into aggressive behaviors.

An analysis of the systemic aspects of anger has dominated the treatment literature on conflicts in couples. Understanding the cyclical nature of anger allows for its systemic analysis, which emphasizes identifying patterns (including communication patterns) within relationships. Lerner (1985) suggested that it is the patterns of actions and reactions, often echoing with intergenerational messages, that create a "circular dance" in couples. This approach acknowledges the interconnection of beliefs and behaviors and focuses on helping couples disengage from their interactive patterns by helping them understand the intergenerational nature of their reactions to relational injury, teaching them to communicate angry feelings effectively, and cultivating effective intimacy skills to manage relationships.

Ironically, these three approaches—cognitive-behavioral, humanistic, and systemic—to understanding and treating anger are basically in agreement on the context in which anger is felt. Anger is felt in the context of power and control. It is felt by people who perceive their rights and boundaries being violated. It is associated with interpersonal situations in which a person feels wronged or unjustly treated (although some would argue these conclusions may be based on distorted cognitions). Anger is felt when an undesired or undeserved outcome is experienced. It is clear that anger is often linked to the potential of violence, hostility, and aggression in interpersonal relationships.

INTIMACY, RELATIONSHIP, AND EMOTIONAL REGULATION SKILLS IN COLLEGE STUDENTS

We know that interpersonal violence exists in the relationships of college students. But in what context does this violence develop? To better understand, we must examine the experience of college students as they struggle to form relationships in general. Levine and Cureton (1998) provide some insights into this context. They suggest that contemporary college students may be more overwhelmed and emotionally damaged than previous generations of students. They may be more likely to come from families isolated from community and family networks and continue this social isolation while attending college. They may be too overworked to have a social life and too fearful to develop intimacy skills. Fewer than ever live on campus because of jobs and part-time attendance. Many of these students begin to form relationship in this context of social isolation and emotional immaturity. Additionally, increasing numbers of college students report that they have never seen a successful adult romantic relationship. More than half of college students come from nontraditional backgrounds that include living with single parents, merged families, and same-sex parents, so that traditional blueprints of successful marriages do not seem to fit (Newton, 1998).

As a result, individual dates seem to have been replaced by group dating that involves large amounts of drinking (Wechsler,

1996). The group may protect students from deeper involvement and intimacy. For many, serious dating does not occur until the junior or senior year when social pressures to find a potential life partner increase and housing options become more varied. Throughout the college experience, casual sex still seems to be a common experience. Levine and Cureton (1998) noted that for today's college students sexual relationships are not meant to have a serious emotional valence and represent another alternative to traditional dating. Consequently, responsible sexual behavior, emotional commitment, and attachment concerns may be issues that partners never have seriously addressed until they begin cohabiting.

Chickering (1969) was the first to acknowledge that increasing one's capacity for mature emotional relationships—specifically the capacity for intimacy—is an important developmental milestone of the college years. Chickering and Reisser (1993) pointed out that development of intimacy skills requires students to make qualitative shifts in the dynamics of their relationship, from relationships maintained by dominance or dependence to ones characterized by interdependence between equals. They specifically noted that this shift includes the ability to discern toxic from nontoxic relationships and the development of conflict resolution skills. Douvan (1981) linked the capacity for intimacy to self-understanding, suggesting that the self-reflection demanded in many higher education courses should aid students in the understanding of their own motives, interests, and aspirations. Students can apply this understanding to identify like-minded peers, which can lead to more intimate, self-revealing relationships.

Other theorists have discussed what can go wrong in the development of relationship skills. According to Kegan (1982), the relationship fusion that characterizes many abusive relationships is due to the absence of intimacy skills. Thus, violence is more likely to become a factor in the relationships of those students who are unable to establish intimacy without losing their sense of an independent self. Contained within this sense of self are the capacities of openness and vulnerability to others as well as the ability to relinquish the need for control. Male college students, in particular, may have difficulties in developing vulnerability, especially with other men, because competitiveness and levity tend to characterize these relationships (Douvan, 1981). How sexual behavior and intimacy blend together can also prove problematic. In fused relationships, some men may regard sexual intimacy with women as implying ownership, and sexual aggression may result from this blurring between self and other boundaries. Additionally, men are also very vulnerable to shame, and these feelings of shame may lead to violence (Allen, 1993). According to Allen (1993), this process is initiated when a young boy is stridently admonished by a physically abusive father that to be worthy he must be strong and always in control. This "mixed message" can engender deep feelings of shame in the boy. Years later when criticized by a wife or girlfriend, these shameful feelings may be evoked—feelings that can be soothed by the power associated with violence. Unfortunately, the woman, unlike the mighty father, is a figure against whom physical retaliation is possible.

Josselson (1996) discussed a common dynamic—what might be regarded as a "pursuer-distancer" dynamic—in damaged love relationships of college students, where one partner is obsessively enamored of the other who reacts with aloofness. Josselson, in her exploration of the patterns and needs that form human relationships, returned again and again to these themes of togetherness and separation. As one member of a relationship, confident in her sense of self, reaches out to develop a relationship with another, she must do so without losing herself and without overwhelming the potential partner with a need to control him.

Kohut (1977) placed mirroring at the center of the development of a healthy self. When others, especially our early caretakers, provide us with empathic mirroring, we feel confirmed in who we are and accepting of our feelings and perceptions. Those parts of ourselves that are not mirrored may get split off. In students who are at risk for relationship violence, it is possible that normal individuation processes are cut off, leaving students feeling alienated from angry or dependent parts of themselves. Kohut (1977) suggested that when parts of the self are kept secret or repressed, "pockets" of shame can form, and these could be the origin of a narcissistic personality style. In his self-psychology system, Kohut linked an enmeshed family style and the absence of empathic parental mirroring to the self-centered (narcissistic) or dependent personality types that predominate in abusive relationships.

Chickering and Reisser (1993) also noted that when some college students cannot soothe their negative emotions such as anger, fear, and sadness this leads to increases in levels of depression, disabling anxiety, and campus violence. Chickering and Reisser (1993) maintained that if students do not manage anger effectively, this anger can lead to aggressive actions. Sexual coercion and violence are one of the problems linked to the inability to manage negative emotions.

Students who have developed emotional regulation skills are able to deal with stressful events. They are aware of their emotional reactions and accept them as part of themselves. They also have emotional independence in the sense that their own emotional reactions are kept separate from the reactions of parents and peers. Kobak and Sceery (1988) stressed the importance of college students' ability to modulate their negative feelings when stressed, and they linked this ability to earlier experiences with loving parents who were available during developmental crises.

SUMMARY

There is serious concern that many of today's students come to college lacking good adult role models for relationships and being relatively unskilled at establishing healthy intimacy. Parenting deficits (e.g., abusiveness, critical lapses in the parental mirroring function) may be responsible, in part, for the narcissistic and dependent personality styles common to victims and victimizers and for anger-prone students' inability to modulate negative feelings effectively. We expect that dysfunctional personality styles and poorly developed intimacy skills should put partners at risk of relating to each other in domineering or dependent fashions and lead to relationships characterized by unhealthy fusion or a pursuer-distancer dynamic.

One of the enormous challenges facing counselors working in institutions of higher learning is to help students accept personal responsibility for angry or anxious feelings and to develop their own flexible coping responses to life stresses. Failure to learn how to regulate emotions in response to stressful life events may give rise to abusive relationships.

ANGER AND ATTACHMENT IN WOMEN AND MEN

To understand more completely anger and aggression in the college student couple, we must include the topic of gender. As we have seen, students at risk for relationship violence tend to have limited intimacy and relationship skills; and they struggle to separate from parents. Additionally, the fighting, controlling, and distancing that punctuate the oscillating nature of these relationships can bring issues of attachment and entitlement to the fore. Before tackling how to treat couples, we need to explore the role gender plays in college students' anger and attachment issues.

For the male college student who is struggling to develop an individuated self, the attachment or closeness experienced in an intimate relationship must not smother his incipient autonomy and independence. Men's sense of identity—their masculinity—does not include the direct expression of emotions; instead, emotions are expressed indirectly through behaviors (Chodorow, 1978). For example, a male college student may react to his cohabiting partner's flirtatious glances at another man by physically punishing her; the physical abuse can be his indirect way of saying, "Now I'm hurting you, like you hurt me!" This acting out often results in people being pushed away, which, in turn, reinforces men's preference for separateness. The abusive male college student, developmentally speaking, likely finds himself in the midst of male gender identity formation (Cullen & Freeman-Longo, 1996). Because the young male in the process of gender identity development tends to deal with emotions by acting them out and is more comfortable with being separate from others, then it follows that anger, almost by default, is his "emotion of choice," because it is easily acted out and results in people being pushed away. Anger creates separation in relationships (Bernardez-Bonesatti, 1978; Horner, 1979), and the young college male may feel comforted by it. That is because the presence of anger bolsters the notion that the young man's self, his identity, can be maintained in the absence of intimacy. In a sense, anger creates more psychological breathing room in which the self can be experienced as whole and complete.

Although feeling angry toward a loved one may produce the distance and separation that many men find comfortable, the abusive man adds aggression to the anger. Jory, Anderson, and Greer (1997) have suggested that abusive men's anger may be triggered by internalized beliefs that justify aggressiveness because it recasts relationships to reflect a distorted perspective on justice and fairness. They conceive a "just" relationship in terms of control rather than empathy and respect. The abusive man may not be able to integrate dimensions of justice—equality, fairness, and caring—to include freedom, reciprocity, empathy, respect, accountability, mutuality, accommodation, attachment, and nurturing. Anger and aggression keep these men from recognizing how gender domination and stereotypes of masculinity and femininity undermine their personal responsibility for abuse and violence (Jenkins, 1990).

Men's anger is often rooted in perceived injustice that stems from a belief that they have "rights" to women and control over their behavior. Boszormenyi-Nagy and Kasner (1986) cautioned that this destructive entitlement can manifest itself in paranoid attitudes, hostility, and rage. They suggested that this sense of entitlement is rooted in the idea that people have an innate sense of justice that demands balance between what they are entitled to receive from a relationship and what they are obliged to give. Damages in family-of-origin relationships can later lead to skewed views of what is "just" in relationships, where this innate sense of justice can manifest as needs for revenge and control.

The young women in abusing couples have their own struggles with boundaries and separating themselves from relationships. Rosen (1996) noted that these women are more vulnerable to the romantic fusion that characterizes abusive relationships, seeing their self-interests as secondary to those of the relationship and their partners. For these women, the relationship is everything. They are also more likely to use relationship-maintenance coping strategies such as avoidance and placation to cope with the abuse; strategies that in turn prevent them from using their anger to escape the damaging relationship. From the developmental perspective, it is easy to see how women could have trouble with angry feelings. Anger is felt when relationships are troubled. This may lead some women to wish to suppress anger rather than to challenge relationships, especially when the relationships are intertwined with their sense of self (Bernardez-Bonesatti, 1978). Horner (1979) suggested that conflicts in relationships are so difficult for women because any separation might evoke in them feelings of disorganization and dissolution of self. As a result, women may deny or minimize their angry feelings to protect their sense of self.

Additionally, women's feelings of responsibility and care for others often lead them to have enmeshed boundaries and to act overly responsible for others (Lerner, 1985; Miller, 1991; Thomas, 1993). Here, angry feelings are denied to protect others or to take the responsibility for change away from others. Hence, these college women are likely to collude with their boyfriends in denying the boyfriend's responsibility for the abuse. They may continue to "over function" in the relationship, somaticize angry feelings into physical complaints, and "stuff" anger expression (Weisinger, 1985). They may have difficulty in communicating angry feelings and in being assertive regarding appropriate boundaries with others.

Women in abusive relationships tend to have traditional feminine sex role socialization and nonegalitarian sex-role attitudes (Rosen, 1996). So, in a sense their problems with angry feelings are rather the opposite of those faced by abusive men. What tends to be the case is that the women are more vulnerable to social messages about the acceptability of expressing anger. Miller (1991) and Lerner (1985) have suggested that traditionally socialized women have been taught that they have no cause to be angry and if they feel anger, something must be wrong with them. Such social messages lead women to believe that their angry feelings are representative of their personal deficiencies. They may believe that they have no right to be angry, and these beliefs inhibit their taking action when anger is felt (Giordano, 1997). College women with these belief systems about anger and its expression will deny their angry feelings, hence discouraging positive self-directed change. The absence of angry feelings in college women may be linked to clinical manifestations deriving from denial of self, such as depression, low self-esteem, eating disorders, and tolerance of abusive relationships (Thomas, 1993).

WHAT CAN COUNSELORS AND STUDENT AFFAIRS PROFESSIONAL DO?

As we see that anger issues are interwoven throughout the abusive dynamics of the cohabitating couple experiencing relationship violence, a final question remains: How can counseling and student affairs staff utilize these anger dynamics to help these couples? This can be accomplished in two ways. First, anger interventions can be used when the couple or an individual member of the couple comes in for psychological treatment. Second, programming on anger issues, communicating angry feelings, and anger and relationships can be presented on campus to trigger couples to enter treatment or to begin the intervention process.

Traditionally, treatment of abusive couples is conducted within counseling services, but student affairs programming can be more effective in many ways. Couples can attend presentations without identifying themselves as abusive. This identification may act as a barrier to treatment. Offering programs to peer-groups such as Greek houses or athletic teams may encourage friends to offer support to the couple or may foster confrontation of them when necessary. Additionally, programming in these areas can be seen as prevention strategies as well as early intervention strategies. Counselors, faculty in women's studies programs, and student affairs staff could work with academic faculty to integrate some of this material into course work focused on family, marriage, or relationship dynamics. Likewise, training can be offered to mentors and academic advisors. Since cohabiting couples live outside the residence halls systems, more indirect and creative ways must be utilized to target programming them. For example, the university's website can contain links to campus support services that could include a page devoted to issues impacting cohabiting students. Additionally, the campus women's studies or women's resource program could facilitate a linkage between off-campus couples and services in the community (see chapter 4). The following section offers treatment interventions and ideas that can be used in a counseling session or as programming topics.

ANGER IDENTIFICATION AND EXPRESSION

The young men and women who live together under a cloud of violence may be having difficulties with anger recognition and expression, although their sex role socialization would suggest that their difficulties represent opposite ends of the continuum. Women underreact to their angry feelings. Although women may be better at recognizing other types of feelings (e.g., sadness and fear) in themselves, they are less likely to recognize anger. Additionally, the women are often more attuned to the feelings of others, especially those of their cohabiting partner. Men, on the other hand, are more likely to overreact to their angry feelings, as noted, and feel anger instead of other emotions. They are also less likely to recognize the range of feelings in themselves and others. Women and men often have opposing styles in the expression of anger. Women "stuff" anger and men escalate their anger (Weisinger, 1985; Spielberger, Jacobs, Russell, & Crane, 1983), often to control their partners. This anger expression difference creates a power imbalance that maintains the damaging relationship.

Often this power imbalance creates a spiraling cycle, where women's lack of awareness of angry feelings leads to suppressed anger that produces frustration and inaction leading to increases in feelings of weakness and low self-esteem. Women may become increasingly "filled" with unacknowledged anger, so that when anger is expressed, it comes out in exaggerated forms, such as screaming and yelling (Miller, 1991). Men have their own spiraling cycle, where overreaction to angry feelings or the expression of anger instead of other feelings leads to verbally or physically aggressive behaviors. Men become increasingly "filled" with unacknowledged fear, sadness, or shame that may lead to increases in feelings of insecurity and thence to increases in controlling behaviors (Cullen & Freeman-Longo, 1996).

The foregoing discussion strongly suggests that both members of the couples must be taught feeling recognition. Activities designed to: (a) evoke angry feelings, (b) develop anger-recognition skills, and (c) explore the effects of suppressed anger may help women who report feeling angry all the time and those who claim to never feel angry. For men, experiential activities are helpful that: (a) evoke feelings other than anger, (b) cultivate awareness of how angry feelings can range in intensity and type, and (c) explore the effects of escalated anger. At this early stage of intervention, counselors need to discourage women from moving on to "taking care of feelings," and simply help the couple build feeling recognition skills. Preventing the exercises from moving prematurely to "action" also encourages men to reflect on their anger, rather than quickly jumping from anger to control. At some point, it may be important to work with abusive men using traditional anger management programs. These programs are designed to identify anger triggers, inhibit impulsive behaviors, and replace them with adaptive coping, assertive, or relaxation responses. (See Furlong & Smith, [1994] or Cullen & Freeman-Longo, [1996] for excellent anger management programs for men and male youth.)

CONFRONTING BELIEF SYSTEMS

After utilizing anger recognition and other feeling identification interventions, confronting belief systems that underlie anger is an important intervention step. Beck (1976) has emphasized the powerful role cognitive appraisal plays in determining a person's emotional response to situations. Therefore, college students' beliefs about the validity of their anger may mediate its expression. Many different types of beliefs prevent, interfere, or distort the awareness and expression of anger. Some of these schemas stem from messages society gives men and women about appropriate sex role behaviors. Others come from family dynamics and parental anger expression modeling. Some schemas are mediated by community sanctions. Exercises that ask students to explore their beliefs about anger and its expression can be useful at this point. These exercises, which can focus on parent/family, community, and society messages about anger, are often more helpful when utilized in a group format.

A counselor facilitating a group can encourage the exploration of beliefs by asking each member of the couple or group how they remember their mother and father expressing anger. A genogram can help to chart family patterns of anger expression and its consequences. Once completed, questions can be posed to the genogram: who in your family was victimized by anger? Did anger lead to divorce or relatives being "cut-off" from their family-of-origin? Are the isolated relatives also the angriest? Students are encouraged to link their anger expression styles and beliefs about anger to those of their parents. For example, men who are hit and/or shamed by their fathers often come to believe that aggressive expressions of anger are the only way to hide shame and protect oneself from hurt (Allen, 1993). Women may see historic family patterns of mothers and grandmothers giving up personal goals for husbands and children, while remaining filled with bitterness and internalized rage. From this pattern, women may conclude that they must give themselves up for others, and that their personal strength will be measured by the sacrifices they made so that others can succeed (Giordano, 1997).

Another useful intervention is social analysis (Russell, 1984). To conduct a social analysis, students are asked to list all the messages they have received, positive and negative, about anger and its expression from their social and cultural influences. Next, the consequences of these messages are investigated. Russell claimed that this process helps clients link feelings of help-lessness or powerlessness to social conditioning, rather than to personal inadequacy. In this sense, beliefs that support psycho-logical health can be reinforced, whereas more restrictive beliefs can be confronted and reframed. As previously indicated, Rosen (1996) and others have suggested that college students with more traditional views of gender roles are at higher risk for bringing abuse into relationships. Traditional sex role socialization has been clearly linked as predictor of dating violence (Bookwala, Frieze, Smith, & Ryan, 1992).

As part of a social analysis exercise it is also important to ask college students about the sort of messages that emanate from the campus community about anger and its expression and how students incorporate these messages into their belief systems. Specifically, students can be asked about what peer groups such as athletic teams, Greek organizations, and others teach to college students about anger expression. For example, some college stu-dent communities may reinforce the belief that men get angry or act out their anger because these that makes them more masculine (see O'Brien, chapter 7, for a discussion pertaining to student-athletes). Peer groups may coalesce around powerful myths pertaining to athletic ability, competitive spirit, and anger expression. As was done with the family, *community* genograms can be sketched to help individuals see the influence of anger and aggression within a community or historic context. The counselor, again, can form detailed questions (Ivey, 1995) that help students tease out community or historic contexts for their influence on anger expression. For example, some African American college students from urban environments may have experienced specific messages linking anger expression to control and as an appropriate reaction to perceived racist behaviors in others (Grier & Cobbs, 1968; Watson, 1989). Angry feelings are also regarded as a critical part of racial identity development (Cross, 1991; Helms, 1990), but it is important to separate adaptive angry feelings from nonadaptive expression and behaviors.

TEACHING COMMUNICATION AND CONFLICT RESOLUTION SKILLS

Another common anger intervention strategy with cohabiting couples is to offer them specific communication, negotiation, and conflict resolution skills training. This type of training derives from research suggesting that violence can be prevented using a communication perspective (Cahn & Lloyd, 1996). In this regard, Carey and Mongeau (1996) studied college student couples for predictors of courtship violence. One of their findings was that specific types of verbal aggressiveness from both partners predicted physical aggression. For example, verbal attacks on the partner's sexual ability and job or academic success were particularly likely to generate a physically violent response. Hence, communication skills training for these couples might interdict cycles of violence interaction.

Carey and Mongeau (1996) found that women used several different strategies to cope with their partners' violence. Escape-avoidant coping strategies were associated with their partners' verbal aggression-coercion and physical aggression-threat. The research revealed that women who used avoidant behaviors to prevent arguments tended to experience greater physical violence. For example, crying, sulking, and stomping out of the room are avoidant behaviors that do not deal directly with conflict. Paradoxically, these behaviors had the effect opposite what the women intended—they led to conflict escalation. Carey and Mongeau also found that the increased use of distancing behaviors (e.g., delaying an argument, changing the subject) as a coping strategy was inversely related to episodes of physical violence in the relationship. This finding suggests that although avoidant behaviors can "overcharge" the situations, distancing behaviors, when practiced by both partners might help to create breathing room during conflict and de-escalate the situation. Carey and Mongeau pointed out that these two apparently conflicting findings offer important information about the type of communication and coping skills that courtship couples may need.

Carey and Mongeau (1996) indicated that physical aggression is likely to occur when partners' perceive problems to be threatening and beyond their coping abilities. Distancing oneself from problems can diminish the anxiety that arises when a problem seems overwhelming, and it can buy time to coolly analyze or defuse a conflict situation. As a result, communication skills that teach couples how to identify problem situations and implement effective problem-solving strategies may help defuse a potential violent situation. The important point here is that encouraging clients to communicate about conflict is not sufficient. This is especially the case when violent individuals have poor impulse control and low frustration tolerance. It is usually more helpful to show these individuals what beneficial actions to take and to teach them practical problem-solving skills. I also recommend communication skills training that helps couples substantially reduce attacking statements. Angry, violent-prone couples are more likely to use confrontation and blame and communicate using negative affect, so teaching two-way, collaborative negotiation styles can increase partner cooperation.

I should caution counselors from encouraging too much direct expression of angry feelings with these couples. Encouraging too much direct anger expression could incite the situation, thereby putting the women at risk (Giordano, 1997). Yet, both members of these couples likely need communication skill training. Using I-messages to express feelings—an almost "generic" communication skills procedure—is helpful. The counselor must be careful to monitor feeling expression so that it does not become attacking. Counselors should not forget that external demands—academic rigors, parental expectations, bill payments, housekeeping responsibilities—can distress the couple. Therefore, helpful interventions to reduce stress on the partners individually and on the relationship include those that teach the couple how to take concrete actions, perform problem-solving techniques, and communicate as team members. When the power dynamics within a relationship are a concern, interventions that increase direct expression of feeling should always be used in conjunction with more cognitive problem-solving, team oriented techniques.

Children victimized by family violence often harbor deep feelings of distrust of others (Boszormenyi-Nagy & Krasner, 1986). From a contextual family therapy perspective, victims then transform their experiences of violations of love and trust into feelings concerning themselves and their relationships in the here and now (Hargrave, 1994). For example, women who stay in abusive relationships are more likely to have histories of violence experiences in childhood and early adolescence that include physical and sexual abuse and witnessing physical conflict between parents (Riggs & Caulfield, 1997). For both men and women, anger feelings are residuals of these damaging experiences that are used to keep others at a distance. In a way, the angry feelings and subsequent aggressive behaviors (especially for men) communicate, "Don't come near me. I've been hurt before." Students can be taught to recognize increasing levels of anxiety and anger from family-of-origin experiences. Communication skill training can include encouraging couples to talk about these past experiences and their relationship to present behaviors.

PROGRAMMING TO BUILD INTIMACY AND RELATIONSHIP SKILLS

Intimacy and relationship skills-building can be offered to prevent a first episode of relationship violence or to help currently abusive couples. Research concerning attachment styles in adulthood offers insights that can be incorporated into developmental programming. In their research on college student attachment, Bartholomew and Horowitz (1991) found four attachment styles: secure, dismissing, preoccupied, and fearful. Securely attached students are comfortable with autonomy and intimacy. Dismissing students are cold and counter-dependent. Fearful types are socially avoidant and afraid of rejection. Preoccupied students are characterized as overinvolved in relationships. Relationships tend to be at higher risk for abuse when there is a nonsecurely attached controlling partner who attempts to keep the relationship from ending. Additionally, the use of disengagement methods of coping with dating violence has also been linked to abusive relationships (Coffey, Leitenberg, Henning, Bennett, & Jankowski, 1996).

One recommendation is for programming that focuses on modal attachment style, relationship loss, and emotional responses associated with that loss (Utterback, Spooner, Barbieri, & Fox, 1995). For example, Bartholomew and Horowitz's (1991) findings suggested that different styles of attachment are associated with different responses to perceived rejection. Fearfully attached students may be fearful of rejection and lack assertiveness skills. Dismissing students often downplay the importance of those who reject them. Preoccupied students tend to blame themselves for the rejection. Utterback et al. suggested that intervention could begin with assessments designed to measure one's attachment style. It may prove useful to help students understand how their early childhood experiences with caretakers serve as prototypes for later relationship experiences outside the family. Didactic activities and discussion could follow to pinpoint problematic attachment styles and offer alternative relationship strategies. For example, students with a preoccupied attachment style tend to be dependent on others but achieve this through being controlling in interpersonal relationships (Bartholomew & Horowitz, 1991). Hence, developmental interventions would help this type of student develop more self-reliance and establish an internal locus for a sense of well-being. The anger work component should include methods of developing coping strategies to deal with the turmoil of detachment in relationships as well as anger expression and management.

Utterback et al. (1995) suggest that enhancing intimacy skills could promote psychological health among all college students.

The key is to design an educational intervention that, on the front end, provides methods for attenuating the angry feelings that give rise to abusive reactions and then to build intimacy skills to combat the abandonment and entitlement beliefs that serve to maintain anger. Designed as developmental programming workshops, they would be most likely to succeed when conducted in naturally occurring college student support systems such as athletic teams, diversity groups, Greek houses, and other types of friendship and peer networks.

Counselors should not overlook the fact that the social support nurtured during these workshops is the last important link in the intervention chain. Negative social support has been found to covary with physical aggression in dating relationships, and men are less likely to seek out positive social support (Carey & Mongeau, 1996). Therefore, it is important to keep couples socially connected. Both members of the couples need friends and role-modeling adults for sharing concerns and seeking information. For this reason, I recommend programming topics for how to develop mentoring or psychologically nourishing relationships with caring adults. College-age men and women—more than they are given credit for—are responsive to interventions by other important adults such as faculty advisors, instructors, and coaches.

SUMMARY

It is clear that relationship violence is an important issue on today's college campuses. Because of the nature of college students and the campus environment, early intervention is paramount, and programming efforts offer a perfect method for strategic prevention. Next, when prevention is not enough, early intervention strategies may deter further damage. Counseling centers and other student affairs staff must be trained to recognize signs of abusive relationships and interpersonal violence and be encouraged to design active and effective interventions. Myths (such as abuse in cohabitating relationships is not as damaging as domestic violence) must be confronted. Mentors and advisors to student groups must be trained. Prevention and early intervention programs can stop long-term damage from occurring and get students back on appropriate developmental pathways.

REFERENCES

Allen, M. (1993). *Angry men, passive men: Understanding the roots of men's anger and how to move beyond it.* Colombine, NY: Fawcett.

Averill, J. R. (1982). *Anger and aggression: An essay on emotion.* New York: Springer.

Bartholomew, K., & Horowitz, L. M. (1991). Attachment styles among young adults: A test of a four-category model. *Journal of Personality and Social Psychology, 61,* 226–244.

Beck, A. (1976). *Cognitive therapy and the emotional disorders.* New York: International Universities Press.

Bernardez-Bonesatti, T. (1978). Women and anger: Conflicts with aggression in contemporary women. *Journal of the American Medical Women's Association 33,* 215–219.

Bookwala, J., Frieze, I. H., & Grote, N. K. (1994). Love, aggression and satisfaction in dating relationships. *Journal of Social & Personal Relationships, 11*(4), 625–632.

Bookwala, J., Frieze, I. H., Smith, C., & Ryan, K. (1992). Predictors of dating violence: A multivariate analysis. *Violence and Victims, 7*(4), 297–311.

Boszormenyi-Nagy, I., & Krasner, B. (1986). *Between give and take: A clinical guide to contextual therapy.* New York: Brunner/Mazel.

Brodbelt, S. (1983). College dating and aggression. *College Student Journal, 17*(3), 273–277.

Cahn, D. D., & Lloyd, S. A. (1996). *Family violence from a communication perspective.* Thousand Oaks, CA: Sage Publications.

Carey, C. M., & Mongeau, P. A. (1996). Communication and violence in courtship relationships. In D. D. Cahn & S. A. Lloyd (Eds.), *Family violence from a communication perspective.* Thousand Oaks, CA: Sage Publications.

Chickering, A. W. (1969). *Education and identity.* San Francisco: Jossey-Bass.

Chickering, A. W., & Reisser, L. (1993). *Education and identity* (2nd ed.). San Francisco: Jossey-Bass.

Chodorow, N. (1978). *The reproduction of mothering.* Berkeley, CA: University of California Press.

Clark, M. L., Beckett, J., Wells, M., & Dungee-Anderson, D. (1994). Courtship violence among African American college students. *Journal of Black Psychology, 20*(3), 264–281.

Cloven, D., & Roloff, M. E. (1993). The chilling effect of aggressive potential on the expression of complaints in intimate relationships. *Communication Monographs, 60*(3), 199–219.

Coffey, P., Leitenberg, H., Henning, K., Bennett, R. T., & Jankowski, M. K. (1996). Dating violence: The association between methods of coping and women's psychological adjustment. *Violence and Victims, 11*(3), 227–238.

Cross, W. (1991). *Shades of black.* Philadelphia: Temple University Press.

Cullen, M., & Freeman-Longo, R. E. (1996). *Men & anger: Understanding and managing your anger for a much better life.* Brandon, VT: The Safer Society Press.

DeRivera, J. (1984). Development and the full range of emotional experience. In C. Malatesta & C. Izard (Eds.), *Emotion in adult development* (pp. 45–63). Beverly Hills, CA: Sage.

Douvan, E. (1981). Capacity for intimacy. In A. W. Chickering and Associates (Eds.), *The modern American college: Responding to the new realities of diverse students and a changing society.* San Francisco: Jossey-Bass.

Felson, R. (1997). Anger, aggression, and violence in love triangles. *Violence and Victims, 12*(4), 345–362.

Furlong, M., & Smith (1994). *Anger, hostility, and aggression: Assessment, prevention, and intervention strategies for youth.* Brandon, VT: Clinical Psychology Publishing.

Giordano, F. G. (1997). Therapeutic interventions for managing anger in women. *Directions in Clinical & Counseling Psychology, 7,* 3–15.

Greenberg, L., & Safran, J. (1989). Emotion in psychotherapy. *American Psychologist, 44,* 19–29.

Grier, W., & Cobbs, P. (1968). *Black rage.* New York: Basic Books.

Hanley, M. J., & O'Neill, P. (1997). Violence and commitment: A study of dating couples. *Journal of Interpersonal Violence, 12*(5), 685–703.

Hargrave, T. (1994). Families and forgiveness: A theoretical and therapeutic framework. *The Family Journal, 2,* 339–348.

Helms, J. (1990). *Black and white racial identity.* Westport, CT: Greenwood.

Horner, A. J. (1979). *Object relations and the developing ego in therapy.* New York: Jason Aronson.

Ivey, A. E. (1995). Psychotherapy as liberation: Toward specific skills and strategies in multicultural counseling and therapy. In J. G. Ponterotto, J. M. Casas, L. A. Suzuki, & C. M. Alexander (Eds.), *Handbook of multicultural counseling* (pp. 53–72). Thousand Oaks, CA: Sage Publications.

Jenkins, A. (1990). *Invitations to responsibility: The therapeutic engagement of men who are violent and abusive.* Adelaide, South Australia: Dulwich Centre Publications.

Jory, B., Anderson, D., & Greer, C. (1997). Intimate justice: Confronting issues of accountability, respect, and freedom in treatment for abuse and violence. *Journal of Marital and Family Therapy, 23*(4), 399–419.

Josselson, R. (1996). *The space between us: Employing the dimensions of human relationships.* Thousand Oaks, CA: Sage Publications.

Katz, J., Street, A., & Arias, I. (1997). Individual differences in self-appraisals and responses to dating violence scenarios. *Violence and Victims, 12*(3), 265–276.

Kegan, R. (1982). *The evolving self: Problem and process in human development.* Cambridge, MA: Harvard University Press.

Kobak, R. R., & Sceery, A. (1988). Attachment in late adolescence: Working models, affect regulation, and representations of self and others. *Child Development, 59,* 135–146.

Kohut, H. (1977). *The restoration of the self.* Madison, CT: International Universities Publications.

LeJeune, C., & Follette, V. (1994). Taking responsibility: Sex differences in reporting dating violence. *Journal of Interpersonal Violence, 9*(1), 133–140.

Lerner, H. G. (1985). *The dance of anger: A woman's guide to changing the patterns of intimate relationships.* New York: Harper & Row.

Levine, A., & Cureton, J. S. (1998). What we know about today's college students. *About campus: Enriching the student learning experience, 3*(1), 4–15.

Lloyd, S. A., Cate, R. M., & Henton, J. M. (1984). Predicting premarital relationship stability: A methodological refinement. *Journal of Marriage & Family, 46*(1), 71–76.

Malatesta, C. A., & Izard, C. E. (1984). Introduction: Conceptualizing emotional development in adults. In C. Malatesta & C. Izard (Eds.), *Emotion in adult development* (pp. 13–21). Beverly Hills, CA: Sage.

McKay, M., Rogers, P. D., & McKay, J. (1989). *When anger hurts: Quieting the storm within.* Oakland, CA: New Harbinger Publications.

Miller, J. B. (1991). The construction of anger in women and men. In J. Jordan, A. Kaplen, J. B., Miller, I. Striver, & J. Surrey (Eds.), *Women's growth in connections: Writings from the Stone Center* (pp. 181–196). New York: Guilford.

Newton, F. (1998). The stressed student: How can we help? *About campus: Enriching the student learning experience, 3*(2), 4–10.

Riggs, D. S., & Caulfield, M. B. (1997). Expected consequences of male violence against their female dating partners. *Journal of Interpersonal Violence, 12*(2), 229–240.

Rogers, C. R. (1961). *On becoming a person.* Boston: Houghton Mifflin.

Roloff, M. E. (1996). The catalyst hypothesis: Conditions under which coercive communication lead to physical aggression. In D. D. Cahn & S. A. Lloyd (Eds.), *Family violence from a communication perspective.* Thousand Oaks, CA: Sage Publications.

Rosen, K. H. (1996). The ties that bind women to violent premarital relationships: Processes of seduction and entrapment. In D. D. Cahn & S. A. Lloyd (Eds.), *Family violence from a communication perspective* (pp. 151–176). Thousand Oaks, CA: Sage Publications.

Russell, M. N. (1984). *Skills in counseling women: The feminist approach.* Springfield, IL: Charles C. Thomas.

Spielberger, C. D., Jacobs, G., Russell, S., & Crane, R. S. (1983). Assessment of anger: The state-trait anger scale. In J. N. Butcher & C. D. Spielberger (Eds.), *Advances in personality assessment* (Vol. 2) (pp. 159–187). Hillsdale, NJ: Erlbaum.

Stets, J. E. (1991). Psychological aggression in dating relationships: The role of interpersonal control. *Journal of Family Violence, 6*(1), 97–114.

Sugarman, D. B., & Hotaling, G. T. (1991). Dating violence: A review of contextual and risk factors. In B. Levy (Ed.), *Dating violence: Young women in danger.* Seattle, WA: Seal Press.

Thomas, S. P. (1993). *Women and anger.* New York: Springer.

Utterback, J. W., Spooner, S. E., Barbieri, J. A., & Fox, S. N. (1995). Gender and ethnic issues in the development of intimacy among college students. *NASPA Journal, 32*(2), 82–89.

Watson, V. M. (1989). Minorities and the legacy of anger. APA *Monitor, 2*(11), 30–31.

Wechsler, H. (1996). Alcohol and the American college campus: A report from the Harvard school of public health. *Change, 28*(4), 20.

Weisinger, H. (1985). *The anger workout book.* New York: Quill.

CHAPTER 9

Sexual Assault: When Victims Are Gay, Lesbian, or Bisexual Students

Beverly D. Tuel

Sexual violence has been conceptualized traditionally as male violence against women. Only recently have the subjects of men as victims and women as perpetrators received scholarly and programmatic attention. Furthermore, as campuses struggle to address the needs of gay, lesbian, bisexual, and transgendered (GLBT) college students, it is imperative that issues related to sexual violence against these students are addressed. Although some college campuses and student personnel professionals have begun to acknowledge problems of violence against gays and lesbians, particularly in the wake of the murder of Matthew Shepard, a University of Wyoming student who was killed in an act of antigay violence, sexual violence has been largely ignored. Slater (1993) outlined the effects that violence targeting lesbians and gays has on young people and college students, but only briefly mentioned sexual violence, and only in the context of lesbians being raped by men. A serious examination of lesbian, bisexual, and gay college students as victims of sexual violence necessitates inclusion of many other issues.

190

PREVALENCE OF SEXUAL ASSAULT ON GAY, LESBIAN, AND BISEXUAL PEOPLE

Estimates of the prevalence of sexual assault against gay, lesbian, and bisexual people are hard to obtain for a variety of pragmatic and methodologic reasons. As a largely invisible population, researchers struggle with defining and identifying whom should be studied. Nearly all studies in this area have utilized nonrandom samples, including age, social, economic, or educational cohorts or snowball samples that begin with one social group and ask its members to identify other potential research participants. Also, although researchers may attempt to study lesbians or gay men, questions emerge about who is included in this group. For example, researchers in one case excluded participants who self-identified as lesbians but acknowledged bisexual behaviors or orientations (Waldner-Haugrud & Gratch, 1997). Virtually no data, either empirical or anecdotal, about sexual assaults of transgendered people exist. Finally, given the stigma and other difficulties with studying sexual violence in any population, research in this field is in its infancy. Nonetheless, a growing body of literature suggests that gay men and lesbians may be victims of sexual assault perpetrated either by strangers or by acquaintances—and even partners—at rates similar to or higher than their heterosexual counterparts.

One of the first large-scale efforts to investigate this problem among gay men occurred in Great Britain. Researchers studied a non-clinic-based cohort of homosexually active men at the beginning of a five-wave, 6-year longitudinal study. As part of the first wave, Hickson, Davies, Hunt, Weatherburn, McManus, and Coxon (1994) collected 930 questionnaires from homosexually active men. Questionnaires included self-report assessments of nonconsensual sexual activity. Of the respondents, 27.6% reported that they had been subjected to nonconsensual sex at some point in their lives. One-third of the men who had been sexually assaulted had been victimized by men with whom they had had a previous or current consensual sexual relationship. In other words, these men had been raped by their partners, lovers, or dates. A small minority of those who had been sexually assaulted (3.9%) had been victimized by female assailants. The type of relationship with assaultive women was not identified.

Another large-scale effort focused on the health needs of lesbians and included questions related to prior sexual victimization. The National Lesbian Health Care Survey (Bradford, Ryan, & Rothblum, 1994) found that of their sample of 1925 self-identified lesbians, 41% reported that they had been raped or sexually attacked at some point in their lives. Twenty-one percent of their sample had been assaulted as children, 15% as adults, and 4% reported assaults in both childhood and adulthood. These reports were more frequent among Latina (46%) and African Americans (51%) than White respondents (40%), suggesting that lesbians of color may be at increased risk for sexual assaults. Women in this survey who reported assaults as adults were violated by lovers (gender unspecified, 10%), husbands (8%), male relatives (5%), other known men (42%), and male strangers (47%). Fewer than 1% reported assaults by female relatives, strangers, or acquaintances. Finally, of the 794 women who reported having been sexually assaulted, only 35% sought help afterwards. Those who did seek help sought the help of friends (19%), police (12%), and counselors (10%).

A study of workplace sexual assaults revealed that lesbians may be sexually assaulted by people they know from work. In a United States sample of 144 self-identified lesbians and 228 self-identified heterosexual women, including 10% women of color, 20% of the lesbians reported attempted or completed sexual assault by someone they knew from work, and 14% of the heterosexual women made such reports. These samples were not comparable, however, so direct comparisons may not be made. Perpetrators in these cases were predominantly bosses or coworkers who used physical or emotional coercion against their victims. Lesbians and heterosexual women were equally unlikely to talk to coworkers, quit, or complain about the assaults. However, lesbians were more likely to have their femininity challenged by assailants and were more likely to report concrete losses as a result of the attacks (Schneider, 1991).

Although the results from the National Lesbian Health Care Survey (Bradford, Ryan, & Rothblum, 1994) suggested that sexual violence perpetrated by female partners may be relatively rare, other research has yielded different results. Domestic violence among gay and lesbian couples has received increasing attention in recent years, and although frequently a part of battering relationships, sexual coercion may be the least understood component of partner abuse (Elliott, 1996). Nevertheless, several recent studies have begun to shed light on this problem.

For example, in a small survey of self-identified lesbians, Lie, Schilit, Bush, Montagne, and Reyes (1991) asked 174 respondents about their history of having experienced and used aggression in their relationships and about their perception of this aggression. Of those respondents who had prior intimate relationships with men, 41.9% had experienced some form of sexual aggression compared with 56.8% who reported having experienced sexual aggression by a prior female partner and 8.9% by a current female partner. Asked about their own use of sexually aggressive behaviors, 31.4% and 10.9% reported such use with past and current female partners, respectively. Over half (51.5%) of the respondents labeled at least one relationship with a past female partner as aggressive, but nearly three-fourths (73.4%) reported experiencing acts defined as aggressive (not limited to sexual aggression). These results suggest that lesbians may utilize denial about violence in their relationships or that they may not perceive aggressive acts as violence or abuse. If this suggestion is correct, it is possible that respondents to the National Lesbian Health Care Survey simply did not perceive sexual aggression by female partners as sexual assault or rape, leading to a potential underreporting of such acts.

An early study (Brand & Kidd, 1986) of same-sex dating violence compared responses of 75 self-identified heterosexuals with 55 self-identified homosexual women, including many college students. Twelve percent of the homosexual women reported attempted or completed rapes by a woman they were dating and 21% by the men they had dated. The prevalence of attempted or completed rapes was not significantly different when sexual orientation and gender of perpetrator were compared. In other words, heterosexual women's reports of assaults by male dates were similar to homosexual women's reports of assaults by female dates. Furthermore, although attempted and completed rapes by men constituted the majority of reported assaults in the study,

29% of the assaults were by women, countering the stereotype that only men commit sexual violence.

Other studies have compared rates of sexual violence in gay male and lesbian relationships. One early study (Waterman, Dawson, & Bologna, 1989) attempted to assess the prevalence of forced sex in same-gender relationships; however, the sample was very small. The sample of college students included 36 women and 34 men, all of whom had been in at least one gay or lesbian relationship. Women appeared more likely to report forced sex by their current or most recent partner than men (31% women vs. 12% men), although the difference between women and men as perpetrators of forced sex was not significant (8.3% women vs. 5.9% men). Unfortunately, the researchers did not clarify the gender of respondents' partners. For example, although respondents had been in at least one gay or lesbian relationship, no attempt was made to ensure that participants' most recent relationships were same-gender. As a result, conclusions about prevalence of sexual violence in same-gender relationships are tenuous.

Attempting to resolve problems with prior research, Waldner-Haugrud and Gratch (1997) hypothesized that sexual coercion would be more common among gay male than lesbian relationships. However, when they compared responses of 162 gay men and 111 lesbians (all of whom were White and well educated), they found that men and women were equally likely to be victims of sexual coercion by their same-sex partners, and further that there were no differences in the type of coercive tactics used. The only difference they found was in the number of coercive acts reported, with men reporting more frequent coercive acts than women. Fifty-two percent of respondents reported at least one incident of sexual coercion by a same-gender partner. On average, women reported 1.2 incidents per person, and men reported 1.6 incidents per person. For both women and men, more extreme forms of coercion were more common than less extreme methods. For example, unwanted penetration was the most frequently reported category of coercive tactics, with 55% of men and 50% of women making such reports.

Three studies have dealt specifically with sexual abuse of gay, lesbian, and bisexual college students. In his survey of 412 college students, Duncan (1990) found that 11.7% of the gay or bisexual men and 30.6% of the lesbian or bisexual women indicated that they had been forced to have sex against their will at some point in their lives. These numbers compared to 3.6% and 17.8% of heterosexual men and women, respectively, a difference that is statistically significant, suggesting that sexual abuse may be more frequent among gay and lesbian students than their heterosexual counterparts. However, the researchers did not clarify the type of abuse experienced, and it is likely that these reports included sexual abuse as well as abuse while an adult.

Baier, Rosenzweig, and Whipple (1991) attempted to answer questions about whether victimization of college students was related to sexual orientation and whether victimization happened prior to or after beginning college. A representative sample of 702 students revealed higher sexual victimization rates among gay and bisexual students (including women) than among heterosexual students. This pattern was statistically significant for assaults in which assailants utilized one of several types of coercive techniques. Types of coercion reported included psychological or verbal coercion (37.1% of gay/bisexual students vs. 19.5% of heterosexual students); the belief that it is "useless" to resist if the partner is aroused (44.1% gay/bisexual vs. 26.2% heterosexual); physically forced attempted rape (11.8 gay/bisexual vs. 10.4% heterosexual); and completed rape (17.6% gay/bisexual vs. 6.1% heterosexual). However, all of the assaults reported by gay and bisexual respondents happened prior to the students entering college, suggesting it is crucial that needs of these survivors are addressed on campuses.

Berrill (1993) reviewed studies of anti-gay violence on college campuses including Yale, Rutgers, Pennsylvania State, and Oberlin. Pennsylvania State's study did not include sexual violence. These studies likely excluded dating and partner violence. However, 12% of students at Yale, 8% at Rutgers, and 18% of the students surveyed at Oberlin reported that they had been sexually harassed or assaulted. It is unknown whether these reports were made of incidents during or prior to attending college.

Most recently, Cortina, Swan, Fitzgerald, and Waldo (1998) examined rates of sexual harassment and assault among a sample of 1037 female undergraduate and graduate students at a large midwestern university, using ethnicity and sexual orientation variables throughout the study. Results revealed that sexual harassment rates were related to sexual orientation, with lesbian and bisexual women much more likely to report some form of sexual harassment compared to heterosexual women. This harassment "had a profound negative impact on both undergraduate and graduate students' educational experiences" (p. 436). Likewise, sexual assault resulted in negative academic consequences for women in their study. Using a conservative definition of rape that only addressed attempted or completed vaginal rape involving physical force, the researchers failed to find differences in sexual assault rates among women with different sexual orientations and ethnicities. In other words, lesbian and bisexual students were just as likely to experience sexual assault as heterosexual women students. Rates of sexual assault increased directly with the length of time spent on campus, with women at their fifth year and beyond reporting sexual assault at seven times the rate of first-year students (28% vs. 4%, respectively).

Despite some limitations of this and other studies, taken together they offer evidence that sexual victimization of lesbian, gay, and bisexual students is a serious problem requiring interventions on college campuses.

PATTERNS AND TYPES OF SEXUAL ASSAULTS AGAINST GAY, LESBIAN, AND BISEXUAL PEOPLE

Research and anecdotal evidence suggest some patterns in how gay, lesbian, and bisexual people are victimized by sexual violence. As in heterosexual violence, sexual assaults against gay, lesbian, and bisexual people take many forms. Certainly, the sexual orientation of the victim may not always be a motivating factor of perpetrators. Indeed, lesbian and bisexual women may face many of the same risks that heterosexual women face, especially to the extent that they have heterosexual relationships with men. However, two forms of sexual victimization may be specific to lesbian, bisexual, and gay people: (a) sexual assault as a bias-related crime and (b) sexual assault by other members of the bisexual, gay, and lesbian communities. A debate has emerged in the literature regarding the prevalence of these two different types of assaults as they apply to gay men. The debate centers on whether assaults on gay men are predominantly heterosexual men who assault in anti-gay motivated crimes or by gay and bisexual men against acquaintances or other known bisexual and gay men.

One foray into this debate was made by Stermac, Sheridan, Davidson, and Dunn (1996). These researchers examined all 29 cases of sexual assault against adult men that were seen by a sexual assault crisis unit in Toronto, Canada over a 16-month period. About 93% of the victims were under age 35, and most (45%) had been brought to the center by police or friends and relatives (31%). Approximately 86% of the reported assaults involved male perpetrators. Half of these male perpetrators were acquaintances of the victims, with victims having known the perpetrator for less than (21%) or more than (29%) 24 hours. Cases in which assailants were known for less than 24 hours tend to be similar to acquaintance sexual assault or "date rape," with victims having met their assailant casually in a bar or other gay cruising area. When information about sexual orientation was revealed by victims, it appeared that they were gay victims of acquaintance sexual assault. In several of these cases, although victims consented to some form of initial contact, they did not consent to subsequent contact. Cases in which victims knew their assailant for more than 24 hours resembled the phenomenon of marital rape in heterosexual couples. In contrast to these acquaintance assaults, perpetrators in half the cases were unknown to the victims. Researchers categorized strangers who assaulted other men as "heterosexual males who rape other males as a means of punishing and degrading them, possibly in an extension of other forms of violence targeted specifically toward subordinate males" (Stermac et al., 1994, p. 62). Victims of stranger attacks may have appeared vulnerable because of perceived sexual orientation, disability, economic hardship, or other variable. This type of assault, the researchers argued, appears rare.

Offering another perspective in this debate, Hodge and Canter (1998) used police reports of 27 heterosexual and 22 homosexual British male perpetrators of sexual assaults against males. They combined these data with self-report data obtained from surveys distributed to victims' groups. Using multidimensional scalogram analyses, they concluded that there are two primary patterns of assaults and perpetrators. They identified the first type as self-identified heterosexual offenders who, often in groups or gangs, attack strangers of any age or sexual orientation in an effort to control and dominate their victims. The second type of offender was homosexuals who usually assaulted individuals with whom they had a relationship, with the coercion involving more psychological manipulation than physical control. In these cases, the victims tended to be males, aged 16 to 25, who were vulnerable because of their youth. Interestingly, the sexual orientation of the perpetrators in the police reports appeared to have been determined by the police officers rather than by the perpetrators themselves, and cases involving bisexuals were dropped from the analyses. Consequently, although this typology may have some validity, it certainly does not capture all forms of male-male sexual assault, and may, in fact, be a typology of perceptions about men who sexually assault other men.

Although research findings into these types of assaults on men remains inconclusive, it does appear that there are some patterns that emerge when considering sexual assaults against bisexual persons, lesbians, and gay men. For purposes of this discussion, two primary types of assaults may be considered. The first involves those assaults committed by presumed heterosexuals against people who are perceived to be gay, lesbian, or bisexual. The second includes assaults by lesbians, gay, or bisexual people against others who are also lesbian, gay, or bisexual.

Assaults against gay, bisexual, and lesbian individuals have at their core issues of power and control. As in both studies cited pertaining to gay men, at least some of the men were victimized because they were perceived to be vulnerable or less powerful based on a variety of characteristics, which may include sexual orientation. In efforts to prove that they are more powerful than gay men, some heterosexual men may engage in antigay assaults. When men are assaulted in this type of bias-related manner, the perpetrators appear to be predominantly male and largely unknown to the victim (Hodge & Canter, 1998).

Research on bias-related assaults on lesbians and bisexual women is scarce. Slater (1993) cited examples of lesbians who were apparently targeted by men because of their sexual orientation. Assaults on lesbian or bisexual women may or may not be motivated by homophobic bias, but misogyny or other biases may be factors. Nevertheless, these assaults are equally motivated by efforts to assert power and control. One would expect attacks on bisexual and lesbian women to mirror assaults on heterosexual women except when homophobia or gender nonconformity is the motive. If this conclusion is accurate, lesbians and bisexual women may be targeted by strangers or known perpetrators in a manner similar to heterosexual women.

An additional dynamic may be at work in cases in which bisexual, gay, and lesbian people are victims of sexual assault by someone of another gender. One service provider (D. de Percin, personal communication, January 11, 1999) noted that bisexual, lesbian, and gay people may be at increased risk for sexual assault because of the perceived need to "prove" that they are not homosexual. This increased risk may be particularly true for youth or for students who have not yet come to terms with their sexual orientation. Research suggests that although most of the heterosexual perpetrators of sexual assault on gay, lesbian, and bisexual people are men, women may also coerce others to perform unwanted sex, either alone or with a male perpetrator.

The other major category of sexual assaults on bisexual, lesbian, and gay people is assaults committed by other bisexual, lesbian, and gay people. In these cases, themes of acquaintance rape and partner violence are prominent. The scarce literature on these types of assaults suggests that in most cases, perpetrators are known to the victims, although the length and nature of the relationship varies from newly met, casual acquaintance to long-term intimate partner. The New York City Gay and Lesbian Anti-Violence Project gave examples of these types of assaults on their internet site: "I picked up this guy at a bar and took him home with me. He made me have a kind of sex that I didn't want. I was too scared to fight back or refuse" ("Male Sexual Assault," 1998, p. 1). This example depicts a recent acquaintance sexually assaulting a man.

As an example of a sexual assault by a partner, this example was offered by a lesbian woman:

> My girlfriend and I were having lots of problems. She was drinking
> a lot and hitting me. One night she stormed out of the house, and

came back hours later even more furious. She pushed me down to the floor, ripped my shorts and started fucking me. I tried to make her stop but she wouldn't. I know it wasn't really violent but I fell [*sic*] disgusting. ("Lesbian Sexual Assault," 1998, p. 2)

Although the literature discusses acquaintance and partner assaults more frequently, stranger assaults by gay and bisexual men do happen. These assaults may happen particularly to men who are in public sex environments or other locations in which one's presence is assumed to imply consent. As with heterosexual women who do not invite assault even though they are in risky situations, being in a highly sexualized environment does not imply consent for men, either. Given the stigma and secrecy involved in these types of environments, however, the prevalence of this type of assault is unknown. Anecdotal reports suggest that such assaults do happen to men by men who are strangers. Whether lesbians or bisexual women engage in stranger assaults of this kind is unknown. However, to the extent that casual or anonymous sex is more prominent in gay male culture than lesbian culture, such occurrences among women may be rare.

ISSUES FOR SURVIVORS

Survivors of sexual violence face a myriad of issues, including physical, emotional, and social effects (Isely, 1998; Koss, Gidycz, & Wisniewski, 1987). For lesbian, gay, and bisexual people, however, these effects can be compounded by heterosexism. Herek (1992) defined heterosexism as "an ideological system that denies, denigrates, and stigmatizes any nonheterosexual form of behavior, identity, relationship, or community" (p. 89) and includes both cultural and psychological heterosexism. According to Berrill and Herek (1990), heterosexism leads to secondary victimization, which occurs when victims are retraumatized by bias in the aftermath of the assault. For example, in secondary victimization, gay or lesbian victims who report assaults may be punished by being "outed" (having sexual identity disclosed without one's consent) and thereby risking stigma, rejection, and discrimination. They may risk "loss of employment, eviction from housing, denial of public accommodations, and loss of child custody" (Berrill & Herek, 1990, p. 401) because of legalized discrimination and heterosexism.

As an example of cultural heterosexism, although all 50 states have legislation that enables heterosexual victims of domestic violence to obtain restraining orders, only four states specifically include same-gender relationship violence in their statutes. Seven states explicitly exclude same-sex relationships from legal protection. Furthermore, three states still criminalize consensual same-sex behavior in so-called sodomy laws. In one of these states, the victim of sexual assault by a same-gender partner could be prosecuted for "sodomy" if the relationship came to the attention of law enforcement officials. The statutes of 37 states are in gender-neutral language but are subject to judicial interpretation as to whether they cover victims of same-sex partners (National Coalition of Anti-Violence Programs, 1998). Given the variability of laws criminalizing same-sex partner violence combined with issues of stigma and shame, low rates of reporting that violence are to be expected.

Bisexual, gay, and lesbian victims of sexual assault need not face discrimination to deter their willingness to seek help or report assaults. The national lesbian health care survey results suggested that reporting of sexual assaults against lesbians is very low, and when victims do tell others about being assaulted, they typically tell friends rather than police or counselors (Bradford, Ryan, & Rothblum, 1994). In fact, Waterman, Dawson, and Bologna (1989) noted that lesbians (including even nonvictims) perceived that counseling for sexual assault would be difficult to obtain. Lesbian victims perceived the availability of counseling as being even lower than did nonvictims. These results suggest that counselors, whom one would suspect to be more sympathetic to lesbian, gay, and bisexual people than law enforcement officials, are not perceived by the community as available to meet the needs of lesbian, gay, and bisexual assault victims.

Although heterosexism in the larger culture certainly affects victims, survivors' needs are further complicated by internalized homophobia, defined as a person's "direction of negative social attitudes toward the self" (Meyer & Dean, 1998, p. 161). The effects of internalized homophobia can range from concealment, internal stress, and fear of disclosure to self-hatred and suicidal ideation and behavior (Slater, 1993). Compounded with the aftermath of sexual assault, the effects of internalized homophobia may be devastating. For example, a woman may believe that she is only a lesbian because she was sexually assaulted by a man (Orzek, 1988). Conversely, a man may believe that being sexually assaulted is punishment for being gay. Furthermore, in cases in which assaults are victims' first same-sex sexual experiences, survivors may develop distorted beliefs and perceptions about their sexual selves, in which the assault becomes the point of reference in a developing sexual identity. Without supporting evidence to the contrary, survivors may develop a sexuality in which being gay or lesbian becomes tied to being a victim, filled with violation, shame, and self-doubt.

Paired with these issues, individuals in the process of developing a bisexual, lesbian, or gay identity may have conflicted feelings about the assault, and where they are in this journey affects how they cope with the assault (Orzek, 1988). On one hand, they may have wanted to experiment with same-sex sexual behavior, but not in that way, at that time, or with that person. This confusion may be complicated by physiological responses. Male victims frequently report erections or ejaculations during the assault, leading to feelings of shame, guilt, and embarrassment, fueling the myth that they "must have wanted it" (Scarce, 1997). Although not as obvious in women, female victims may experience physiological arousal and subsequent confusing emotions.

Several other myths may affect lesbian, bisexual, and gay sexual assault victims. Myths such as "women aren't aggressive," "men don't get raped," and "men always want sex" contribute to the way victims make sense of what happened to them and the willingness of others to help. Many male victims, for example, do not consider an assault to be a rape unless they are physically injured during the assault (Mezey & King, 1987). Lesbians may fear ridicule or disbelief by service providers who do not believe that women are capable of sexually assaulting other women. Given the heterosexual bias in most writing on sexual assault, these fears are not unfounded.

The type of assault may also influence the effects it has on its victim. Hickson et al. (1994) noted the particular significance of anal sex and forced anal sex to gay men. Although perhaps not having the same salience as vaginal rape to women (because of women's traditional definitions in the context of marriage and virginity), forced anal sex is loaded with interpersonal significance to gay men. In this age of AIDS, unprotected anal sex is a highly risky behavior, and men who are forced to be a receptive participant in anal sex without a condom face additional trauma because of the risk of HIV infection. This removal of one's choice to engage in unsafe sexual behavior adds a layer of trauma not present in the days prior to the AIDS epidemic.

Another factor affecting victims is the continued contact with a known perpetrator. Many gay and lesbian communities are small, interwoven networks, and particularly on college campuses, victims and perpetrators are likely to have mutual friends and acquaintances. This continued contact with a perpetrator, in addition to retraumatizing a victim, may render a victim without support as friends are forced to "choose sides" or become estranged from a small and cohesive community. Furthermore, denial of the problem of violence within the community may cause victims to internalize their feelings or leave the community or campus, adding to their isolation. Finally, victims of lesbian relationship violence have noted that being victimized by a woman was a profound betrayal "(b)ecause women aren't supposed to do that to other women" (Tuel & Russell, 1998, p. 358).

Additional factors of racism and gender identity confusion may come into play. Others have explicated some of the issues by people of color who are also gay, lesbian, and bisexual (e.g., Greene, 1997; Mendez, 1996; Waldron, 1996). Service providers need culturally relevant knowledge to provide adequate services that take into account victims' cultural contexts and the ways in which their sexual identities interact with their ethnicities. Gender identity may be misunderstood by services providers, too, leading, for example, to a "butch" lesbian being perceived as a man and denied services or the refusal of others to respect a transgendered individual's gender identity.

DEVELOPING CAMPUS PREVENTION EFFORTS

In recent years, sexual assault prevention programs have proliferated on college campuses. Roark (1987) described three levels of prevention that programs require to be successful: primary, secondary, and tertiary. Programs to prevent sexual assault of lesbian, gay, and bisexual students may be considered from this three-tiered perspective.

Primary prevention programs are those that target an entire population. Creation of a campus environment that is safe for gay, bisexual, and lesbian people is of utmost importance. People of all sexual orientations must feel respected and valued if any prevention efforts are to be successful. Heterosexism and homophobia can create a hostile campus culture in which violence against lesbian, gay, and bisexual people is condoned (Slater, 1993). Creation of an open and supportive environment can go a long way toward ending homophobic stigma and antigay bias that lead to hate crimes. Two excellent sources for creation of a campus environment that is safe for GLBT people are *Working with lesbian, gay, bisexual, and transgender students: A handbook for faculty and administrators* (Sanlo, 1998) and *Lesbian, gay, bisexual, and trangender campus organizing: A comprehensive manual* (Shepard, Yeskel, & Outcalt, 1995). Sanlo's comprehensive handbook includes sections on the developmental needs of GLBT college students; career, counseling, and health issues; curricular and classroom applications; concerns unique to specific groups (e.g., fraternities, residence halls, student organizations, alumni groups, religious entities, athletics); administration and policy; technology use; and sample programs. The campus organizing manual serves as an excellent how-to book for campuses beginning to organize around GLBT issues. Both resources discuss the importance of addressing GLBT issues at many levels across the institution, from interpersonal interactions to institutional policies.

Primary prevention efforts that target the campus at large should be inclusive of lesbian, gay, bisexual, and transgender people and acknowledge that one does not have to be a woman to be raped. This recommendation does not imply that gender should be ignored in trainings. As Renzetti (1996) notes, "Intimate violence *is* gendered, as are individual and institutionalized responses to that violence" (p. 215). However, assuming that all cases of sexual assault are heterosexual in nature and involve male perpetrators and female victims does a grave disservice.

Acknowledgment that sexual assault can happen to bisexual, lesbian, and gay people and to men of all sexual orientations can help break the stigma associated with being a victim. These acknowledgments need to be made each time sexual assault is discussed.

Programs aimed at general audiences such as residence halls or fraternities often include role plays of dating situations. These programs could be expanded to include scenarios of same-sex relationships along with heterosexual examples. Facilitators would need to be prepared to address homophobic attitudes and comments, but if handled well, these types of programs have two effects: (a) increasing awareness of sexual assault as it affects all people in all types of relationships; and (b) addressing homophobic attitudes by confronting once taboo issues. A more subtle way to reach gay, lesbian, and bisexual students is to include examples and resources in all publicity and literature about sexual assault and to make this literature widely available for students.

Secondary prevention efforts target a specific subset of a population who may be considered at risk. In this context, besides changing the overall campus environment to make it safer for GLBT people (primary prevention), specific programming needs to be developed to address sexual assault prevention within the gay communities. Examples of secondary prevention programming are a self-defense course for bisexual, gay, and lesbian students or a workshop on same-gender violence. Programs on sexual responsibility and decision-making should be tailored to the specific population targeted, keeping in mind that the concerns of gay men, lesbians, and bisexual men may be quite different from each other. Hickson et al. (1994) noted that the eroticization of violence is a prominent theme in gay male subculture, so programs need to promote healthy forms of sexual expression when addressing this group. Programs for women might focus on recognizing red flags in intimate relationships as well as assertiveness and self-defense training. Red flags or warning signs may include indicators such as feeling nervous, confused, or depressed in the relationship, feeling insulted by a partner, or putting the partner's needs ahead of one's own. Prevention efforts aimed at students questioning their sexuality should be safe, affirming, and confidential and should provide the students a setting to explore sexual identity and expression and decision-making and self-care skills during this confusing time.

Sexual assault prevention programs and departments can also have designated liaisons with the gay, lesbian, bisexual, and transgender communities who can provide important support for community members. These liaisons should be trusted individuals who serve as role models of responsible behavior. Although targeted programs may have significant benefit, they should not be seen as substitutes for making entire programs and staffs aware of and comfortable with bisexual, gay, and lesbian issues. Not all students who either identify as bisexual, gay, or lesbian or who engage in same-gender sexual behavior will identify with the campus's visible gay organizations or communities.

Finally, tertiary intervention programs are those that target individuals who have been sexually assaulted to reduce or limit the amount of distress they experience subsequent to the assault. To meet this need, all victim and offender services must be sensitive to the needs of transgendered, bisexual, gay, and lesbian students. Law enforcement officials, court personnel, victim advocates, counselors, medical personnel, paraprofessionals, and others with whom victims come in contact should receive extensive training on multicultural issues and issues facing GLBT assault victims and students in general. They should be taught to avoid assumptions of heterosexuality in language, definitions of sex, and identity. Finally, people who work with victims need to examine their own biases and homophobia, recognizing that challenging societal definitions of sex and gender may bring up personal issues and confusion (Orzek, 1988).

Although it is important for victim services to actually be a safe place for lesbian, gay, bisexual, and transgendered victims, these services also need to proactively communicate their support for the people they serve. Without information to the contrary, many GLBT people assume that services will not be available to them or will be hostile to their lifestyles or experiences. Therefore, efforts need to be made to identify services and providers as allies. For example, posters in offices and waiting rooms could include themes supportive of gay and lesbian identities; public statements can include language inclusive of gay, bisexual, lesbian, and transgendered people; and gender-neutral language can be used when describing sexual assault or when interviewing victims. Because members of sexual minorities are often hidden or closeted unless they know they are in supportive environments, these types of interventions need to be implemented with all victims, not merely those who are known to have a homosexual or bisexual orientation. Furthermore, individual providers, even those in hostile environments, can communicate their support to bisexual, lesbian, gay, and transgendered people and help them negotiate an otherwise hostile system.

MODEL PROGRAMS

Universities are increasingly recognizing the need for creation of campus climates that are safe and respectful for gay, lesbian, bisexual, and transgendered people. However, attention to gay and lesbian issues in sexual assault programs on college campuses has been largely absent. Rankin, a senior diversity analyst at Pennsylvania State University, reviewed 30 university campus climate surveys and reports from around the country. Her review (Rankin, 1998) states that themes of invisibility/ostracism, isolation/self-concealment, and university consequences were prominent in these reports.

In summarizing the recommendations of these reports, Rankin found four primary areas in which campus climate may be changed: structural transformation, policy inclusion, curricular integration, and educational efforts. Structural transformation includes:

> (c)reation of an office for LGBT concerns; (c)reation and identification of a designated safe, social meeting place; (i)ntegration of LGBT presence in university documents/publications . . . ; (a)ctive recruitment and retention of LGBT persons and allies; (c)reation of an LGBT alumni group within the existing alumni organization . . . ; (c)reation of documentation forms in police services for reporting of hate crimes against LGBT persons; and (c)reation of a standing LGBT advisory committee. (Rankin, 1998, p. 283)

Including sexual orientation in institutions' nondiscrimination statements and providing domestic partner benefits represent policy inclusion (Rankin, 1998). Curricular integration involves developing "queer studies" programs, expanding library holdings, and integrating sexual orientation issues into existing courses. Development of educational programs targeting the Greek system, residence life, student orientation, faculty and staff orientation, peer education programs, campus health care staff, and safety officers are additional recommendations (Rankin, 1999).

A secondary prevention program was developed by The Ohio State University in the form of a self-defense course for gay, lesbian, and bisexual people (Ault, n.d.). The model used for this program, which they claim is the first of its kind in the United States when it was initiated in 1991, reflects feminist and "queer" perspectives. Although the course was described as a gay, lesbian, and bisexual self-defense class, it was open to whomever wished to participate, regardless of sexual orientation. Designed as five 2-hour sessions across 5 weeks, the course was both interactive and didactic, with each session divided into a theoretic/substantive component and a physical skills training component. The didactic sections were further subdivided into a brief lecture on some facet of violence and scenarios for role-playing experiences for participants. Opening and closing rituals for each session included personal sharing of self-defense experiences and guided imagery.

In the first of the five sessions, instructors offered a feminist perspective on the sexism and heterosexism aspects of violence against gay men, lesbians, and bisexuals and "the 'continuum of violence' in queer terms" (Ault, n.d., p. 6). The second session examined sexual harassment and verbal bashing of lesbian, gay, and bisexual people that occurs both within the community or that it perpetuated by straight people. Role-plays included opportunities for students to defend themselves against verbal harassment. "Gay bashings" were the topic of the third session, and role-plays depicted increasingly threatening scenes of verbal harassment or physical assault.

The fourth session consisted of discussion of intimate partner violence, the cycle theory of domestic violence, and role-plays in which students could defend themselves against an abusive partner. The final session culminated in discussions of sexual assault and included issues of consent, power, and community norms. Presenters noted that in this final session gender differences became most salient, and they stressed the importance of respect for diversity and tolerance for ambiguity, while stressing the central purpose of the session:

> to raise awareness of sexual assault against gay, lesbian, and bi people perpetrated by nongay strangers or acquaintances, GLB acquaintances, dates, and same-sex partners; to offer people opportunities to have their experiences validated; and to provide them with some means of identifying and resisting sexual assault situations. (Ault, n.d., p. 7)

The Ithaca Rape Crisis (IRC) program, although not university affiliated, works closely with members of the campus communities in this town with two universities. As do many rape crisis units, the IRC maintains a 24-hour hotline for victims of sexual assault. However, they also have done an excellent job of reaching out to the gay, bisexual, and lesbian communities through articles in the local gay newspaper, educational forums, support groups, and outreach/publicity items targeting the Ithaca community. For example, bookmarks distributed throughout the community invite gay men or lesbians to call or come to the center to discuss sexual violence. "For lesbians," one bookmark reads, "the person who assaults you may be another woman or a man. More than likely they will be a friend, a lover, an ex-lover, an acquaintance. They may also be a stranger." Verbal, physical, and emotional sexual violence are defined, and resources are included. Similar bookmarks are available for gay men. In addition to these outreach efforts, staff members receive training about gay, lesbian, bisexual, and transgender issues surrounding sexual assault, including coming out, age of victim, sexual identity development, community support, homophobic violence, and gender confusion (C. Tague, personal communication, December 1, 1998).

At the University of Colorado at Boulder, the CU Rape and Gender Education Program (COURAGE) and the Gay, Lesbian, Bisexual, Transgender Resource Center have collaborated to ensure that lesbian, bisexual, and gay students' needs are met through the campus's prevention programs. Initial projects have included revision of the peer education training program and manual to include gay, bisexual, and lesbian sexual assault issues. As part of the COURAGE peer training program, students participate in a 20-hour training, which now includes a section working with GLBT students. Peers are asked to examine their assumptions and beliefs about heterosexuality and homosexuality before learning about issues of specific relevance to GLBT students. They are invited to explore how recognition of same-gender sexual violence challenges their notions about violence, and they are led through a visualization exercise that allows heterosexual peer educators a chance to envision the life of a gay or lesbian student. The training program is supplemented by the training manual, which has been revised to include special sections on gay and lesbian sexual assault issues and highlighting of these issues throughout the text. For example, a page with common myths and facts about sexual assault has been revised to address myths such as "men can't be sexually assaulted" and "lesbians have perfect relationships." Peers are encouraged to critique the manual and suggest ways in which it may become more inclusive.

A different but related program under development at the University of Colorado at Boulder uses interactive theater to address issues of sexual violence (Brown & Tuel, 1999). Interactive theater programs are being created to address a variety of topics that deal with such student issues as safety, substance abuse, and diversity. One vignette has been developed to present a confidential discussion group for gay, bisexual, and questioning men that meets on campus. This scenario, called the "Four Is," depicts a prevalent pattern occurring in acquaintance sexual assault. Intoxication, ignoring, invasion, and isolation are all factors that singly, or in combination, contribute to sexual assault. The goals for the presentation are to: (a) introduce the four Is; (b) raise awareness about male rape and sexual assault, particularly in the gay community; (c) explore issues related to men's responses to sexual assault by another male; and (d) provide resources for male victims of sexual assault.

The presentation depicts two male students and includes two scenes, one taking place in a local gay bar at night and the second occurring the following day in the students' homes. The first scene portrays the events leading up to a sexual assault and the second portrays the two students having phone conversations with friends about their experiences the previous evening. A facilitator invites the audience to ask the actors questions and guides discussion to highlight different aspect of sexual assault, communication, and safety. The actors, who stay in role and pretend not to hear each other's answers, are trained to make appropriate responses, including common perpetrator and victim responses to sexual assault, factual information, and myths.

RECOMMENDATIONS

Hopefully, as the various constituents on college and university campuses become more aware of sexual assault and the needs of GLBT students, they will move toward developing programs to meet those needs. These programs require addressing all levels of prevention—primary, secondary, and tertiary. Many community agencies, including both sexual assault agencies and antigay violence programs, have begun to take into account some aspects of the needs of GLBT community members, and collaboration with these agencies is essential. In addition to avoiding duplication of services, collaboration between campus and community agency can ensure that all members of the community receive appropriate services. Also, since students are community members, too, collaboration means tending to the needs of the whole student.

Involving the entire campus community in prevention is of utmost importance. Programs that only serve "out" and visible gay students will neglect a large segment of the GLBT community, perhaps the group that is most in need. In addition to entire campus involvement, however, it is important to ensure that there are visible "safe" people who are identified and known as advocates of GLBT concerns. As one service provider noted, with a good advocate, victims can have a positive experience even in a less-than-adequate system. However, faced with an unsympathetic individual even in a system that is generally supportive to GLBT people, victims will have poor experiences.

Existing sexual assault prevention programs must be reviewed for both homophobic and heterosexist content. For example, one educational curriculum called "The Men's Program" was produced by a national organization and first used at the University of Maryland as a way to sensitize men to women's experiences of rape. This workshop and guidebook have been severely criticized as overtly homophobic and revictimizing to male survivors (M. Scarce, personal communication, December 10, 1998). New and existing workshops, programs, and written materials should be scrutinized to avoid these problems. Training for all members of the campus community engaged in sexual assault response and education should include sexual orientation as a variable when addressing sexual assault. Peers and professionals need to challenge heterosexist norms and assumptions in their attitudes and responses to sexual violence.

Campus services should also be assessed for inclusiveness. Tague, a staff member at Ithaca Rape Crisis Center in New York, developed the following list of questions to consider when attempting to create spaces and services that are welcoming to lesbian, gay, bisexual, and transgender (LGBT) people:

> Is the language on your intake/client forms inclusive of LGBT people and their experiences? Is it a policy to use inclusive language such as partner/significant other? Do your office and other areas have LGBT focus and positive materials displayed such as stickers, posters, videos, books, etc.? Do your outreach materials reflect a sensitivity and awareness that not all perpetrators of violence against women are men, that sometimes it is other women? Do you have specific materials that address gay men, lesbians, bisexuals and transgendered people and sexual assault issues? When possible does your agency participate in LGBT picnics, gatherings, and other community events? Is an evaluation of homophobia done with potential staff and volunteers? Is training on LGBT issues, homophobia, and sexual violence part of your training with new volunteers and staff? Are you aware of individuals in your community who could be of help to you by being a connection to the LGBT community? What community links do you have to the LGBT service organizations? Is same sex rape/sexual assault brought up for discussion in education programs? Does your agency receive newsletters, magazines, etc. that are LGBT focus? Are all of the staff and volunteers expected to provide effective services to LGBT people, or is the lesbian/bisexual on staff expected to handle those situations? Do you currently provide and advertise services to the

LGBT community? Is posting and distribution of materials done at LGBT locations/events? Does your agency participate in an ongoing dialog through articles in LGBT and "mainstream" media on sexual violence in the LGBT community? Is ongoing value clarification for staff/volunteers encouraged? If your agency does produce outreach materials for the LGBT community, are they well thought out and specific to issues related to LGBTs? Or, are they simply general information flyers that are provided to the general community with only the words LGBT put in at various places? (Tague, n.d., p. 1)

Finally, theory and practice in the prevention and treatment of sexual violence must be expanded beyond simple gender analyses. Although gender often plays a role in the perpetration and response to sexual assault, other factors such as heterosexism and homophobia may be just as important. Issues of power and control, not simply male socialization, need to be conceptualized as roots of sexual violence. Gay, lesbian, bisexual, and transgendered students must be fully welcomed into the fabric of the university community and into our understanding of sexual violence.

INTERNET RESOURCES

An excellent list of internet resources for individuals and institutions working to create campuses that are safe for lesbian, transgender, gay, and bisexual students can be found in Barnett and Sanlo (1998). Because internet addresses and sites change frequently, the Barnett and Sanlo chapter and updated information can be found at: www.uic.edu/orgs/lgbt/internet.chapter.html.

Internet sources for GLBT sexual assaults are few. However, a few sites deserve mention for their inclusion of these issues.

The web site for Rutgers University's sexual assault services mentions sexual orientation as a possible factor in sexual violence. The page also includes a pointer to another page on gay and lesbian dating violence. It is located at www.rutgers.edu/SexualAssault/

The Coalition for Positive Sexuality maintains a site that promotes sex-positive, responsible decision making among youth. See www.positive.org/~cps/Home/index.html.One subpage includes a candid discussion of sexual orientation and sexual assault in an inclusive and nonjudgmental manner. See www.positive.org/~cps/JustSayYes/respect.html.

The New York Anti-Violence Project maintains statistics on sexual assault reports made to the project. See www.avp.org/sa/avp_sexual-_assault_statistics.html. For a list of members of the National Coalition of Anti-Violence Programs, a coalition of programs that combat violence against gay, lesbian, bisexual, and transgendered people see www.avp.org/ncavp/members.html.

The website for Advocates for Abused and Battered Lesbians includes resources and links to other related sites. See www.aabl.org.

REFERENCES

Ault, A. (n.d.). *Self-defense for gay, lesbian, and bi people.* (Available from the Rape Education and Prevention Program, The Ohio State University, 408 Ohio Union, 1739 North High Street, Columbus, OH 43210).

Baier, J. L., Rosenzweig, M. G., & Whipple, E. G. (1991). Patterns of sexual behavior, coercion, and victimization of university students. *Journal of College Student Development, 32,* 310–321.

Barnett, D. C., & Sanlo, R. L. (1998). The lavender web: LGTB resources on the internet. In R. L. Sanlo (Ed.), *Working with lesbian, gay, bisexual, and transgender college students* (pp. 403–412). Wesport, CT: Greenwood Press.

Berrill, K. T. (1993). Anti-gay violence and victimization in the United States: An overview. In G. M. Herek & K. T. Berrill (Eds.), *Hate crimes: Confronting violence against lesbians and gay men* (pp. 19–45). Newbury Park, CA: Sage.

Berrill, K. T., & Herek, G. M. (1990). Primary and secondary victimization in anti-gay hate crimes. *Journal of Interpersonal Violence, 5,* 401–413.

Bradford, J., Ryan, C., & Rothblum, E. D. (1994). National lesbian health care survey: Implications for mental health care. *Journal of Consulting and Clinical Psychology, 62,* 228–242.

Brand, P. A., & Kidd, A. H. (1986). Frequency of physical aggression in heterosexual and female homosexual dyads. *Psychological Reports, 59,* 1307–1313.

Brown, R., & Tuel, B. D. (1999). *GLBT sexual assault presentation.* Unpublished manuscript.

Cortina, L. M., Swan, S., Fitzgerald, L. F., & Waldo, C. (1998). Sexual harassment and assault: Chilling the climate for women in academia. *Psychology of Women Quarterly, 22,* 419–441.

Duncan, D. (1990). Prevalence of sexual assault victimization among heterosexual and gay/lesbian university students. *Psychological Reports, 66,* 65–66.

Elliott, P. (1996). Shattering illusions: Same-sex domestic violence. In C. M. Renzetti & C. H. Miley (Eds.), *Violence in gay and lesbian domestic partnerships* (pp. 1–8). Binghamton, NY: Haworth.

Greene, B. (Ed.). (1997). *Ethnic and cultural diversity among lesbians and gay men.* Thousand Oaks, CA: Sage.

Herek, G. M. (1993). The social context of hate crimes: Notes on cultural heterosexism. In G. M. Herek & K. T. Berrill (Eds.), *Hate crimes: Confronting violence against lesbians and gay men* (pp. 89–104). Newbury Park, CA: Sage.

Hickson, F. C. I., Davies, P. M., Hunt, A. J., Weatherburn, P., McManus, T. J., & Coxon, A. P. M. (1994). Gay men as victims of nonconsensual sex. *Archives of Sexual Behavior, 23,* 281–294.

Hodge, S., & Canter, D. (1998). Victims and perpetrators of male sexual assault. *Journal of Interpersonal Violence, 13,* 222–239.

Isely, P. J. (1998). Sexual assault of men: College-age victims. *National Association of Student Personnel Administrators Journal, 35,* 305–317.

Koss, M. P., Gidycz, C. A., & Wisniewski, N. (1987). The scope of rape: Incidence and prevalence of sexual aggression and victimization in a national sample of higher education students. *Journal of Consulting and Clinical Psychology, 55,* 162–170.

Lesbian sexual assault. (1998). *New York City gay and lesbian anti-violence project* [On-line]. (Available: http://www/avp.org/sa/lesbian-assault.htm).

Lie, G., Schilit, R., Bush, J., Montagne, M., & Reyes, L. (1991). Lesbians in currently aggressive relationships: How frequently do they report aggressive past relationships? *Violence & Victims, 6,* 121–135.

Male sexual assault. (1998). *New York City gay and lesbian anti-violence project* [On-line]. (Available: http://www.avp.org/sa/male-assault.htm).

Mendez, J. M. (1996). Serving gays and lesbians of color who are survivors of domestic violence. In C. M. Renzetti & C. H. Miley (Eds.), *Violence in gay and lesbian domestic partnerships* (pp. 53–61). Binghamton, NY: Haworth.

Meyer, I. H., & Dean, L. (1998). Internalized homophobia, intimacy, and sexual behavior among gay and bisexual men. In G. M. Herek (Ed.),

Stigma and sexual orientation: Understanding prejudice against lesbians, gay men, and bisexuals (pp. 160–186). Thousand Oaks, CA: Sage.

Mezey, G., & King, M. (1987). Male victims of sexual assault. *Medicine, Science, and the Law, 27,* 122–124.

National Coalition of Anti-Violence Programs. (1998, October). *Annual report on lesbian, gay, bisexual, transgender domestic violence.* (Available from Community United Against Violence, 973 Market Street, Suite 500, San Francisco, CA 94103).

Orzek, A. M. (1988). The lesbian victim of sexual assault: Special considerations for the mental health professional. *Women and Therapy: A Feminist Quarterly, 8,* 107–117.

Rankin, S. R. (1998). The campus climate report: Assessment and intervention strategies. In R. L. Sanlo (Ed.), *Working with lesbian, gay, bisexual, and transgender college students* (pp. 277–284). Westport, CT: Greenwood Press.

Rankin, S. R. (1999). Queering campus: Understanding and transforming climate. *Metropolitan Universities: An International Forum, 9*(4), 29–38.

Renzetti, C. M. (1996). On dancing with a bear: Reflections on some of the current debates among domestic violence theorists. In L. K. Hamberger & C. M. Renzetti (Eds.), *Domestic partner abuse* (pp. 213–222). New York: Springer.

Roark, M. L. (1987). Preventing violence on college campus. *Journal of Counseling and Development, 65,* 367–371.

Sanlo, R. L. (Ed.) (1998). *Working with lesbian, gay, bisexual, and transgender college students.* Westport, CT: Greenwood Press.

Scarce, M. (1997). Same-sex rape of male college students. *Journal of American College Health, 45,* 171–173.

Schneider, B. E. (1991). Put up or shut up: Workplace sexual assaults. *Gender & Society, 5,* 533–548.

Shepard, C. F., Yeskel, F., & Outcalt, C. (Eds.) (1995). *Lesbian, gay, bisexual, and transgender campus organizing: A comprehensive manual.* Washington, DC: National Gay and Lesbian Task Force.

Slater, B. R. (1993). Violence against lesbian and gay male college students. *Journal of College Student Psychotherapy, 8,* 177–202.

Stermac, L., Sheridan, P. M., Davidson, A., & Dunn, S. (1996). Sexual assault of adult males. *Journal of Interpersonal Violence, 11,* 52–64.

Tague, C. (n.d.) *Some things to think about concerning LGBT friendly spaces and services.* (Available from the Ithaca Rape Crisis Center, 308 W. State Street, Ithaca, NY 14850).

Tuel, B. D., & Russell, R. K. (1998). Self-esteem and depression in battered women: A comparison of lesbian and heterosexual survivors. *Violence Against Women, 4,* 344–362.

Waldner-Haugrud, L. K., & Gratch, L. V. (1997). Sexual coercion in gay/lesbian relationships: Descriptive and gender differences. *Violence & Victims, 12,* 87–98.

Waldron, C. M. (1996). Lesbians of color and the domestic violence movement. In C. M. Renzetti & C. H. Miley (Eds.), *Violence in gay and lesbian domestic partnerships* (pp. 43–52). Binghamton, NY: Haworth.

Waterman, C. K., Dawson, L. J., & Bologna, M. J. (1989). Sexual coercion in gay male and lesbian relationships: Predictors and implications for support services. *Journal of Sex Research, 26,* 118–124.

CHAPTER 10

Sexual Assault and the University Judicial Process

Douglas R. Pearson *

The most challenging student violation that any university judicial office confronts is a sexual assault by one of its students against another. Few issues can polarize a university campus community more quickly, or tap into a wider array of emotions, than this allegation. Since the university has the obligation to serve both the alleged perpetrator and the alleged student-victim in a sexual assault case, administrators can often feel torn while fulfilling their responsibilities. Moreover, the obligation of the university judicial officer to maintain a safe and secure campus community during the period of dealing with the allegation further complicates matters.

The university judicial process, in its simplest form, serves two primary purposes: (a) to educate students by making them aware of, and holding them responsible for, the university's expectations, as detailed in the student code of conduct; and (b) to protect the university community. University administrators

*The author wishes to acknowledge the material suggestions made by Dr. Barbara Varchol and the contributions of Ms. Mary Pearson, Dr. Jennifer Buchanan, Dr. K. C. White, Mr. David Klemanski, and Ms. Cheryl Brown.

vested with the responsibility of overseeing judicial processes can find themselves challenged when trying to balance these often perceived competing purposes, especially when dealing with allegations of sexual misconduct. Cases involving sexual assault are particularly complex because they encompass a wider range of constituents and issues than most cases of minor violations of the student code of conduct. This chapter outlines some key issues inherent in this topic. Because institutions differ in size and nature, as well as the frequency of reported cases, the ability to deal effectively with sexual assault charges varies from institution to institution. Each college must adhere to its unique set of state laws and institutional guidelines when adjudicating a sexual misconduct violation. This chapter provides the reader with some judicial fundamentals inherent in dealing with cases involving sexual assault and illuminates some dilemmas that may confront administrators as they attempt to accommodate the needs of charged students and alleged victims. I recommend ways to balance or resolve these potential dilemmas. Finally, I present the reader with a proposed "walk-through" of the process and the vital decision-making junctures faced by administrators who must resolve sexual misconduct charges within the confines of our nation's university systems. Although not specifically stated throughout this chapter, one should interpret the charged student to be the "alleged" perpetrator, and the victim to be the "alleged" victim. Until a hearing is held to determine the facts of the case, administrators should constantly check and affirm their neutrality when working with individuals involved in sexual misconduct.

INSTITUTIONAL RESPONSIBILITY AND DUE PROCESS

The basis for a university to take disciplinary action against a student can be traced back to the *in loco parentis* era of college life. Under the *in loco parentis* philosophy, the college, in essence, stood in "the place of the parent" with regard to decisions affecting all major aspects of college students' lives. Most researchers on the subject (Alstyne, 1969; Bickel & Lake, 1994; Brittain, 1971; Edwards, 1994) generally credit Sir William Blackstone in 1770 with the first application of the phrase *in loco parentis* to education. Blackstone wrote:

> The father may also delegate part of his parental authority, during his life, to the tutor or schoolmaster, of his child; who is then "*in loco parentis*" and has such a portion of the power of the parent committed to his charges, that of restraining and correction, as may be necessary to answer the purposes for which he was employed. (Blackstone, 1770, p. 413)

The appearance of the *in loco parentis* philosophy in the American judicial process can be traced back to at least 1837 in the case of *State v. Pendergrass* (Bickel & Lake, 1994), but *Gott v. Berea College* (1913) is most often cited as the case that provided the legal basis for colleges to maintain and enforce rules and regulations regarding student behavior:

> College authorities stand *in loco parentis* concerning the physical and moral welfare and mental training of the pupils, and we are unable to see why, to that end, they may not make any rule or regulation for the betterment of their pupils that a parent could for the same purpose. . . . [T]he courts are not disposed to interfere, unless the rules and aims are unlawful or against public policy. (p. 206)

This unbridled authority of institutions over student conduct was challenged during the student rights movements in the late 1950s and early 1960s and eventually tempered by a series of court decisions that began in 1961 with *Dixon v. Alabama State Board of Education.* In *Dixon*, the U.S. Court of Appeals concluded that students did not give up their basic Constitutional rights simply by enrolling in a public institution. The U.S. Court of Appeals in *Dixon* put forth that an institution must provide minimal due process rights of notice and an opportunity to be heard before taking judicial action against a student. These due process standards were later expounded on in several cases, most prominently in the case of *Goss v. Lopez* in 1975. Due process in a university judicial system simply means providing adequate procedural safeguards to protect the university from acting arbitrarily and capriciously in its dealings with students. Gehring and Young (1977) asserted that:

> Due process is a concept of fundamental fairness. It is not a fixed or inflexible concept unrelated to time and circumstances. Rather than attempting to formulate a precise definition of the term, the courts have preferred to define it as the 'gradual process of judicial inclusion and exclusion . . . ' It is well settled that the greater the right or interest sought to be deprived, the greater the procedural safeguards should be. (p. ix)

Notice can take many forms. Picozzi (1987) asserted that proper notice includes informing the student of:

> (1) the precise charges lodged against him, (2) the name(s) of the person(s) accusing him, (3) the specific regulations under which he is being charged, (4) the identity of the prosecuting authority, (5) the forum in which the prosecution will take place, (6) the date and the place of the hearing, (7) the names of the witnesses testifying against him, (8) a summary of their testimony, (9) a statement of his rights at the forthcoming hearing, (10) the possible sanctions he faces, (11) his right to appeal any adverse decision. (p. 248)

Although this may be a daunting list, most of these provisions can be accomplished simply by providing the charged student with a copy of the institution's student code of conduct. All codes of conduct should provide students with information on the process utilized by the institution for resolving judicial charges, the rights of students within that process, the range of possible sanctions, and relevant information on the process for initiating an appeal. Once this basic information has been made available to the student, the institution should maintain a process for notifying its students in writing about the specifics of their violations. This should include outlining the specific infraction(s) that will be reviewed at the hearing and the allegations on which each infraction is based. The allegations should include information on both the time and location of the incident, as well as the name of the victim in sexual assault cases. (In most states, identifying information beyond the victim's name, including social security number and address may be excluded to protect the victim.) Notice should be provided in a timely fashion, meaning that the charged student has adequate time to prepare for the hearing and gather any information or witnesses relative to his or her defense. Dannells (1997) found that court requirements for this period of time generally ranged from providing 2 days notice to 10 days.

"Hearing" means providing a student with a fair opportunity to address the charges in front of an unbiased hearing body. Picozzi (1987) asserted that

> a proper hearing should (1) consider only the charges and evidence of which the student has formal notice, (2) be open or closed to the public according to the student defendant's choice, (3) allow the student the assistance of counsel, (4) require witnesses to testify under oath, (5) provide the student with a chance to confront and cross examine his accusers, (6) provide the student with an opportunity to present evidence and witnesses on his own behalf, (7) not require a student to testify against himself, (8) provide the student with a compulsory process over people, objects and documents with the university community, except those otherwise covered by privileges of confidentiality under law, (9) require the university to prove its charges by clear and convincing evidence, (10) be recorded and transcribed, and (11) provide a written finding of the facts by the jurors. (p. 249–250)

Although this provides the reader with a good overview of many of the components necessary for a fair hearing, not all of these safeguards are required or universally accepted, and some are in need of explanation.

Procedural safeguards vary from institution to institution and from state to state. Some of the key procedural protections provided at most institutions include the right to a hearing before an impartial hearing body, the right to confront witnesses, and the right to some form of advisement. The right to advisement can take many forms, including the allowance of an attorney at the proceedings. However, the role the advisor plays in the judicial process can dramatically alter the nature of a university's judicial proceeding, especially in cases involving sexual assault. Institutions can, and should, note the distinction between an advisor's role to "advise" as opposed to "represent." Many attorneys believe that they should be allowed to represent the student and speak on the student's behalf during hearings. It is imperative that an institution weigh the merits of allowing an advisor to become the student's "mouthpiece" against the philosophy and purposes of the university judicial process. Swen (1987) pointed out that "most courts do not find due process violations where university officials permit students to be represented by legal counsel, but several courts have rejected the assertion that due process entitles a student to legal counsel at a disciplinary hearing" (p. 373).

Although most researchers who have studied the institutional-student relationship agree that *in loco parentis* is no longer tenable as a guiding philosophy (Brittain, 1971; Zirkel & Reichner, 1986), several legal decisions in the 1980s suggest that a movement back toward an expanded responsibility for universities and colleges to protect students may have occurred (*Bullock v. Board of Governors of the University of North Carolina*, 1989; *Mullins v. Pine Manor College et al.*, 1983). In cases in which an institution is aware of a "foreseeable risk," the institution has an obligation to take action to prevent students from being harmed. This duty appears to be particularly true in cases in which landlord-tenant relationships exist, as courts appear to be upholding liability in these situations based on "special duty relationships" (Pearson, 1998). These cases suggest that institutions may not only have the right to take action in cases involving student conduct, but may have a legal obligation to do so in order to avoid liability.

DIFFERENCES BETWEEN CRIMINAL AND JUDICIAL PROCESSES

The university's right to take judicial action against a student in an allegation involving sexual assault often confuses students, attorneys, and professionals alike, when criminal action has also been sought. The question of double jeopardy arises. Since a sexual assault involving a student can, and often does, result in criminal charges being filed against the student, it may appear that the student has been charged twice for the same crime. However, the law is established on this issue, and a university's judicial action against a student who violates a university policy does not violate the double jeopardy standard when the student has already been charged criminally. Double jeopardy refers to being tried twice for the same offense. As Dannells (1997) noted " . . . it is well established in the law that the prohibition against double jeopardy applies only to successive criminal proceedings, which campus actions, based on violations of institutional rules rather than criminal statutes, are not" (p. 22).

Violations of the law related to sexual assault and violations of university policies and regulations differ in many key ways, primarily in relation to how the violation is defined and adjudicated. Criminal charges involving sexual assault fall under state legislative definitions of rape and battery, while universities can define sexual misconduct violations for their own community. For instance, Pavela (1997) pointed out that Duke University defines sexual assault as:

> By stranger or acquaintance, rape, forcible sodomy, forcible sexual penetration, however slight, of another person's anal or genital opening with any object. These acts must be committed either by force, threat, intimidation or through the use of the victim's mental or physical helplessness of which the accused was aware or should have been aware.

Florida State University defines sexual misconduct primarily as "Any sexual act that occurs without the consent of the victim or that occurs when the victim is unable to give consent" (*Florida State University Handbook*, 1998/1999, p. 85). Although both Duke University and Florida State University include other specifics of sexual misconduct within their violations, these definitions illustrate the differences that may exist between institutions when defining this violation.

Administrators need to review their institution's definitions to ensure that they are specific enough to provide students with adequate notice of what is considered appropriate and inappropriate, without making the definitions so narrow that they do not encompass all of the misconduct deemed necessary. In their research on student disciplinary conduct codes, Stoner and Cerminara (1990) recommend the following encompassing definition:

"Physical abuse, verbal abuse, threats, intimidation, harassment, coercion and/or other conduct which threatens or endangers the health or safety of any person" (p. 100). As Pavela (1997) made clear, no definition is going to be without controversy.

Criminal and university charges are also adjudicated in separate venues with distinct rules governing their procedures and often require different weights of evidence to find a student guilty, thereby creating further distinctions with regard to double jeopardy. For instance, in most university judicial proceedings written statements and hearsay evidence are admissible, whereas in most criminal proceedings they are not. As previously noted, university judicial proceedings can also limit the degree to which a student's advisor can participate. For example, a student does not have a constitutional right to legal representation in most university judicial proceedings; however, the use of an advisor/attorney in criminal proceedings is not only necessary, but imperative in most venues.

Finally, the weight of evidence used in judicial and criminal proceedings can vary a great deal. Criminal proceedings employ what is known as the "beyond a reasonable doubt" standard, commonly interpreted to mean that all other avenues, other than that the charged individual committed the crime, have been ruled out. College and university judicial proceedings, on the other hand, most commonly utilize one of two weights of evidence: (a) the "preponderance of evidence," or (b) the "clear and convincing" standard suggested by Picozzi (1987). The "preponderance of the evidence" standard means that the evidence, taken as a whole, shows the fact sought to be proved is more probable than not; this has often been interpreted to mean that there is a greater than 50% likelihood that an event occurred. The "clear and convincing" standard falls somewhere between the "preponderance" standard and that of "beyond a reasonable doubt," and has often been interpreted to mean about the 75% likelihood of occurrence.

THE RIGHTS AND ROLE OF VICTIMS

Cases involving sexual assault can be particularly sensitive when the alleged victim is a university student. The last two decades have witnessed a dramatic increase in both state and federal legislation to protect victims of crimes. Today, every state in this country has laws protecting victims' rights (Tomz & McGillis, 1998). They stated that "Although states have not established one standard set of rights for victims, most bills of rights contain basic provisions for victims to be treated with dignity and compassion, to be informed of the status of their case, to be notified of hearings and trial dates, to be heard at sentencing and parole through victim impact statements, and to receive restitution from convicted offenders" (p. 3). These laws are primarily focused on the rights of victims within the criminal process. However, an awareness of the legislative mandates that apply in each school's state, and a familiarity of victimization issues as a whole, are both vital to administrators when creating university policies and procedures for dealing with victims of sexual assault. Some of the key issues related to working with victims and developing policies and procedures are listed below.

THE ROLE OF THE VICTIM IN THE CHARGING DECISION

Depending on the design of the institutional judicial process, the role of the victim in the process can vary widely. The initial issue that poses one of the greatest challenges to institutions is determining if the victim or the institution should have the final say about the decision to pursue judicial action in a sexual assault case. To make an appropriate decision on this issue, administrators need to be aware of the dynamics of victimization and balance those dynamics against the moral and legal obligations of the institution regarding community safety and security.

Institutions can approach this dilemma from two perspectives. One suggests that the victim should have the final decision on whether the university should charge. Proponents of this philosophy argue that going forward without the consent of a victim potentially victimizes the individual further and removes that essential component of control often lost by a victim because of the assault. Further, disregard for the victim's wishes may also alienate the victim and, thus, greatly jeopardize the case because the testimony of a victim is so pivotal in a sexual misconduct charge. That the university should have the final decision with regard to the charging decision is the other perspective. This perspective argues that the university has a legal and moral obligation to take action against students alleged to have committed a sexual assault. Once an administrator is aware of a potential attack on a student, this perspective asserts that the institution has the moral and legal obligation to take steps to protect the community and its students from a potential danger.

THE ROLE OF AN ADVISOR

As with a charged student, the institution should consider clearly delineating the rights and limitations of advisors for the victim during disciplinary procedures. The degree of participation of the victim's advisor should be considered and balanced against the rights and limitations outlined in the judicial process for the advisor of the charged student. The goal is to ensure fairness in the proceedings for both parties. The purpose of an advisor for victims is threefold: (a) to aid them in preparing and participating in the judicial process, (b) to help them deal with the emotional aspects of the victimization as they proceed in the hearing, and (c) to protect the victim's case related to any outside criminal matters that may still be pending.

Who the advisor should be is often impacted by the status of any pending criminal charges. If criminal charges are still pending, a victim would be wise to have legal counsel accompanying him or her to protect his or her interests. However, at many institutions, the role of advisor is often assumed by a victim advocate. This could be a good choice if the victim is in need of emotional support, because these professionals are trained to deal with these issues. But having a victim advocate serve as a victim's advisor can place the victim advocate and the institution in a precarious position. A victim advocate is a professional whose primary purpose is to work with victims by outlining options and advocating for the choices made by the victim as he or she deals with the emotional and physical ramifications associated with the assault. "Advising," especially in a judicial process, can often be at odds with this purpose, and can be outside the realm of the advocate's expertise. More importantly, victim advocate services are often supported by and housed within the institution, sometimes within the same department as the judicial office. Utilizing victim advocate services as an advising body for a student-victim could jeopardize the integrity of the judicial process and the perception of fairness. It is important to remember that the university becomes the charging agent in a sexual assault case. The institution should consider the ramifications of providing advisement services from a university victim advocate office in light of this role.

THE ROLE OF THE VICTIM IN THE HEARING

Victims need to be made aware early on that they may be asked to provide supporting testimony in front of a judicial hearing body if charges are pursued. Since the victim's testimony is so crucial to a hearing body in reaching conclusions about sexual assault violations, every effort must be made to keep the victim informed and involved in the process. Most university judicial processes allow the charged students to question individuals who bring forth information against them. This includes the victim of a sexual assault.

The role of the victim at the hearing is to provide as much information as possible to the hearing body and to answer questions about the incident from both the hearing body and the charged student. This may be very traumatic for victims in light of what they have been through. Answering questions about a forced sexual encounter to a judicial hearing body and the person accused of the violation is, obviously, a daunting request for anyone. Thus, many institutions have found ways to ease this burden without jeopardizing the ability to gain information and follow up with questions about the testimony.

Some of the methods employed include allowing victims to testify from another room by phone or by two-way audio/video hook-up. This approach allows for instantaneous questioning and testimony. Another method has been to allow the victim to answer preset questions from the panel and charged student on audio-tape that can later be played back for the panel and the charged student. Once the taped testimony is heard, both the panel and charged student are allowed to draft follow-up questions that are again posed to the victim and taped for playback. This can continue until there are no more questions from either party. In exploring these options, it is imperative to involve the university legal counsel and scrutinize the wording of the institution's conduct code before deciding how to proceed. Many conduct codes state that the charged student simply has the right to "confront" witnesses. "Confront" may be defined as simply hearing testimony, or it may be defined as both hearing and *seeing* the victim. The interpretation of "confront" can be a source of legal conflict if there is disagreement between the charged student and the university when making arrangements for a victim; therefore, involving the university counsel when making any accommodations for a victim would be wise.

Another issue that often arises with sexual assault cases is the presence of the victim during the hearing. Keeping in mind that the charged student should be present when any information regarding his or her case is obtained by the hearing body, the question then becomes what rights does the victim have with regards to being present during the hearing. Although this may appear to be a simple issue, it is important to keep in mind that the victim is not the charged individual, and, as a result, may not maintain the same degree of rights as the charged student during the hearing. In cases involving sexual assault, the decision of responsibility often hinges on an evaluation of credibility between the charged student and the victim. As information from witnesses is gathered, a victim may be asked by the panel to come back and to provide additional information or clarify previous testimony. Having the victim present when witness information is gathered may "taint" crucial follow-up testimony needed from the victim. Therefore, great care must be used when making this decision.

THE ROLE OF THE VICTIM IN THE DECISION

Obviously, a victim should not participate in the decision-making process regarding the university charges. However, in many processes, a victim is allowed to provide input to the hearing body regarding sanctions imposed on the charged student if the student is found "responsible." This can be facilitated by allowing the victim to provide a concluding statement at the end of the hearing. Frequently, however, this input takes the form of an impact statement. An impact statement is written by the victim and is a sealed document given to the hearing body. The statement includes information from the victim on how the sexual assault has affected him or her and what particular sanctions the victim would like to see implemented by the board. The hearing body uses it only after a determination of responsibility has been reached. The panel is not bound to the victim's recommendations, and generally does not read the impact statement if the student is found "not responsible."

DEALING WITH A SEXUAL ASSAULT ON YOUR CAMPUS

This section provides readers with fundamental steps and suggestions for dealing with a sexual assault violation on their campus. Again, administrators must be fully aware of the state and administrative laws that apply to their specific campuses and of the subtle differences that exist within their own specific codes of conduct when dealing with an assault. Where conflicts arise between these suggestions and your procedures, legal counsel should be sought. As in any critical situation, it is essential that all university administrators dealing with a sexual assault keep detailed notes on their work with the case, including any and all contacts with either the victim or the charged student.

STEP ONE: INITIAL INFORMATION AND ADMINISTRATIVE ACTION

An administrator may first become aware of a sexual assault from many different sources, including the media, the police, residence life staff, or various counseling services. Therefore, the first step in dealing with a sexual assault is to identify the source and evaluate the reliability of the information received. At most institutions, campus police should be able to help with this assessment. Official police reports taken directly from victims and witnesses are much more reliable and helpful to an administrator than information reported in the media or taken from indirect sources. The primary concern for an administrator at this stage should be to assess the health and safety of the alleged victim. It is at this juncture that victim advocate or university counseling personnel can be helpful in establishing a rapport with the victim by offering support and advice and trying to identify the victim's needs. Most law enforcement agencies and counseling services are trained to deal with victims of sexual assault and encourage the victim to seek medical treatment to assess his or her health and obtain potential evidence. At many institutions, safe apartments or rooms are available for victims who may be fearful of staying in their apartments or residence hall rooms after the incident.

Once the immediate needs of the victim have been met, the next step is to obtain as much information as possible on the incident and evaluate what administrative action, if any, is necessary. Whenever possible, the gathering of information should be done by trained law enforcement agents who are familiar with investigative techniques and can assess potential criminal charges. However, at most institutions, statements provided directly by the victim to the university judicial office can also be the basis for a charge. Regardless of the source, the information as a whole should, at a minimum, include: (a) clear identification of the suspect and the alleged victim, any previous criminal or judicial history on the suspect, and their student standing (i.e., identifying if they are currently enrolled students); (b) the nature and location of the alleged incident, including whether it took place on or off campus, and whether there are any potential mitigating circumstances (e.g., if the victim or suspect are minors, if there were multiple assailants); (c) feedback from the victim on what his or her preference may be in pursuing university judicial action, criminal action, or both; and (d) relevant information from law enforcement agencies, if necessary, on the status of the investigation and any potential criminal charges that might be pending. All of the information should be in writing prior to taking any university action to limit possible errors and discrepancies, and to protect the institution from acting prematurely or recklessly.

Once this information is gathered, the university needs to do two things. First, it must assess if the information is sufficient to pursue charging a student with a violation of the student code of conduct. Second, the university should evaluate the need for immediate administrative steps to be taken to protect the victim or the campus community from any potential danger posed by the suspect. This administrative action generally takes the form of an interim suspension (also known as a temporary suspension). An interim suspension, in essence, removes the student from the campus community until a hearing can take place to determine the facts of the case. Interim suspensions are permissible [see *Goss v. Lopez* (1975)] in cases in which a student may pose a threat to the property or welfare of others at the institution, as long as the institution's student code of conduct allows for such action. In these situations, a student can be prohibited access to certain areas of campus or the entire campus altogether prior to a hearing on his or her case. Stoner and Cerminara (1990) emphasized that the requisite notice and hearing on the incident should follow an interim suspension as soon as practicable. Many institutions allow for an appeal hearing on the decision of the imposed interim suspension. The hearing on the interim suspension should be separate from a hearing held later to determine the validity of student conduct charges in the case and should focus solely on the merits of the interim suspension decision.

STEP TWO: THE CHARGING DECISION

It is important to note that in student judicial cases involving potential criminal charges, the receipt of police reports or statements can often be delayed while prosecutors evaluating the information review and pursue legal strategies. Each institution must evaluate when it has received enough information to take immediate action, such as an interim suspension, and when to initiate conduct charges. Because the charge letter must provide enough notice to allow the student to know the specifics of the charges, it is strongly recommended that the university administrator get the *complete* copy of the written record that has been compiled *prior* to charging a student. This step will allow the university to focus the scope of the charges and prevent overcharging on violations that may be proven unfounded after receiving the entire docket of information. As noted earlier, interim suspension decisions can be made at any point that the university can justifiably defend that it believes the student poses a danger to the campus community. Since there can be gaps in time between when an interim suspension decision is made and when a charging decision is made, interim suspension decisions should not be made lightly.

The charge letter should provide the student with as much of the information outlined previously in the section on due process. It is necessary to include the following points:

- A listing of the specific student code violations alleged to have been breached.
- The allegations on which these charges are based (including the date, time, and the location of the alleged incident).
- Information on the judicial process and the charged student's rights within that process.
- A list of the witnesses who will be requested to attend the hearing.
- The time and location of the hearing and the person(s) presiding over the hearing.

It is also wise for the university's judicial officer to meet with the charged student and the alleged victim, separately, prior to the hearing to review the hearing process, ensure that both parties are fully informed, and resolve any logistical questions that may exist.

STEP THREE: THE HEARING

Because hearing procedures differ greatly in many ways from institution to institution, it is difficult to provide specific recommendations in this area. However, prior to any judicial hearing, several steps should occur. First, hearing bodies should be trained on institutional judicial procedures and victimization issues. This training will enable the hearing body to focus primarily on the task of determining the facts of the case during the hearing. It is imperative to protect against bias within the hearing board. Therefore, hearing bodies should be as diverse as possible and composed of individuals who have not had any prior involvement in or knowledge of the case. Because of the serious nature of adjudicating sexual assault cases and the challenge of determining "responsibility" for these charges, it is recommended that hearings be conducted by hearing panels as opposed to single judicial officers. Many institutions utilize panels that represent a cross-section of the university community, with either a faculty member or a staff administrator and a student. Dannells (1978, 1990) found that this was the most common composition of hearing boards for campus judicial boards.

Identifying and resolving the logistical problems of the hearing ahead of time is key. For instance, the hearing should occur in an area that ensures maximum privacy for the charged student, the victim, and any witnesses. If the hearing is closed, separate waiting rooms should be reserved and designated for the various parties. All potential witnesses should be contacted and provided information related to their involvement in the hearing. The judicial hearing body should be provided ample time to review the materials related to the case prior to the hearing and have a thorough understanding of the charges related to the incident. Issues of an open and closed hearing, who may accompany the charged student and the alleged victim in the hearing, and any modifications regarding the questioning of the victim should be reviewed and determined in advance. Inevitably, procedural questions will arise. Therefore, it is wise to make sure that the staff member with the most experience or knowledge regarding student judicial procedures be available during the time of the hearing.

The purpose of the hearing is to gain as much information about the alleged violation as possible, from as many sources as possible. As such, the alleged victim, the charged student, and any witnesses should be given ample opportunity to provide their testimony to the hearing body. Often, however, pertinent sources of information arise during a hearing that were unforeseen, yet relevant. Any available information, relative to the determination of responsibility, should be sought as long as it does not jeopardize the integrity of the process. During these times, the hearing panel should decide how to pursue obtaining this information in the fairest way possible to both the victim and the charged student.

STEP FOUR: THE DECISION AND SANCTIONS

After the hearing body has reviewed all the information and testimony it deems relevant to the proceedings, the hearing is concluded. The hearing body, utilizing the standard of evidence outlined in the institution's code of conduct, must determine the validity of the charges. The decision must include a clear finding of fact, the evidence supporting or refuting the charges, and any sanctions recommended by the panel. Sanctions should be applied only in cases involving a finding of "responsible."

Prior to making a sanctioning decision, the hearing body must take into consideration several factors: (a) any prior judicial record(s) of the charged student; (b) input from the victim (usually in the victim impact statement); (c) prior similar cases that have occurred on the campus and the sanctions imposed in those cases; and (d) any mitigating circumstances in the case that would warrant increasing or decreasing the sanctions. To ensure that the hearing body's determination of "responsibility" is based solely on the merits of the case, the judicial history of the charged student is generally not shared with the hearing body until after a determination of responsibility has been reached. Furthermore, a review of prior similar cases that have occurred at the institution is intended only to maintain some sense of consistency from case to case and should not prohibit the judicial body from implementing sanctions that it believes are justified based on the facts and circumstances of the particular case they are hearing—unless the system has a prescribed set of sanctions for each offense. Providing specific information in the decision letter on mitigating circumstances relating to the case can demonstrate the university is not arbitrary in upholding decisions that contain harsher or weaker sanctions than in previous cases.

Stoner and Cerminara (1990) offered a rather extensive list of possible sanctions that a university could choose to apply in judicial cases. The list includes warnings, probation, loss of privileges, fines, restitution, residence hall suspensions and expulsions, and university suspensions and expulsions (p. 114). Additional sanctions, such as restrictions on contact with the victim, completion of classes or programs on violence or sexual assault, and counseling, can also be included. It should be noted, however, that counseling is not universally accepted as an appropriate sanction to impose from a disciplinary hearing (Dannells, 1997; Gilbert & Sheiman, 1995). Many believe that forced counseling is unethical and ineffective. All final sanctions should be clear and specific, particularly with regard to due dates of sanctions.

STEP FIVE: APPEALS AND READMISSION

The criteria under which a student can appeal a decision and the number of times a student can appeal varies from institution to institution. Stoner and Cerminara (1990) pointed out that "Although there is some authority for the proposition that students need not be given the right to appeal from a decision rendered as a result of a hearing, providing an appellate process promotes an image of fairness" (p. 118). Information on institutional appeals should be provided in the initial hearing decision letter provided to the student. The most common bases for appeals are evidence of bias in the decision-making process, compromise of student's due process rights, and disproportionate sanctioning. Two other considerations include the discovery of new evidence relative to the decision and the sufficiency of the evidence presented at the hearing to meet the standard of evidence cited in the institution's hearing procedures. Many institutions qualify the "discovery of new evidence" standard by adding that it must be new information that was unavailable *at the time of the hearing*.

Often, a finding of "responsible" for charges of sexual assault results in a sanction that separates the charged student, either permanently or for a specified period of time, from the institution. In cases in which students are allowed to reapply to the institution, it is important for the institution to review the process for readmission. Although the final decision of readmission should be made by the Office of Admissions, the process should include receiving clearance from the judicial office, and, if feasible, the university police. This review allows the institution to accomplish two objectives. First, by receiving clearance from the judicial office, the institution can guarantee that any and all sanctions imposed, including the suspension, have been completed. Secondly, by working with law enforcement, the institution can try to reasonably verify that no new incidents resulting in criminal charges involving the student have occurred while the student was separated from the institution.

WHEN THE RIGHTS OF THE VICTIM AND THE CHARGED STUDENT COLLIDE

Despite the best efforts to maintain a sense of fairness and balance within the judicial process, there will be times when an institution will have to compromise to move forward with the process. Many of these potentially conflicting junctures between the alleged victim and the charged student have been outlined in this chapter. The following information reflects Florida State University as an example of one university's response to these conflicts. It is in each institution's best interest for an administrator to meet with the university's legal counsel, victim advocate services, police agency, and judicial office to review these issues and reach a consensus on the best way to proceed prior to dealing with a sexual misconduct charge.

MEETING WITH THE VICTIM OR PERPETRATOR PRIOR TO CHARGING

As noted previously, it is recommended that the university meet with the alleged victim prior to charging, whenever possible, to gain input into the charging decision. However, this meeting can create the impression that the victim is getting "special treatment" or, conversely, receiving "pressure" from the university. It may also appear that the university is listening to only one "side" before proceeding.

At Florida State University, a representative from the Office of Student Rights and Responsibilities (the judicial office) meets with the alleged victim prior to charging, but in a limited capacity only. This meeting is usually coordinated with the Office of the Victim Advocate to have representation from that office present as well. The purpose of this meeting is to demystify the judicial process and allow the victim input with regard to going forward with charges. It is not to investigate the case; this investigation is left to the institution's investigative agency or the local police. A representative from the Office of Student Rights and Responsibilities at Florida State University may also meet with the alleged suspect, prior to the charging, to provide balance to the process. This meeting would be used to update the charged individual about what is occurring, provide information about the judicial process, and impose any restrictions on contact with the alleged victim, if necessary.

THE CHARGING DECISION

As outlined earlier, one of the most complex issues in these cases is whether the alleged victim or the institution should have the final determination about going forward with charges. A parallel issue centers on whether the university should charge the *victim* of any conduct code violations in cases where misconduct is also alleged on his or her part, such as underage alcohol consumption or use of illegal drugs.

Florida State University goes forward with charges of sexual misconduct only when the victim consents, unless there is a compelling reason for the university to go forward without that consent. One compelling reason may be knowledge of prior incident(s) by the alleged suspect. Every institution must carefully weigh the available evidence, the potential impact associated with going forward without the victim's consent, and safety of the campus environment as a whole, before making this decision. Ramifications of this decision can affect the effectiveness of the case, the sense of well-being of the victim, as well as potentially discourage future victims from coming forward

Florida State University only charges the suspect of the assault in a case of sexual misconduct and attempts to avoid charging the victim with lesser offenses, such as underage consumption of alcohol, whenever possible. This falls under what has been termed the "greater good" approach to the dilemma, meaning that the willingness of the victim of sexual assault who may have violated the alcohol policy coming forward outweighs the goal of maintaining a totally consistent alcohol charging policy. However, we often follow up with a discussion with the victim regarding health/lifestyle decisions when appropriate.

SUPPORT SERVICES

Often, the student charged with an assault feels that he or she is the real "victim," claiming to be the "victim of false charges." On more than one occasion, these charged students have requested the services of the Victim Advocate Office. This can create an obvious dilemma, especially when the Victim Advocate Office is providing services to the original alleged victim. By denying the charged student access to this service, the institution may be perceived as supporting the victim of the sexual assault over the charged student.

At Florida State University, victim advocate services are primarily available for victims of sexual assault, physical violence, and stalking—not for charged students who believe they have been falsely accused. Advisory services are made available for the charged students elsewhere in the institution, through our Student Government Association.

PRESENCE OF THE VICTIM WHILE PROVIDING TESTIMONY DURING THE HEARING

As outlined previously, the alleged victim of a sexual assault often does not want to testify in the same room with the student who allegedly assaulted him or her. This concern creates logistical problems for obtaining testimony and sharing information with the charged student. In many states, seeing, as well as hearing, the victim is considered a legitimate part of cross-examination.

At Florida State University, the victim is allowed to testify in what is called "limited privacy." This can include testifying from another room as long as the charged student can both hear and see the victim. This can be accomplished by two-way audio/video hook-up. (Where finances may make this difficult, two home-video cameras, two televisions, and several long cables can make this a reality at any institution.) Modifications must not interfere with the charged student's ability to fully cross-examine the victim.

OPEN OR CLOSED HEARINGS

The charged student often decides to have an open hearing, while the victim prefers the proceedings to be closed. The institution must then strike a balance between respecting the privacy and wishes of the alleged victim and defending itself from charges that it is holding "secret" hearings on offenses.

The solution to this dilemma is largely dictated by state laws and the institution's code of conduct. At Florida State University, the hearing is closed unless the request is made by the charged student to open the hearing. If a request is made by the charged student to open the hearing, the hearing will be opened only after receiving the consent of any and *all* victims involved in the case. In some states, however, recent court decisions have required hearings to be open (see *Red & Black Publishing Co. v. Board of Regents*, 1993).

PRESENCE OF THE VICTIM DURING THE HEARING

Many victims request to be present during the hearing. This is not as simple an issue as it may first appear. If the victim is asked to provide follow-up testimony during the course of the proceeding, his or her presence at the entire hearing could potentially create problems and jeopardize the victim's case. In addition, many times the charged student does not wish the victim to be present during the hearing except when the victim is testifying.

As a general rule, the process is less contaminated if victims are not present when testimony from other witnesses is obtained.

Should the victim be called back to clarify any questions for the hearing body, there is less possibility that he or she would be aware of the specifics behind questions if he or she were not present earlier, thereby limiting credibility issues for the hearing body. However, recognizing the legitimate need of some victims to know what is being said regarding their case, provisions could be made to allow the victim to be present if admissible under your code of conduct. Often, the victim only wishes to be present to hear what the charged student has to say about the incident. Therefore, an acceptable middle ground may be found where the victim is present only during this part of the hearing.

At Florida State University, the victim can ask the hearing body if he or she can be present during the entire hearing or portions thereof. This request is made to the hearing body only after the benefits and drawbacks have been explained to the victim by the director of the judicial office. The charged student is also allowed to provide his or her input regarding this issue to the hearing body prior to a decision being made. The final determination is then left up to the hearing body chair.

CASES INVOLVING GREEK ORGANIZATIONS AND ATHLETES

There are many circumstances that can add to the complexity of dealing with a sexual assault on a college campus. Two of the most challenging factors that confront university administrators are when a sexual assault involves a student organization or when an athlete is the suspected perpetrator. Both of these situations create unique dynamics that warrant attention. Although this section concentrates primarily on the elements of a fraternal organization involved in a sexual assault, administrators should note that these points also apply to any student organization. This focus is not intended to indict the fraternity system in relation to the occurrence of sexual assaults, but rather to recognize that fraternity involvement in sexual assault allegations is sometimes an unfortunate reality in higher education.

Greek organizations can offer students a wealth of positive experiences and leadership opportunities not found elsewhere in campus life. At many colleges, fraternities and sororities also often provide the majority of the social outlets available to students. When not maintained responsibly, the fraternal environment can contribute to a culture that increases the risks of sexual assault on women (Warshaw, 1988; Koss & Gaines, 1993). Warshaw (1988), assessing the factors that contribute to gang rapes in fraternities, asserted that "The culture of many fraternities instills in members a group ethos which objectifies and debases women through language and physical aggression, which lauds heavy drinking and other drug use, and which reinforces group loyalty through united behavior—especially antisocial and sometimes illegal behavior" (p. 107). Warshaw reported that of the 50 incidents of gang rape that occurred in 1985 on U.S. campuses, the majority occurred at fraternity parties. Whether one believes that fraternal organizations contribute to the risk of a sexual assault, or rather that the media tends to report cases of sexual assault associated with fraternities more prominently than other assaults is not the real issue. The fact of the matter is that assaults can and do occur within fraternities, and administrators need to be aware of certain dynamics when dealing with such cases.

An assault occurring in or involving a fraternity can affect a case in two key ways: (a) when a suspect or victim, or both, is a *member* of an organization and (b) when the assault involves multiple perpetrators, thereby, potentially implicating the organization as a whole as the violator of university policies. Under the first situation, the mere fact that a suspect or victim is a member of a Greek organization does not, by itself, mandate additional action by the university. However, because of the close-knit nature of most Greek communities, steps should be taken by the university to assess the needs of the groups involved, including counseling, and to keep the community appraised of as much information as legally and ethically possible regarding the handling of the case. Violations that occur during a fraternity function or that are committed by members of a fraternity have the potential to implicate the entire organization. Therefore, one of the first assessments that needs to be made by an administrator is whether an infraction actually involved the organization as a whole, or whether it involved individuals who merely happened to be part of that organization. This distinction is important in determining what course of action the university may pursue; that is, will there be charges against the organization, charges against an individual, or both? How this assessment is made may appear to be an imprecise endeavor, but specific criteria should be outlined in either the institution's student code of conduct, policies governing student organizations, or its Greek constitutions. Some factors that may be considered when evaluating organizational versus individual charges are the following:

1. Whether the suspects involved in the misconduct are actual members of the organization;
2. Whether the incident occurred at a function hosted by or attended by the organization;
3. Whether any officers of the organization were involved in the infraction or had any knowledge of the misconduct;
4. Whether a significant number of members from the organization were involved in the infraction;
5. Whether the event was announced or planned at organizational meetings;
6. Whether the event was financially sponsored by the organization in any way;
7. What steps the organization took after becoming aware of the violation.

The manner in which organizational cases are initiated and adjudicated at one's institution should be clearly defined by its conduct code or organizational policies. At many institutions, the policies governing individual students in the institution's code of conduct also apply interchangeably to student organizations. Therefore, the same rights, responsibilities, and procedures applicable to individual students would also apply to the charged organization.

Because the determination of organizational charges can be a difficult task, it is crucial that the police department does a thorough investigation, even if it means one-on-one interviewing and questioning. As with cases involving individuals, the institution's judicial process should allow for immediate action to be taken against the organization, such as a temporary suspension, if the activities of the organization pose a threat to the members of that organization or the university community as a whole. However, unlike temporary suspensions involving individuals, suspensions governing organizations would most likely focus on curtailing activities and meetings held by the suspended organization over prohibitions of class attendance.

At Florida State University, we have instituted a collaborative model to assess charges involving Greek organizations. In cases involving fraternities, a student member of the Interfraternity Council Judicial Board, an administrative representative from the Office of Greek Life, and the Director from the Office of Student Rights and Responsibilities (the student judicial office) meet on a weekly basis to review police reports involving Greek organizations. At this meeting, a determination is made by the group as to whether any of the reports involving a particular group merit disciplinary charges. If it is determined that charges are appropriate, the same process outlined earlier involving individuals takes place, in this case utilizing the organization as the charged body. At Florida State University, the president of the charged organization is expected to coordinate a response to the charges. Within our process, the Student Code of Conduct allows for an Interfraternity Council Judicial Board to hear cases involving fraternities and make recommendations to the university regarding findings of fact, responsibility, and sanctions. Other groups are adjudicated by the appropriate governing boards that oversee them as designated for in the Code.

In some instances, there maybe charges against an organization while at the same time the institution is adjudicating charges against an individual. The most common example of this is when a sexual assault happens to take place at a fraternity party involving the underage provision and consumption of alcohol by students. In such a case, the fraternity is often faced with organizational charges for the alcohol violations, although an individual may be faced with the charges related to the sexual assault. This situation forces the question of which case should take priority. In addition, the fact that some or all of the parties may also be facing criminal or civil action adds to the complexity of this situation.

There is no completely right or wrong answer about how to proceed in these instances. Most often, cases involving criminal proceedings will either result in one of two situations that will impact the university's determination of whether to proceed before or after criminal action is taken. The first situation usually involves the State Attorney's Office not releasing key or pertinent information related to the case that impacts the institution's ability to initiate judicial action. Without a complete report or access to key information, the university may not be able to adequately ascertain charges even if it wishes to go forward. Conversely, criminal proceedings can also be drawn out and move at a pace that makes delaying institutional action unfavorable. Although institutions can choose to wait until criminal proceedings have concluded, they are not required to do so by law in most states. Many institutions would prefer to move the case forward and resolve the allegation in a timely fashion and not delay until after possibly lengthy criminal proceedings. As noted previously, these decisions should be made only after consulting with one's institutional legal counsel and scrutinizing the case at hand.

When trying to decide to pursue/adjudicate individual or organizational charges first, it is suggested that a thorough review is made of both processes and the possible outcomes. Some questions helpful in assessing this issue are as follows:

1. What are the laws regarding confidentiality in each case, and how would they impact the decision regarding which to pursue first? In some states, cases involving organizational charges are public record, while in most states cases involving individual students are confidential. Will pursuing one case prior to the other be impacted by these laws?
2. Does pursuing one before the other jeopardize or unfairly penalize the other charged body that must go second? If so, in what way(s)?
3. Which is the more important case to resolve for the institution?
4. What happens if information brought out during the adjudication process in one case is germane to the other case? How would that information be shared?
5. Does pursuing charges against the organization jeopardize the victim's rights to confidentiality in any manner?

6. At what point is there enough information to justify taking action against either of the charged bodies? Does taking action at that point limit the hearing body's ability to completely investigate the case or the charged body's ability to defend itself?
7. What is the cost to each of the charged bodies in delaying their case?

Hopefully, by reviewing the situation in light of these questions, readers will be able to make an appropriate determination regarding the fairest course of action for their institution and the students involved.

Because cases involving an organization can involve a larger number of constituents, it is vital to keep in contact with several key people within the organization. The contacts should include the president of the organization, the advisor, and any national offices that the group may be affiliated with. Because rumors in organizational cases tend to fly fast and furiously, it is critical to move quickly and to communicate with the appropriate governing bodies before misinformation is disseminated.

Many of the same issues inherent in dealing with Greek organizations are also found in cases involving student athletes. Some of the same group dynamics that contribute to the occurrence of assaults apply to both groups. Research supports that men in sex-segregated groups like fraternities and sports team are more likely to commit acts of group sexual assault (Koss & Gaines, 1993). A study in 1996 that looked at male college student athletes at Division I institutions suggests that varsity athletes may account for a significantly higher percentage of sexual assault complaints on college campuses (Crosset, Ptacek, McDonald, & Benedict, 1996). Warshaw (1988) also contended that:

> Like fraternities, athletic teams are breeding grounds for rape, particularly gang acquaintance rape. They are organizations which pride themselves on the physical aggressiveness of their members, and which demand group loyalty and reinforce it through promoting the superiority of their members over outsiders. Athletic teams are often populated by men steeped in sexist, rape-supportive beliefs. (p. 113)

If there is one overriding suggestion to offer administrators dealing with a sexual assault involving an athlete, especially in high-profile situations, it is *not* to deviate from the standard practice and procedures unless common sense or fairness dictates otherwise. Too often, administrators can become deluged with lawyers, coaches, interested alumni, and others who have an "interest" in an athlete's case and who are too willing to share their thoughts about how to best resolve the complaint. These suggestions can be very tempting in an environment that reveres student athletes. However, the best course of action, both legally and ethically, is, most often, to follow the process that is in place and let it run its course to determine the appropriate outcome. Whether a coach decides a player should sit out a game or a season is a determination most appropriate for those in the athletic domain. On the other hand, the determination of responsibility a student athlete has for a violation of the student code of conduct is a separate issue and should be determined by those vested with that responsibility at the institution. Like any case, this determination should be made only after a full investigation and hearing on the facts has been conducted. To do otherwise would be unfair to the student-athlete, the victim, and the student constituency of the university.

As with cases involving fraternities, media scrutiny will likely increase with complaints involving athletes. Administrators need to anticipate this interest and respond appropriately (see "Dealing with the Media"). Some form of contact from the judicial office with the university athletic department may be warranted out of professional courtesy as athletic departments and staff are often the focus of media contact during incidents involving athletes. Keeping them informed and educated on the judicial process can be beneficial to all involved. However, this contact should be done on a need-to-know basis only and not compromise the rights of the victim, the rights of the student athlete, or the judicial process.

STUDENT RECORDS AND LEGISLATION

Administrators who work with student records and information involving sexual misconduct need to be aware of the laws governing the confidentiality and release of these records, both at the federal and state level. Chief among these statutes is the Family Educational Rights and Privacy Act of 1974 (20 U.S.C. 1232g), often referred to as FERPA or the Buckley Amendment. In essence, FERPA prevents institutions from releasing student records or information maintained by colleges and universities without student consent. "Student records" is broadly defined as any record related to the student that is maintained by the institution. Historically, many institutions have not interpreted this protection to restrict an administrator from sharing the final judicial outcome of a university disciplinary proceeding with the alleged victim of a sexual assault. It should be noted that policies governing the confidentiality of student judicial records have been under considerable scrutiny in recent years by the media, the courts, and the legislature. Pressure from parents and victim advocate groups have challenged the perception that students charged with serious violations in the university judicial processes have the right of confidentiality. After considerable debate, FERPA was amended by the Higher Education Amendments of 1998 (20 U.S.C. §1232g(b)). Under this amendment, barring any state provisions, institutions taking disciplinary action against students for violent conduct or nonforcible sex offenses now have the discretion to release specified information to the public in cases in which a student perpetrator is found "responsible." This information includes the charged student's name, the conduct violation(s) alleged to have been committed, and any sanctions imposed by the university on the student. Administrators would be wise to thoroughly review this act and the recent changes made to it in light of state laws that apply to their institution when assessing what information may be released.

In addition to laws concerning the confidentiality of student records, institutions dealing with sexual assault need to also be aware of at least two other federal acts: the Crime Awareness and Campus Security Act of 1990 (20 U.S.C. §1092(f)) and the Campus Sexual Assault Victims' Bill of Rights Amendment to the Higher Education Reauthorization Act of 1992 (20 U.S.C. §1092(f)7). The Crime Awareness and Campus Security Act of 1990 requires that institutions in which students receive federal funds track and report statistics on specified crimes occurring on their campuses. Recent amendments in federal law have expanded the geographic reporting requirements of this act to include the reporting of noncampus crimes in areas "related" to institutions and used by students. It has yet to be determined exactly how this expansion will be interpreted in practice. The Campus Sexual Assault Victims' Bill of Rights Amendment to the Higher Education Reauthorization Act (1992) requires that institutions of higher education develop educational programs to promote awareness of sexual assault offenses and to have in place formal procedures for dealing with sexual assaults. Finally, every institution must ensure that it is adhering to its own policies set forth within its individual student code of conduct in regard to the maintenance, release, and expungement of student records.

DEALING WITH THE MEDIA

Although this chapter is not intended to be a guide on media relations, the severity of sexual assault, combined with the public's natural curiosity and right to know makes addressing media inquiries a practical concern. To this end, the following suggestions are offered to help administrators deal with this issue;

- Before dealing with a media request, identify one person on your campus who will act as the point person for addressing such inquiries. This will decrease the chance of conflicting information being released from your institution. Institutions with media relations offices may already have people trained and in place for dealing with this. It is important that the point person has been informed of the facts, educated on the university's judicial process, and aware of the parameters of confidentiality related to the case.
- Remember that great care should be taken to protect the confidentiality of the alleged victim and the suspect in each case. Although police records, depending on the status of the investigation, may be public, universities and colleges in most states have an obligation to protect the rights of the students involved in the campus judicial process by federal and/or state law.

- Don't fear the media. Instead, view media inquiries as an opportunity to educate the public on your judicial process and to allay any fears that your institution may not be responding to the assault. Although you may be limited in your ability to share details about the case, nothing prevents you from outlining the process that your institution takes when dealing with a sexual assault allegation.
- Whenever possible, make sure that both the alleged victim and charged student are informed of any media inquiries and of the information that will be shared with the media before it is released. The primary focus of the institution must remain on addressing the needs of the students involved in the case rather than the needs of the media. Every effort should be made not to alienate these students by releasing information to the media prior to the students being made aware of the information.
- Prior to talking with the media, try to identify two or three main points that you want to share with them. Rather than getting drawn into discussions with reporters, frame your responses around these talking points.
- You can control the setting by initiating meeting times and locations. It is also not unreasonable to ask for questions in advance to prepare.

SUMMARY

As administrators of higher education become better educated on the issues of sexual assault, they will become more adept at identifying and responding to the challenges these incidents pose to student-victims, their campus judicial process, and the campus community as a whole. There has already been a dramatic increase in educational programming, victim advocate services, and the promulgation of victim's rights within campus disciplinary processes across this country. Administrators must realize, however, that these changes, if managed responsibly, will most likely result in an increase in the number of cases reported to the institution, not a decrease. Sexual assault continues to be an underreported crime, and as services and agencies within institutions become more adept at handling these violations, they should create an environment that encourages the reporting of these incidents.

Because of the severity of sexual assault, administrators must continue to work with local law enforcement to foster a process that encourages victims to pursue both campus *and* criminal proceedings whenever possible. It is imperative that administrators remember that they are not in the business of prosecuting criminals, but rather, adjudicating student conduct code violations. The primary purpose of the college judicial process is to educate students, not to adjudicate violations of the law. However, if college and university administrators are truly committed to providing safe environments for their students, they must recognize that there may be times when they have the sole responsibility for reviewing sexual assault allegations. For a variety of reasons, victims of sexual assault may be reluctant to pursue criminal action, and the university judicial process may provide the only alternative available for the institution to fully investigate an incident. By evaluating your institution's process in light of the issues raised in this chapter, institutions can become better prepared to deal with this challenge. By doing so, higher education can make positive strides toward increasing the safety of students.

REFERENCES

Alstyne, W. (1969). The tentative emergence of student power in the United States. *The American Journal of Comparative Law, 17,* 403–415.

Bickel, R., & Lake, P. (1994). Reconceptualizing the university's duty to provide a safe learning environment: A criticism of the doctrine of *In Loco Parentis* and the restatement (second) of torts. *Journal of College and University Law, 20*(3), 261–294.

Blackstone, W. (1770). *Commentaries on the Law.* Vol. 1. Oxford: Clarendon Press.

Brittain, K. R. (1971). Colleges and universities: The demise of *In Loco Parentis. Land and Water Law Review, 6,* 715–741.

Bullock v. Board of Governors of the University of North Carolina, I.C. No. TA-10433, North Carolina Industrial Commission (1989).

Crosset, T. W., Ptacek, J., McDonald, M. A., & Benedict, J. R. (1996). Male student-athletes and violence against women: A survey of campus judicial affairs offices. *Violence Against Women, 2*(2), 163–179.

Dannells, M. (1978). *Disciplinary practices and procedures in baccalaureate-granting institutions of higher education in the United States.* Unpublished doctoral dissertation, University of Iowa, Iowa City.

Dannells, M. (1990). Changes in disciplinary policies and practices over 10 years. *Journal of College Student Development, 31,* 408–414.

Dannells, M. (1997). *From discipline to development: Rethinking student conduct in higher education.* ASHA-ERIC Higher Education Report Volume 25, No. 2. Washington, DC: The George Washington University Graduate School of Education and Human Development.

Dixon v. Alabama State Board of Education, 294 F. 2d 150 (5th Cir., 1961) *cert. denied,* 286 U.S. 930 (1961).

Edwards, A. (1994, November). *In loco parentis: Alive and kicking, dead and buried, or rising phoenix?* Paper presented at Association for the Study of Higher Education, Tucson, AZ.

Florida State University Handbook (1998/1999). Florida State University student code of conduct. Tallahassee, FL: Author.

Gehring, D., & Young, D. (1977). *The college student and the courts.* Asheville, NC: College Administration Publications.

Gilbert, S., & Sheiman, J. (1995). Mandatory counseling of university students: An oxymoron? *Journal of College Student Psychotherapy, 9*(4), 3–21.

Goss v. Lopez, 419 U.S. 565. (1975).

Gott v. Berea College, 161 S. W. 204 (156 Ky. 376) (1913).

Koss, M., & Gaines, J. (1993). The prediction of sexual aggression by alcohol use, athletic participation, and fraternity affiliation. *Journal of Interpersonal Violence, 8,* 94–108.

Mullins v. Pine Manor College et al., 389 Mass. 47, 449 N.E.2d 331 Supreme Judicial Court of Massachusetts, Norfolk (1983).

Pavela, G. (1997, February). Defining sexual assault. Paper presented at the Association for Student Judicial Affairs Conference, Clearwater, FL.

Pearson, D. (1998). *Negligent liability in United States colleges and universities: A legal-historical analysis.* Unpublished doctoral dissertation, Florida State University, Tallahassee.

Picozzi, J. M. (1987). University disciplinary process: What's fair, what's due and what you don't get. *Yale Law Journal, 96*(8), 2132–2161.

Red & Black Publishing Co. v. Board of Regents, 427 S.E. 2d 257 (1993).

Stoner, E. N., & Cerminara, K. (1990). Harnessing the 'Spirit of Insubordination': A model code of disciplinary conduct. *The Journal of College and University Law, 17*(2), 89–121.

Swen, L. (1987). Due process rights in student disciplinary matters. *The Journal of College and University Law, 14*(2), 359–382.

Tomz, J., & McGillis, D. (1998). *Serving crime victims and witnesses* (2nd ed.). Washington, DC: U.S. Department of Justice.

Warshaw, R. (1988). *I never called it rape.* New York: Harper & Row.

Zirkel, P. A., & Reichner, H. F. (1986). Is the *In Loco Parentis* doctrine dead? *Journal of Law and Education, 15*(3), 271–283.

CHAPTER 11

Group Counseling for Survivors
of Sexual Assault

Jamie R. Funderburk

It is not surprising that college campuses, as microcosms of society, have serious problems with sexual violence. Several factors contribute to the vital need for colleges and universities to provide help to the victims. Obviously, the heinous nature of the violence and its traumatic aftermath drive victims toward helping resources. Research indicates that assault victims use mental health services at twice the rate of individuals who were not victimized (Koss & Harvey, 1991). Kilpatrick and Resnick (1993) reported that the lifetime prevalence rate for posttraumatic stress disorder among rape victims is 80%. Moreover, the alarming incidence of sexual assault and dating violence among college students would overwhelm almost any campus's helping capacity. In this regard, Lederman (1993) found that nearly 25% of the 2016 college women surveyed had experiences that met the legal definition for rape. Almost all college counselors have anecdotal evidence of a client revealing that her first experience of sex was an assault.

Another factor that complicates the picture is that many victims do not recognize that they were victims of rape (Koss, Gidycz, & Wisniewski, 1987; Warshaw, 1988). Some victims who fail to ac-

254

knowledge the experience as rape have been found to possess mental rape scripts that portray rape as something that must be more violent and perpetrated by strangers (Kahn, Mathie, & Torgler, 1994). In a similar vein, Koss (1985) found that unacknowledged rape victims were more likely to have been acquainted with their attackers, and a majority had had previous intimacy with them, factors that, as Koss reported, seemed to have "disqualified the experience as rape in the victim's mind" (p. 210). Unacknowledged victims are at greater risk of continuing in a relationship with their assailant. Layman, Gidycz, and Lynn (1996) found that nearly one third of the rape victims in their study maintained a relationship with the assailant, and of those, 90% had not acknowledged their experience as rape.

In addition, the reactions of significant others to disclosure about the rape experience are mediators in the victim recognizing the experience as rape. One acquaintance rape survivor reportedly told her girlfriend that she was assaulted by a date. The girlfriend then talked to the date and believed his contention that "she wanted it." Another client told no one of her experience for 2 years, believing it was her fault and denying it to the point of continuing to date the perpetrator, excusing him by believing that he didn't know what he had done. She did not define the experience as rape, blaming herself for the bad situation, and later was confused by her phobias and nightmares. Thus revictimization is a real danger for many unacknowledged victims of acquaintance rape (Rosen, 1996) and a factor that complicates the recovery process.

Given the high incidence and prevalence of sexual assault among college women, with the majority of assailants being known to the victim and the dual dilemma of many victims not reporting the crime and others not even identifying or acknowledging themselves as having been raped, it is imperative that treatment approaches start with accurate identification and recruitment of survivors (Dye & Roth, 1990). For this reason, both rape prevention and awareness educational programming on college campuses are essential to decrease student vulnerability as potential victims and perpetrators of sexual assault, and to help those students who have been raped acknowledge the experience and seek counseling services to facilitate their recovery process.

Group counseling is a treatment modality that is especially applicable for women's recovery. With this in mind, I present in this chapter a three-part model for group treatment of survivors of sexual violence on campus. The chapter, as a whole, consists of four sections. I begin with an overview of rape trauma, including symptoms, diagnostic considerations, and factors influencing recovery. The second section discusses the work of Judith Herman and her conceptualization of complex posttraumatic stress disorder and its appropriateness for comprehensive, multiphase recovery group treatment. Next, I demonstrate how this model can be applied for each phase, including the important issues of initial interviewing and screening. The chapter concludes with a section on alternative paths to recovery.

RAPE TRAUMA RESPONSE

Fear, anxiety, and terror are well-documented, universal responses to rape. Feelings of helplessness and terror are reported in 90 to 95% of rape cases (Calhoun, Atkeson, & Resick, 1982; Kilpatrick, Veronen, & Resick, 1982). Immediately following the assault victims are distressed, although they may show this in different ways. Some victims may be emotionally expressive and tearful, while others become withdrawn, refusing to talk to anyone.

Based on research, Burgess and Holmstrom (1974) proposed a model of victim response to rape that they termed the "rape trauma syndrome." Rape trauma syndrome describes two phases of victim response to rape, an acute phase lasting from a few days to several weeks, and a longer-term reorganization phase that may last several years. Ruch and Leon (1983) described rape reactions as being determined by two distinct components: the effect on the victim and the level of the trauma. Using a longitudinal view, they proposed that postrape adjustment is impacted by several factors, including social support, coping mechanisms, and preexisting life stressors. Developmental stage of the rape victim at the time of the assault is another important consideration. Building on these concepts, the American Psychiatric Association developed diagnostic criteria for acute stress disorder

(ASD) and posttraumatic stress disorder (PTSD), which were inclusive of the rape trauma experience.

ACUTE STRESS

Victims of all forms of trauma experience intense fear, helplessness, or horror. The fourth edition of the *Diagnostic and Statistical Manual of Mental Disorders* (American Psychiatric Association, 1994) defines rape trauma responses that occur within 2 days to 4 weeks of the trauma as acute stress disorder (ASD). To meet the criteria for ASD, victims of rape trauma, either during or immediately posttrauma, display at least three of the following dissociative symptoms: an absence of emotional responsiveness or detachment, a subjective sense of numbing, derealization, dissociative amnesia, or a reduction in awareness of their surroundings. In addition, ASD victims persistently reexperience the traumatic event, avoid stimuli that may trigger memories of the trauma, and experience marked anxiety. One client's reexperiencing of the painful event of being raped on the beach during spring break came back to her vividly when she smelled suntan lotion in a grocery store. These symptoms occur to the degree that they interfere with normal functioning. When symptoms continue 1 month beyond the trauma, the DSM-IV diagnosis changes from ASD to PTSD.

POSTTRAUMATIC STRESS

The many symptoms of PTSD are similar to those of ASD and fit into three categories. These categories are intrusion, constriction, and hyperarousal. As described in the *DSM-IV* (APA, 1994), characteristic features of PTSD involve "persistent re-experiencing of the traumatic event, persistent avoidance of stimuli associated with the trauma and numbing of general responsiveness, and persistent symptoms of increased arousal" (p. 424). As Judith Herman (1992) noted, "Hyperarousal reflects the persistent expectation of danger, intrusion reflects the indelible imprint of the traumatic moment; constriction reflects the numbing response of surrender" (p. 25).

The *DSM-IV* (APA, 1994) stipulates further that PTSD may be particularly severe and long lasting when the stressor is of human design, as in rape. PTSD is defined as *acute* when the duration of symptoms has been less than 3 months, *chronic* when symptoms have lasted more than 3 months, and *delayed* when at least 6 months have past between the rape and the onset of symptoms.

THE EMOTIONAL AFTERMATH OF RAPE

The inhumane contact between humans that defines rape is a truly devastating experience. Use of denial and minimization in recalling the experience is a common coping strategy of acquaintance rape survivors (Kelly, 1988). Painful guilt feelings are also common. For rape victims, guilt is often related to shame about what they had to do to survive, and may serve to decrease feelings of helplessness and vulnerability. Unfortunately, the minimization, denial, and self-blame acquaintance rape survivors often use to cope may also make it difficult for them to get the support that they need during the recovery process (LeJeune & Follette, 1994).

Needless to say, depression is a common response to rape. Seventy-five percent of rape victims report depression during the first month after the assault (Atkeson, Calhoun, Resick, & Ellis, 1982; Calhoun & Atkeson, 1991). Other researchers have found that acquaintance rape victims have significantly more trauma symptoms and lower sexual self-esteem in the areas of moral judgement, adaptiveness, and control than women who were not victims (Shapiro & Chwarz, 1997).

Responses to rape trauma might include self-destructive and impulsive behavior such as substance abuse and risk taking, somatic complaints, feeling damaged, hostility, social withdrawal, a loss of previously sustained beliefs, feelings of ineffectiveness, feeling constantly threatened and hypervigilant, difficulty concentrating, hopelessness and despair, and suicidal ideation or attempts (APA, 1994; Burgess, 1991; Cohen & Roth, 1987).

Anger is an inevitable response to rape as well (Burgess, 1991). However, due to female socialization, which often discourages expression of anger, and the predominance of fear, which occurs in response to life-threatening trauma, anger often is not overtly expressed and may even be turned inward toward self. Obsessive-compulsive behaviors may develop, such as washing and cleaning rituals, cognitive rituals, binge/purge behavior, or self-cutting (Calhoun & Atkeson, 1991). Overeating as efforts to self-nurture and provide temporary relief can result in weight gain, which then may serve a protective function by decreasing the survivor's perceived vulnerability as a target of rape.

Sexual dysfunction is a common consequence of rape (Becker, Abel, & Skinner, 1979; Becker, Skinner, Abel, Axelrod, & Chichon, 1984). Survivors of sexual violence react on a continuum in terms of their sexual functioning. At one extreme is avoidance and pho-bia—not wanting anything to do with sex. Sexually compulsive behavior or indiscriminant sexual behavior is at the other end. Many rape victims respond to the experience by initiating sexual contact with partners with whom they are not emotionally inti-mate. This enables them to feel in control and avoid intimacy and vulnerability to trust issues, while also fulfilling negative beliefs they may have developed about their worth postassault. Along the continuum of sexual behavior are survivors who have sexual intimacy but may disassociate during the experience, or survivors who avoid certain sexual acts due to traumatic reexperi-encing. All of these responses can be framed as attempts on the part of the survivor to cope with posttrauma symptoms of hyperarousal, reexperiencing, and avoidance, and these re-sponses may vary over time.

FACTORS INFLUENCING RECOVERY

Several researchers have examined causal attributions and cop-ing strategies of rape victims as they impact recovery. Frazier (1993) found that postrape distress levels remained high for vic-tims who blamed themselves and victims who blamed external forces, and that recovery was facilitated and distress levels were lower when a victim has a sense of future control and a belief that future assaults could be avoided. In a study examining factors in persistent as compared to recovered PTSD, Dunmore, Clark, and Ehlers (1997) found that victims with more persistent symptoms of PTSD were less likely to engage in mental planning during the assault and more likely to have experienced mental defeat than those who had recovered. In other words, victims who did not mentally give up during the assault but thought about ways to escape or survive while being assaulted had less persistent PTSD than those who surrendered mentally as well as physically during the assault. Perhaps this mental defeat engendered in victims a sense of powerlessness and self-blame that later contributed to PTSD. In support of this hypothesis, victims with more persistent PTSD symptoms also reported more negative appraisals of their actions during the assault, of others' reactions after the assault, and of their initial PTSD symptoms. Given the potential of developing persistent posttrauma PTSD symptoms and other negative coping strategies, it is crucial to emotionally process the experience, challenge cognitive distortions, and get support for the victim at the earliest opportunities.

COMPLEX POSTTRAUMATIC STRESS DISORDER: A PROPOSAL

Judith Herman's (1992) proposed diagnosis of complex PTSD provides valuable guidance in designing a comprehensive rape recovery group treatment program for survivors for whom the diagnosis of simple PTSD may not be sufficient. Herman's proposed diagnosis addresses the profound impact of intimate violence and trauma on survivors' global perceptions of self, others, and the meaning of life, important clinical considerations that go well beyond disturbances in affect and consciousness regulation caused by the trauma. Besides the posttraumatic stress categories common to all trauma victims that involve difficulties with affect regulation (depression, anxiety, intrusive memories) and with consciousness regulation (dissociation, possible amnesia for traumatic events), Herman's proposed complex PTSD includes diagnostic categories encompassing alterations in self perception, perception of the perpetrator, interpersonal relationships, and systems of meaning.

These additional diagnostic categories attend to the interpersonal nature of the trauma and its impact on self. For example, the betrayal of trust is a critical factor characteristic of repeated sexual assault by an acquaintance, such as date rape or incest. The resultant struggle to make meaning of the experience leads to changes in perceptions of self, the perpetrator, and relationships in general.

Alterations in self-perception can encompass a sense of helplessness or paralysis of initiative and feelings of shame, guilt, and self-blame, as well as a sense of defilement or stigma. There may be a feeling of complete difference from others that may be experienced as being special or utterly alone. There may be alterations in the victim's perception of the perpetrator, especially if he or she is a romantic partner, which may include preoccupation with the relationship. Preoccupation with the relationship may be manifested in a number of ways: the victim may be consumed by thoughts of revenge, attribute total power to the perpetrator, idealize or feel paradoxical gratitude to him or her, or accept the perpetrator's belief system and rationalizations (Herman, 1992).

As mentioned earlier, sometimes the victim of acquaintance rape, as a way to feel in control and rationalize the rape, continues in a consensual sexual relationship with the perpetrator. This is more likely if the victim has not acknowledged the experience as rape. These alterations in self-perception can also be seen in survivors of relationship violence involving physical and emotional abuse.

In the aftermath of sexual assault trauma, victims' relationships may undergo significant alterations. The victim may become isolated or withdraw, repeatedly search for a rescuer, display persistent distrust, or make repeated attempts at self-protection.

Finally, alterations in systems of meaning may include a loss of sustaining faith or hopelessness and despair. For college-age victims the impact of these alterations can lead to profound questions and doubting about their purpose in life, values, and goals. College students struggling to recover from rape and intimate violence often falter in critical areas of self-growth, including reduced academic motivation and performance, disruptions in intimate relationships, and arrested identity and career development. It is as if victims of interpersonal violence disconnect from their lives in an effort to survive and decrease painful feelings.

TRAUMA RECOVERY THEORY: A THREE-STAGE PROCESS

In her groundbreaking book, *Trauma and Recovery*, Judith Herman (1992) described three developmental stages of an individual's response to interpersonal trauma: (1) disconnection, (2) remembering and mourning, and (3) reconnection. These stages of trauma recovery are consistent with previous conceptualization of rape trauma response (Burgess & Holmstrom, 1974), battered women's syndrome (Walker, 1979) and conceptualizations of responses to trauma in general (APA, 1994). According to Herman, successful resolution of interpersonal trauma involves movement through these stages. Without support, a feeling of safety, and "witnessing" from others, survivors are less likely to move successfully through the recovery process. Survivors can get stuck in the disconnected stage, not feeling safe enough to acknowledge the pain and loss related to the trauma even to themselves. Or they can get stuck at the remembering and mourning stage. Stuckness at this stage manifests itself as an all-consuming identification with being a victim/survivor to the point where victims fail to appreciate other aspects of themselves or trust connecting with others. Without support, safety, and witnessing from others, trauma survivors can become caught in a vicious cycle: they vacillate between feeling disconnected from themselves and others, to intense remembering, which feels overwhelming, and then they cope by disconnecting again, with the result that they are never able to move through mourning and, finally, reconnection to others.

STAGE ONE: DISCONNECTION

In Herman's first stage, the victim uses denial, numbing, dissociation, and disconnection from others as ways to protect self and survive. This is referred to as the shock phase. Seen in the context of the fear and powerlessness of trauma, this is a very functional response to being trapped in a painful situation. The DSM-IV diagnostic criteria for PTSD and ASD that most closely match this phase are symptoms of withdrawal and isolation and avoidance of trauma-related stimuli such as emotional numbing and phobic avoidance. At the disconnection stage the victim is attempting to master or mask acute stress response symptoms of fear and anxiety.

One client gave this description of her experience of acquaintance rape and resulting shock and detachment from her body:

> The experience moved from heavy petting to forcing intercourse on me. I realized that a fly on the wall watching would have seen two people making love. But inside I was horrified and remembered thinking to myself that this can't be happening to me. I felt like throwing-up, and I shriveled up inside of myself, so that the outside of my body and the parts he was touching were just a shell.

Often when recent victims who are in the acute, disconnected phase present for counseling services, they have been referred by others, and therefore they are not yet motivated to explore their trauma. Other survivors may have experienced the trauma in the more remote past but still can be viewed as being in a chronic, disconnected phase. Some of these survivors may not even identify the rape or physical abuse as an issue to work on. Their presenting concerns may be more related to depression, generalized anxiety, difficulties with intimacy, or poor academic motivation and difficulty concentrating. For this reason, intake forms should have specific questions about sexual or physical assault to facilitate identification of victims. For example, at the University of Florida Counseling Center the general intake form that all clients complete prior to intake includes a check list of 27 concerns. Clients are asked to rank the three most important concerns they wish to discuss in the intake and then check any other concerns that apply. Items included in the list of 27 concerns are: sexual assault/rape; physical assault/relationship violence/ stalking; childhood abuse (emotional, physical, or sexual); and oppression/discrimination. Later on in the intake form, to gather more historic data, clients are also asked whether they have ever been a victim of rape, incest, sexual molestation as a child, physical and/or emotional abuse as a child, and physical and/or sexual abuse by their partner. Although asking these specific questions is important and helpful in uncovering interpersonal violence, the intake counselor should be aware that clients may not define their experience as rape, particularly if it was coercive acquaintance rape not involving physical injury.

Stage Two: Remembering and Mourning

Rape and interpersonal violence victims are more likely to seek counseling services specifically for trauma recovery when they are in the remembering and mourning stage. At this stage, intrusive memories are causing anxiety and distress, and awareness of losses sustained from the rape experience or physical abuse contributes to depression and anger. During the remembering and mourning stage, the intrusive symptoms described in the *DSM-IV* diagnosis of PTSD are salient. Specifically, the victim often has a reexperiencing of the trauma (e.g., flashbacks, nightmares, and psychological distress). Foa, Hearst-Ikeda, and Perry (1995) found that 90% of rape victims met symptom criteria for PTSD 2 weeks after the assault and that 3 months later, 50% still met the criteria. Often, it is at this point that victims seek mental health services.

How quickly or how willingly victims move to the second stage of trauma recovery, remembering, and mourning, depends, in part, on how safe they feel. Issues of safety are paramount for survivors of sexual assault who are experiencing intrusive symptoms. Factors impacting the survivor's perception of safety include both current situational and historic factors. At this acute stage of trauma response, the goal of support services is to establish and maintain as much safety for the survivor as possible. Issues that need to be assessed include:

- Is the victim still in a relationship with the assailant?
- Does the victim have a support system of family or friends she feels she can confide in?
- How does the victim's cultural background impact the significance of the trauma (and its aftermath)?
- How does the victim's cultural background affect her comfort with the counseling experience?
- If she did confide in someone was the response positive?

- How empowered does the victim feel to be able to avoid danger in the future?
- What is the victim's history in terms of secure attachment?
- What are the issues of trust and efficacy?
- Is their any previous history of abuse?
- Does "institutional privilege" (e.g., favored status for athletes or members of Greek organizations) play a possible complicating role in the victim's recovery process?

All of these factors, as well as the actual circumstances of the assault, will impact the survivor's timing and nature of movement from the disconnection to the remembering and mourning stage.

STAGE THREE: RECONNECTION

Herman's (1992) final phase of trauma recovery is reconnection. Once survivors feel safe enough to remember and mourn the trauma and losses associated with it, they can start to reconnect with self, others, and spirit. A focus toward the present and future and away from the past is also part of the reconnection phase. A trauma recovery group is an ideal place to start the process of reconnecting with self and others following the trauma of acquaintance rape and intimate violence.

To alleviate the immediate adverse reactions to the trauma and to promote positive coping, crisis intervention and rape recovery groups have long been advocated for survivors of rape (Burgess & Holmstrom, 1979; Cryer & Beutler, 1980; Forman, 1980). Group counseling is very helpful and empowering because it offers a safe and supportive environment for exploring trauma-related concerns with other survivors who have had similar experiences. Initially, the group facilitator should focus on stress reduction training (e.g., deep muscle relaxation and breathing, stress inoculation through guided imagery, and systematic desensitization) and on safety planning to increase each survivor's sense of control and safety within and outside the group. The group facilitator's goal at this stage is to achieve a balance between directively helping survivors manage anxiety and intrusive symptoms and encouraging their mutual support to increase connectedness and foster self-efficacy. Group members' active participation in the group is an important component of the empowerment process as the survivor starts to feel less isolated and powerless.

A THREE-PHASE GROUP COUNSELING MODEL FOR RECOVERY FROM INTERPERSONAL VIOLENCE

A three-phase recovery group model is proposed to address the complex nature of rape trauma response and the differing needs of survivors at different points in the recovery process. The theoretic framework for this model involves an integration of trauma and loss theories as well as feminist, psychodynamic, self-development, and cognitive-behavioral approaches to treatment and is supported by research (Bryant, Harvey, Dang, Sackville, & Basten, 1998; Foa et al., 1995; Foa, Rothbaum, Riggs, & Murdock, 1991; Resick & Schnicke, 1993).

The three-phase trauma recovery group model is based on the distinct differences between the trauma recovery needs for survivors of interpersonal trauma at different stages of the recovery process. The three recovery groups proposed for survivors are (a) an acute trauma stabilization group, (b) a trauma recovery group, and (c) a women's therapy/empowerment group.

In this chapter section, I provide a brief overview of the three types of recovery groups, address essential issues for interviewing and screening potential group members, and discuss the roles of the group leader-facilitator. In the sections that follow, I describe in detail the format and process of each of the groups.

THE THREE RECOVERY GROUPS: AN OVERVIEW

Survivors of recent, single incident, interpersonal violence or rape trauma who acknowledge the experience as rape or abuse can benefit from a *time-limited acute trauma stabilization group.* If not enough survivors of recent incidents are available to form a group, acute trauma stabilization can be done on an individual basis. Obviously, this is preferable to having a student wait for an acute trauma stabilization group to form. Often, these survivors will still be in the disconnected phase of trauma response, experiencing alternating intrusive memories and numbing symptoms, leading to generalized anxiety and confusion.

Those who identify themselves as rape survivors with trauma-related issues, but who are no longer experiencing predominantly acute intrusive and numbing symptoms and hyperarousal can benefit from the second phase *trauma recovery group*. Recent rape victims who have progressed through the crisis stabilization phase as well as those who were raped in the remote past can benefit from this group. In this group there is greater opportunity for members to actively remember and mourn their trauma experience. This is the case because by now survivors' acute trauma responses related to overpowering memories and alternating with disconnecting and emotional numbing have been attenuated. Because they feel less vulnerable and out of control, members are better able to hear and support each other's mourning process. Survivors of other forms of intimate violence involving physical abuse can also benefit from the trauma recovery group. Both survivors of single incident and repeated victimization are appropriate for this group. Survivors have the opportunity in this group to begin the remembering and mourning process and to connect with others who have had similar experiences.

Finally, an ongoing *women's empowerment/therapy group* is offered for any female student who feels oppressed as a woman or who wants to better understand the impact of gender issues on her current struggles and personal growth. For women who are either acknowledged or unacknowledged victims of gender-related oppression—acquaintance rape, sexual harassment, relationship violence, sexism and family-of-origin concerns—this group is a safe place to explore feelings, perceptions and experiences, raise consciousness levels and find support. This group can meet the trauma recovery needs of victims whose experience with acquaintance rape or dating violence: (a) may still be unacknowledged, (b) occurred recently or in the remote past, (c) involves repeated episodes, or (d) includes a history of previous victimization.

At the University of Florida Counseling Center, our staff provides acute trauma stabilization and ongoing women's empowerment/therapy groups. Occasionally, we offer sexual assault/

abuse trauma recovery groups, but fortunately, we have a specialized service on campus, the Center for Sexual Assault and Abuse Recovery and Education (CARE), that regularly provides this service. I worked at CARE for several years, and this is where I received most of my intensive experience with sexual abuse and assault survivors. At the UF Counseling Center, we work closely with CARE to coordinate services. We have found that it benefits students to have the choice of two campus counseling services for interpersonal trauma recovery. Often a student may feel more comfortable going to a specialty service for sexual assault/abuse trauma; conversely, other students are comfortable seeking services at a general counseling center, when, for example, minimizing the reality of acquaintance rape victimization is an issue for them. I have had many clients in the women's empowerment/ therapy groups become aware of acquaintance rape experiences that they had minimized or denied, realizations that had a profound impact on their self-esteem and trust in relationships. Often in these cases, the client has disconnected from a part of herself and in the safety of the group is able to remember, mourn, and reclaim that part. For these clients, disconnection served a protective function against overpowering feeling and had become a chronic way of life.

In summary, given individuals' varying responses to interpersonal trauma based on characteristics of the assault (e.g., acquaintance vs. stranger, ongoing vs. single incident) and varying coping responses of the victims over time (denial and minimization, intrusive symptoms/hyperarousal, numbing symptoms/dissociation, constricting symptoms/avoidance, and secondary elaborations such as disordered eating, substance abuse, suicidality, low self-esteem, and sexual dysfunction), a multifaceted, three-stage model for trauma recovery support and counseling services provides a comprehensive and sensitive intervention to issues survivors face.

INITIAL INTERVIEW AND GROUP SCREENING

During the initial interview it is appropriate for the counselor to gather information about the assault, current functioning and symptoms, support system, and previous victimization. Asking the victim what she did and is doing to survive can help the victim begin to recognize her strength in surviving and elicit information about current negative coping strategies (e.g., substance abuse, withdrawal, isolation, disordered eating), as well as positive strategies such as seeking support, assertively setting limits, exercising, or journaling. Suicidal ideation is a common strategy to cope with overwhelming negative feelings and should be assessed.

Survivors who are suicidal may need individual counseling to stabilize prior to group participation. This will decrease the chances of one group member monopolizing group time. A victim who is still trapped in an abusive relationship should receive individual counseling that facilitates safety planning and ending the relationship prior to group participation. For some survivors, there is great ambivalence about ending the relationship with the assailant. In this case, if the counselor feels the victim is reasonably aware of safety issues while in the relationship, and is avoiding violence, then group participation may be appropriate. Hearing other members' stories of escape can provide the support and motivation needed to get out. Through group members' stories, acquaintance rape survivors can finally realize that submission is not the same as consent.

There are numerous factors that the intake counselor should take into consideration when planning a course of treatment with survivors. For example, survivors with severe posttrauma intrusive symptoms leading to debilitating anxiety and fear should either attend the acute trauma stabilization group or receive individual counseling prior to referral to the general trauma recovery group. Survivors who experience high levels of shame about their rape or physical abuse may need individual counseling before they are willing to expose themselves in a group. Survivors with a history of incest or child sexual abuse may be combating painful, unresolved memories of their past victimization triggered by the current trauma. These clients may benefit more from a group for survivors of childhood sexual abuse, following initial stabilization of acute symptoms. Survivors who are self-medicating alcohol or other drugs to the point of severe impairment may need individual or group counseling for the substance abuse problem before they are able to participate in a trauma recovery group. In these cases the counselor needs to work concurrently on both the trauma issues and the substance abuses; they cannot be separated.

At the end of the individual screening interview it is important to educate the student about the norms and rules of the group and about the group process. This alleviates anxiety and instills in the survivor a positive expectation about group participation. I list a number of important points to address during the individual screening appointment:

- The group is time limited (a semester), meets at a certain day and time, and members need to make a commitment to attend group
- It is normal to have some anxiety about participating in group. This tends to dissipate as group members learn to trust and as group cohesion builds
- Realizing you are not alone is a powerful healing force
- Everything shared in group is confidential, including the identity of other members
- Members are not expected, and will not be pushed, to share more than they are ready to share
- Group facilitators are there to provide a balance of structure and support to ensure the group remains a safe environment
- The more members are willing to put into group through honest sharing, the more they will get out of group
- It is important for members to commit to attending all meetings and to inform the group if they are unable to come due to illness
- Feeling safe in the group is critical for members, and therefore, they are encouraged to share their experiences and reactions in nonjudging ways

Psychoeducation about the group can help prevent anxiety and empower the student to take an active role in the group. This information also provides clear expectations and boundaries that can instill an important sense of control for a trauma survivor.

ROLE OF THE FACILITATOR

The role of the facilitator in the first phase of group is more active and directive than in the later phases, and the group is initially more structured to increase a sense of safety. Because the survivor of interpersonal trauma is especially vulnerable to the power dynamics inherent in any helping relationship, it is imperative that a collaborative relationship develop between client and counselor, within an intervention model that is empowering to the survivor.

The feminist therapy model provides this empowering framework. The survivor is seen as an active participant in her own healing process, and the interpersonal trauma is conceptualized within the broader context of the destructive consequences of imbalances in power relationships (Laidlaw, Malmo, & Associates, 1990). The client is regarded as the expert on her experience, and the counselor serves as guide or coach, with specific skills, knowledge, and expertise in the recovery process. As with a marathon runner, an injured athlete, or a woman in labor, the support, advocacy, and encouragement of coach, physician, or counselor is invaluable, but it is the survivor herself who must make the painful, but healing and rewarding journey.

Pacing is an important consideration. Since the journey of recovery from trauma involves alternating numbing and intrusive symptoms and concomitant approach/avoidance reactions on the part of the survivor, the therapist-facilitator must take cues from the client about how quickly to proceed. There are times for expression of emotional pain and pushing, and there are times for building strength, resting, and increasing a sense of security. The facilitator can use her own level of detachment as an indication of the survivor's detachment. It is imperative that the survivor be the creator and director of her own healing process and feel in control of it.

ACUTE TRAUMA STABILIZATION

The first component of group intervention involves a short-term group intervention consisting of two 2-hour sessions for survivors of interpersonal trauma who are experiencing acute trauma stress responses (dissociation, shock, confusion, and intrusive symptoms such as nightmares, flashbacks, and anxiety). This component of group recovery work (a) focuses on normalizing and educating about trauma response and the recovery process, and (b) adopts cognitive-behavioral treatment interventions to decrease PTSD intrusive symptoms. Additionally, group members have an opportunity to tell their stories and receive support and validation. The survivors in this group are likely to be recent victims of trauma, self-referrals for rape recovery counseling due to serious posttraumatic symptoms, or referred by authorities or rape victim advocates after having reported the crime. For this subgroup of trauma survivors experiencing acute stress, the issue of acknowledging and identifying the experience as rape or abuse is not the focal issue, rather it is the need for safety, support, and stabilization.

Survivors are asked to bring an audio tape and cassette player to the first and second group sessions to record relaxation exercises, which they can then practice at home. Survivors are also encouraged to bring a small notebook or journal to group.

The first session starts with an introduction. Information that normalizes and educates group members about trauma response is provided. I might begin this process by saying:

> All of you are here today because you have experienced an interpersonal trauma that has likely created a crisis in your senses of control, trust, and security. It is natural for you to have a strong response to the trauma that may include feeling numb, disoriented, and confused or feeling fearful and overwhelmed. You may feel fearful around other people or feel afraid to be alone. You may question your judgment or the trustworthiness of others. Painful memories of the trauma may arise uninvited, or you may be unable to remember the event. Certain sights, sounds, smells, or physical sensations may trigger a memory. You may feel ashamed, as if somehow you caused or deserved the trauma you experienced. All of these are normal reactions to trauma. You're not crazy, and it is important to try to understand what you're going through, to be self-nurturing, and to get support. You have a lot you can learn from each other.

To the extent that they are comfortable, members can share some of their reactions to the introduction or ask questions about being in group at this time. Group norms and rules regarding confidentiality and safety can be discussed at this time, and members can exchange first names.

The introduction and group norming is followed by an audio-taped relaxation exercise. The goal of the relaxation is to empower members' sense of control over their own bodies and to gain access to inner resources for calming and healing. Group members are told they are in control of how far they want to go with the relaxation, and they can stop at whatever point they wish. At first, group members may feel less vulnerable with their eyes open, and this is allowable. I recommend progressive muscle relaxation (Benson, 1975; Tubesing & Tubesing, 1983) because the directives to breathe deeply and focus on tensing and relaxing specific muscle groups help the group members stay grounded in their bodies and in the present moment. Group members can then describe their experience of the relaxation, identifying bodily reactions and blocks to relaxation such as intrusive thoughts and memories.

Next, I invite members to share their stories. Sharing stories might trigger emotional reactions in both speaker and listeners; therefore it is important that the group facilitator normalize such reactions and reframe them as important parts of the recovery process. Members are encouraged to take responsibility for how much they share, and I remind them that they can use breathing, focusing on the present, and relaxing their bodies if needed. They are to take only 5 minutes to tell their stories and not to respond or interrupt while another member is talking. Members, however, can jot down notes of their reactions to the sharing to not forget important insights. I find that the no-interruption guideline allows boundaries to form and fosters a feeling of containment that increases the sense of safety in the group. It also minimizes the pressure on members to play the "caretaker" role for each other and possibly get distracted from their own feelings. After sharing, I invite reactions and processing with an emphasis on members supporting each other. I find it helpful to remind members of their strength in surviving and to normalize the trauma recovery process, especially normalizing and predicting the common survivor experience of alternating intrusive and numbing symptoms.

Group ends with a brief relaxation that focuses on breathing and imagining a safe place where one could find haven when needed. In anticipation of the next group session, I encourage members over the week to identify and write down their emotional triggers, including their thoughts and behaviors in response to the triggers. They may also journal about the trauma. I remind them to practice progressive muscle relaxation and to imagine their safe place every day, to apply normalization principles to trauma responses they might experience, and to identify and seek out safe support resources.

I start the second group session by asking members to briefly share their current status (feelings, thoughts, behaviors) and reactions from the past week, including reactions to our group session and homework. Next, members share their trauma experience again, with a focus on what they did to survive. The process of retelling trauma stories in a safe environment tends to decrease the power of the memories to elicit strong emotion. Unlike the first session with its 5-minute restriction, this sharing is less time-limited and more interactive; the intent is to foster members coalescing around a common survival experience and associated feelings and thoughts. These feelings and thoughts can include guilt, anger, fear, self-blame, numbness, and shame. I continually reframe (and, hence, normalize) members' behaviors during and after the assault as efforts to survive. I model ways to challenge (supportively) cognitive distortions such as self-blame, while simultaneously validating feelings of loss, anger, and hurt to facilitate members' grieving processes. Postassault survival behaviors (e.g., isolating, remaining with one's assailant, substance abuse, sexual acting out) are examined for their self-protective meaning. As members hear others' stories they feel less alone and judge themselves less harshly. In one group, for example, a member who had been raped several years earlier disclosed that she constantly initiated sexual contact with her boyfriend to feel in control and avoid emotional intimacy. She realized this decreased her feelings of vulnerability but put much pressure on her boyfriend.

I close the second session with a relaxation. After breathing and muscle relaxation, positive guided imagery is used to evoke a safe place, and I leave members with suggestions about positive inner resources, self-control, and empowerment. I encourage the use of coping strategies such as active support-seeking, journalling, self-nurturing, and progressive muscle relaxation. Once again, I try to normalize (and predict) the cyclical nature of intrusive and numbing symptoms by explaining that they are inherent to the recovery process.

TRAUMA RECOVERY GROUP

Following crisis stabilization, the second phase of group begins. This group can include members from the acute trauma stabilization group as well as new members. During this trauma recovery phase, members are usually characterized by a decreased levels of trauma-related anxiety, confusion, and intrusive symptoms. As security concerns recede into the background, different issues become salient; these include feelings of trust, control, and loss, as well as the meaning of the assault to the survivor. Depression, anger, and self-blame continue as themes. Members' use of detachment, dissociation, and minimization continue to be normalized and framed in the context of trauma response and survival. The group format at this point is less structured and more interactive. Increasingly, members take responsibility for supporting and challenging each other, using the normalizing principles they have learned about trauma response and the recovery process. Stories continue to be shared to undercut the trauma memories' power to elicit strong emotions. Once fear and anxiety is less prevalent, deep grieving often occurs about the losses and pain, and group members serve the function of bearing witness to each others' experiences by providing support and validation. Group content naturally alternates between remembering and mourning, problem-solving, and coping in the present, and understanding the meaning of the survivor's experience. One client, who was a virgin and very religious at the time of the acquaintance rape at age 18 during her first semester at college, realized she had changed her perception of herself from "good" to "bad" as a result of the rape. She started to abuse substances and become sexually active, something she had never done. Through the support and challenge of group members, she came to appreciate that she was the same person she had been before the rape. She even realized that her dichotomous views of the world and herself had been unrealistic, although developmentally understandable. As a result, she developed more compassion for herself and others, and no longer saw herself as "bad."

Thus, challenging cognitive distortions that induce self-blame and engender feelings of insecurity in the here-and-now is an important component of group. The challenging enables members to work toward gaining perspective on the trauma and integrating it into their experience. The healing process begins to firmly establish itself when members regard the trauma as an unforgettable experience certainly, *but also one that does not control them.* At some point a critical shift occurs where remembering the trauma and mourning the associated losses give way to an exploration of the *meaning* of the trauma to the individual and to her worldview.

The goals of the trauma recovery group are fourfold: to (a) facilitate grieving and mourning the losses associated with the trauma; (b) deconstruct and realistically reconstruct and reframe the trauma to decrease anxiety, depression, and isolation; (c) challenge cognitive distortions; and (d) increase connectedness to others and group members in the present. Members start to find a meaning for the trauma experience that puts it in perspective and allows for personal growth, instilling hope for the future. Often this journey results in greater compassion for others and increased self-awareness and acceptance.

WOMEN'S EMPOWERMENT/THERAPY GROUP

The third type of group intervention is designed to be more of a general empowerment/therapy group for women. Women appropriate for this group may have experienced sexual harassment, relationship violence, and other forms of sexism *but are not currently experiencing acute traumatic stress responses.* Its membership is drawn from the large number of women who may not yet have defined their experience as rape or abuse trauma and who are not yet ready to attend a trauma recovery group.

Specifically, for whom is this group intended? Its members are women who could have experienced sexual assault or interpersonal violence recently or in the remote past. Whether they have

always defined the experience as rape or not, they all have con-
sciously struggled with issues of safety, control, and trust in
relationships or with issues of self-esteem. Members of these
groups have included survivors who have never told anyone of
their experience, and other survivors who did tell someone only
to be disbelieved or blamed. Some sought help at the time of the
trauma but discovered that unresolved feelings related to the
interpersonal trauma triggered conflict around the developmental issue of balancing independence and intimacy. Given that
61% of rape victims in a 1990 National Victim Center survey of
4000 women were under 18 at the time of the attack, many women
come to college already burdened by the experience (National
Victim Center and the Crime Victims Research and Treatment
Center, 1992). For any of these women who are not experiencing
acute trauma response, this group is an appropriate healing
vessel.

The group provides some essential ingredients toward empowerment. It is a safe place where members can acknowledge and
share the oppression they have experienced. This is accomplished through the support from other women. The support
and sharing are crucial. Without supportive witnessing, trauma
responses "go underground," perhaps outwardly invisible, but
nevertheless dwelling within the survivor and impacting her
worldview, sense of self, and relationships. Through acknowledgment and witnessing, the women are invited to take steps to
become reacquainted with their "true" selves and to regain
their lives.

ALTERNATIVE PATHS OF RECOVERY, EMPOWERMENT AND ENLIGHTENMENT

There are many paths to recovery from interpersonal trauma,
group counseling being one. In recovery, the important therapeutic ingredients are a safe place for acknowledging the trauma,
time to focus on oneself, and the survivor's courage. College
campuses should provide multiple avenues for healing. Making
a public expression of one's trauma experiences empowers the
individual by validating that interpersonal violence and its trau-

matic aftermath are systemic issues for which individual *and* systemic responses are needed. Many campuses provide forums where survivors can publicly speak out against violence. Besides being a therapeutic experience in its own right, speaking out helps transform self-blame to anger and can galvanize the campus to making a commitment to social change through education and awareness.

Just as humans have great potential for inflicting pain, great, too, are the human resources for healing. Many survivors find healing through art. Often, words cannot express what painting, sculpting, photography, and dance can—often profoundly. At the University of Florida an annual Survivors' Art Exhibit has enabled over 100 survivors of interpersonal violence over the past 3 years to have a voice and share their work (Funderburk, 1998). Besides allowing survivors to connect with each other, the exhibit increases public awareness about trauma. Women's wilderness programs are wonderful opportunities for survivors of interpersonal violence to reconnect with their bodies and benefit from the healing power of nature. Spiritual and meditation practices serve as personal safety havens and as rituals for healing and self-acceptance. Self-defense training, especially when incorporated into counseling groups such as Kick-Boxing for Empowerment, can provide avenues for healing for trauma survivors (Edgerly, 1996).

Finally, I should emphasize that it is important to be sensitive to relationship boundaries with survivors. For example, if a survivor/client decides to speak out publicly, that should be the client's sole decision, and not influenced by the needs of the counselor. Care should be taken to minimize dual role conflicts, and if some role overlap is inevitable, the situation should be processed with the survivor/client. For example, a possible overlap in roles could occur when a client wants to be part of a speak-out or art exhibit that the counselor is coordinating. From a feminist perspective, the need to minimize dual roles with clients whenever possible is balanced with a commitment to and belief in the benefit of participating in social action and change. Interpersonal violence is both an individual and a social problem; the two cannot be separated. To do so leaves survivors alone in their pain, questioning their own experience, apart from others.

SUMMARY

This chapter's focus is on recovery from interpersonal violence through the empowerment of the survivor. The recovery model I put forth is a three-phase group counseling model, based on Herman's (1992) developmental stages of victims' responses to interpersonal trauma. Survivors at the various phases of the recovery process present with different needs. I describe group interventions that address these needs, beginning with an acute stabilization group that meets the needs of survivors of recent trauma who are experiencing symptoms of alternating fear and numbing that are characteristic of the disconnected phase of trauma response. Other counseling groups and group interventions are described for working through the grief and anger of the remembering and mourning phase as well as for helping the survivor explore the meaning of the trauma and reconnect with self and others. The essential ingredients for healing from interpersonal trauma that manifest themselves in group counseling appear to be a safe therapeutic environment, time to focus on self, and support and witnessing of others.

There are certain critical interventions at each of the group phases. These are normalizing the reality of interpersonal violence and individuals' responses to trauma and validating the survivors' inner resources and strengths in surviving. The group facilitator is personal counselor/coach, social change agent, and advocate.

Finally, I included examples of alternative approaches to healing that included speaking out, creative expression through art, wilderness programs, and self-defense training groups.

REFERENCES

American Psychiatric Association. (1994). *Diagnostic and statistical manual of mental disorders* (4th ed.). Washington, DC: Author.

Atkeson, B. M., Calhoun, K. S., Resick, P. A., & Ellis, E. M. (1982). Victims of rape: Repeated assessment of depressive symptoms. *Journal of Consulting and Clinical Psychology, 50*(1), 96–102.

Becker, J., Abel, G., & Skinner, L. (1979). The impact of sexual assault on the victim's sexual life. *Victimology, 4,* 229–235.

Becker, J. V., Skinner, L. J., Abel, G. G., Axelrod, R., & Chichon, J. (1984). Sexual problems of sexual assault survivors. *Women and Health, 9,* 5–20.

Benson, H. (1975). *The relaxation response.* New York: William Morrow.

Bryant, R. A., Harvey, A. G., Dang, S. T., Sackville, T., & Basten, C. (1998). Treatment of acute stress disorder: A comparison of cognitive-behavioral therapy and supportive counseling. *Journal of Consulting and Clinical Psychology, 66*(6), 862–866.

Burgess, A. W. (1991). *Rape and sexual assault III: A research handbook.* New York: Garland Publishing.

Burgess, A. W., & Holmstrom, L. L. (1974). Rape trauma syndrome. *American Journal of Psychiatry, 131,* 981–986.

Burgess, A. W., & Holmstrom, L. L. (1979). *Rape: Crisis and recovery.* Bowie, MD: Robert J. Brady.

Calhoun, K. S., & Atkeson, B. M. (1991). *Treatment of rape victims: Facilitating psychosocial adjustment.* New York: Pergamon Press.

Calhoun, K. S., Atkeson, B. N., & Resick, P. A. (1982). A longitudinal examination of fear reactions in victims of rape. *Journal of Counseling Psychology, 29,* 655–661.

Cohen, L. J., & Roth, S. (1987). The psychological aftermath of rape: Long-term effects and individual differences in recovery. *Journal of Social and Clinical Psychology, 5,* 525–534.

Cryer, L., & Beutler, L. (1980). Group therapy: An alternative treatment approach for rape victims. *Journal of Sex and Marital Therapy, 6,* 40–46.

Dunmore, E., Clark, D. M., & Ehlers, A. (1997). Cognitive factors in persistent versus recovered post-traumatic stress disorder after physical or sexual assault: A pilot study. *Behavioural and Cognitive Psychology, 25*(2), 147–159.

Dye, E., & Roth, S. (1990). Psychotherapists' knowledge about and attitudes toward sexual assault victim clients. *Psychology of Women Quarterly, 14,* 191–212.

Edgerly, C. (1996, October). *Untaming the tamed woman: Kickboxing for empowerment.* Paper presented at the meeting of the Association of Women in Psychology Southern Regional Conference, Hilton Head, SC.

Foa, E. B., Hearst-Ikeda, D., & Perry, K. J. (1995). Evaluation of a brief cognitive-behavioral program for the prevention of chronic PTSD in recent assault victims. *Journal of Consulting and Clinical Psychology, 63*(6), 948–955.

Foa, E. B., Rothbaum, B. O., Riggs, D. S., & Murdock, T. B. (1991). Treatment of post-traumatic stress disorder in rape victims: A comparison between cognitive-behavioral procedures and counseling. *Journal of Consulting and Clinical Psychology, 59*(5), 715–723.

Forman, B. (1980). Psychotherapy with rape victims. *Psychotherapy: Theory, Research, and Practice, 17,* 304–311.

Frazier, P. A. (1993). A comparative study of male and female rape victims seen at a hospital based rape crisis program. *Journal of Interpersonal Violence, 8,* 65–76.

Funderburk, J. R. (March, 1998). *A survivors' art exhibit: A feminist-informed approach to healing.* Paper presented at the meeting of the Association of Women in Psychology, Baltimore, MD.

Herman, J. L. (1992). *Trauma and recovery.* New York: Basic Books.

Kahn, A. S., Mathie, V. A., & Torgler, C. (1994). Rape scripts and rape acknowledgment. *Psychology of Women Quarterly, 18,* 53–66.

Kelly, L. (1988). *Surviving sexual violence.* Minneapolis: University of Minnesota Press.

Kilpatrick, D. G., & Resnick, H. S. (1993). Posttraumatic stress disorder associated with exposure to criminal victimization in clinical and community populations. In J. R. T. Davidson & E. B. Foa (Eds.), *Posttraumatic stress disorder: DSM-IV and beyond* (pp. 113–143). Washington, DC: American Psychiatric Press.

Kilpatrick, D. G., Veronen, L. J., & Resick, P. A. (1982). Psychological sequelae to rape: Assessment and treatment strategies. In D. M. Doleys, R. L. Meredith, & A. R. Ciminero (Eds.), *Behavioral medicine: Assessment and treatment strategies* (pp. 473–498). New York: Plenum.

Koss, M. P. (1985). The hidden rape victim: Personality, attitudinal, and situational characteristics. *Psychology of Women Quarterly, 9,* 193–212.

Koss, M. P., Gidycz, C. A., & Wisniewski, N. (1987). The scope of rape: Incidence and prevalence of sexual aggression and victimization in a national sample of higher education students. *Journal of Consulting and Clinical Psychology, 55,* 162–170.

Koss, M. P., & Harvey, M. R. (1991). *The rape victim: Clinical and community interventions.* Beverly Hills, CA: Sage.

Laidlaw, T. A., Malmo, C., & Associates. (1990). *Healing voices: Feminist approaches to therapy with women.* San Francisco: Jossey-Bass.

Layman, M. J., Gidycz, C. A., & Lynn, S. J. (1996). Unacknowledged versus acknowledged rape victims: Situational factors and posttraumatic stress. *Journal of Abnormal Psychology, 105,* 124–131.

Lederman, D. (1993, July 14). Colleges report 7,500 violent crimes on their campuses. *Chronicle of Higher Education, 39,* A32.

LeJeune, C., & Follette, V. (1994). Taking responsibility: Sex differences in reporting dating violence. *Journal of Interpersonal Violence, 9*(1), 133–140.

National Victim Center and the Crime Victims Research and Treatment Center. (1992). *Rape in America: A report to the nation* (Research Report No. 1992-1). Washington, DC: Author.

Resick, P. A., & Schnicke, M. K. (1993). *Cognitive processing therapy for rape victims: A treatment manual*. Newbury Park, CA: Sage.

Roark, M. L. (1987). Preventing violence on college campuses. *Journal of Counseling and Development, 65,* 367–371.

Rosen, K. H. (1996). The ties that bind women to violent premarital relationships: Processes of seduction and entrapment. In D. D. Cahn & S. A. Lloyd (Eds.), *Family violence from a communication perspective* (pp. 151–176). Thousand Oaks, CA: Sage.

Ruch, L. O., & Leon, J. J. (1983). Sexual assault trauma and trauma change. *Women and Health, 8,* 5–21.

Shapiro, B. L., & Chwarz, J. C. (1997). Date rape: Its relationship to trauma symptoms and sexual self-esteem. *Journal of Interpersonal Violence, 12*(3), 407–419.

Tubesing, N., & Tubesing, D. (Eds.) (1983). *Structured exercises in stress management: A whole person handbook for trainers, educators and group leaders. Vol 1.* Duluth, MN: Whole Person Press.

Walker, L. (1979). *The battered woman syndrome*. New York: Springer.

Warshaw, R. (1988). *I never called it rape*. New York: Harper & Row.

Chapter 12

Summary Remarks: Emerging Themes and Implications

Kathy Hotelling

Each chapter in this book stands as a somber reminder that sexual aggression is a chronic and serious problem on our college campuses. The seminal study of Koss, Gidycz, and Wisniewski (1987) indicated that approximately 83 of every 1000 women in their sample were victims of rape and attempted rape, and that of these, 57% were assaulted by their dates and 84% of the women knew their assailants. Subsequent studies have not challenged these findings substantially. In viewing the statistics of any one campus, it is important to remember the estimation that no more than 1 in 5 sexual assaults are reported (FBI Uniform Crime Reports, 1995), and that date rape is even less likely to be reported that stranger assaults.

An analysis of this situation on our campuses appropriately includes examination of the psychological factors of the actors (in sexual assault, of the perpetrators) that operate within the sociocultural context. Throughout all of the chapters, we are reminded of the power of the culture, of the group, within which perpetrators operate, within which preventive efforts must take place, and within which survivors must heal. As Ottens pointed out in chapter 1, only some individuals will exploit the windows of opportunity that are provided by the culture. Yet, these individuals can create a hostile and unsafe environment for all students, an environment within which these same students are expected to mature, to develop identities, and to learn. The costs are great to the victim, the secondary victims, the perpetrators, and the institution. Through understanding the complex interplay between the individual's personality and group norms, it is possible to craft interventions that have the potential to make a positive impact on the incidence of sexual violence on campus and to help healing begin.

Chapter authors sought to provide answers to the many questions related to sexual assault on college campuses. How does an institution impact the motivations that abuse and rape require? How do we change rape-supportive myths? How do we obliterate the tolerance of men's violence that remains a strong force on our campuses? How do we empower potential and actual victims? How do we set up effective judicial systems and counseling options to assist victims? How can the university be a resource for cohabiting couples at risk for relationship violence? The answer to these questions, as evidenced by the array of topics covered in the chapters of this book, lie within a variety of approaches. The reality of university staff addressing any issue within the college environment is that efforts must be *continually renewed* because the population is constantly in flux and the students are so geographically and culturally diverse. The task facing college personnel and faculty is doubly challenging: not only must our educational efforts make inroads against society's "conventional wisdom" about sexual relationships, but that once informed, we must insure that students will retain this information and convey it to peers, colleagues, and family.

Despite the varied professional affiliations and perspectives of the contributors, certain themes can be extracted that tend to collectively influence their thinking and guide their work. Although the themes are presented separately, when woven together they form a patchwork that advances our ideas for designing prevention efforts and for refining existing effective programs.

EMERGING THEMES

One notable theme is the contrast between the contributors' rich descriptions of contemporary intervention programs and how the problem of sexual violence was addressed on campuses a quarter century ago. In the past, the responsibility for the prevention of rape fell totally on women as illustrated by the messages: "Don't go out alone," "Don't take night classes or go to the library at night," and "Avoid certain areas of campus." Women were advised to restrict their range of behaviors and to be on the lookout at all times to protect themselves from strangers jumping out of bushes. These messages implied that women are responsible for their own behavior, as well as that of men. A different message (discussed thoroughly in chapter 5) is that women need to take personally protective precautions without foregoing the social and academic opportunities that enrich their college experiences. Concurrent with this attitudinal shift has been the change in treatment of sexual assault survivors. Police officers, judicial officers, counselors, and other professionals providing service to these individuals are trained to recognize that blaming the victim is not appropriate, but rather that the survivor needs to be treated with dignity and respect.

Other changes have occurred. In the late 1970s, women were encouraged to empower themselves by learning self-defense and by becoming outspoken critics of the patriarchy that encourages men to rape. Although rape prevention does require women to be physically equipped to the fullest extent possible and to speak out against societal conditions that engender rape, now it is acknowledged that acquaintances and friends pose the greatest threat when it comes to sexual assault. The grave problem of gang rape has been fully recognized, and prevention and education efforts have been specifically developed for the groups of men, members of fraternities and athletic teams, considered most likely to perpetrate this kind of rape. (see especially chapters 6 and 7). In this vein, the old adage, "boys will be boys," is no longer an acceptable excuse for rape: men must be held responsible for their actions. Furthermore, it is recognized that men can be victims of sexual assault (see chapter 9).

Sexual Assault Is a Complex Issue

In chapter 1, Ottens effectively guides us through the maze of issues that underlie the existence of campus sexual assault. He challenges us to consider the windows of opportunity that exist within our culture: dating rules, rape-supportive myths, the use of alcohol, and institution laxity, all of which contribute to sexual assault. Realistically, it is a small proportion of any campus's population that actually commits rape. Thus, Ottens also asserts that the sociocultural variables related to heterosexism and gender inequality account for some, but not all of the sexual violence that occurs, suggesting that we must also examine the personality characteristics of the perpetrators.

The role that alcohol plays in campus sexual violence is also more complex than might be expected. In chapter 2, Marchell and Cummings recognize that although alcohol may be a catalyst, sexual assaults would occur even without alcohol because of misperceptions of intent, situational variables, and personality attributes of the assailant. Thus, changing communication patterns, minimizing exploitable opportunities, and holding assailants accountable are just several approaches that must be utilized, in conjunction with raising awareness of alcohol's role, to combat sexual assault. Marchell and Cummings speak to the limitations of the traditional, individual approach to preaching responsible drinking. Complicating matters further, Zorza (chapter 3) alerts us to the growing menace of drug-facilitated rape. This places additional burden on potential victims to be alert to risky situations and also places extra responsibility on the institution to educate its constituency about how to respond to this threat. Moreover, the devastating aftermath of a drug-facilitated rape complicates the recovery process for the survivor and requires a high level of compassion and sensitivity from the campus medical, housing, judicial affairs, counseling, and security personnel. The information presented in chapters 2 and 3 provides further evidence that sexual assault prevention on campuses requires a multipronged effort informed by wisdom, endurance, creativity, compassion, and awareness.

Schuiteman in chapter 4 reminds us that the problem of sexual violence on campus is too urgent and complex to be handled only by departments under the purview of student affairs. Obviously, faculty must weigh in against the problem, and Schuiteman shows us the essential role that women's studies faculty can play as advocates, consultants, and educators.

POWER AND CONTROL NOT SEX

It is only recently that rape has come to be reconceptualized as an illegitimate outgrowth of power and control. Although feminists have long promulgated this point (see, for example, Brownmiller, 1975), it has taken some time for it to become essential to the understanding of sexual assault. Feminism seeks to challenge relationships that are forged on power and control, and in chapter 4, Schuiteman effectively articulates how feminist scholarship can and must be combined with antiviolence efforts. Tuel (chapter 9) also underscores the importance of widening the field of our perspective on rape by viewing it not as an aberration in male socialization but as attempts to inappropriately wield power and control. This latter perspective prevents us from being "blind" to victims from the sexual minority population on our campuses and to reach out to them in the ways Tuel has so eloquently described.

COLLABORATION IS ESSENTIAL

The chapter authors' backgrounds and professional affiliations attest to how essential collaboration looms in combating campus sexual assault and in assisting survivors. The example set by Michigan State University (see chapter 4) demonstrates how Women's Studies faculty and service providers can work together to eradicate sexual assault. Certainly no one person or office can offer the range of interventions that are needed for either prevention of sexual assault or for the services needed by survivors of sexual assault. Campus administrators must understand the importance of drawing on the expertise of a wide range of professionals in the design and implementation of interventions on campus. Even only moderately ambitious intervention plans require that professionals be given time and resources to conceive, formulate, and pilot them. Services for survivors and for those at risk of being perpetrators or victims must also be well planned and coordinated across departmental lines. This is *not* a task for one person, or even one office.

EMPOWERMENT THROUGH EDUCATION, DIALOGUE, AND ACTIVISM

It is clear that prevention of sexual assault and aid to the survivors requires empowerment—whether that be empowerment of groups of individuals or single individuals. Empowerment takes many forms. For example, students can be presented with the reality that others may not drink as much as assumed, which may influence students to drink less and thus be at less risk for being involved in an episode of sexual violence (see Marchell & Cummings, chapter 2). Empowering bystanders (see Fouts & Knapp, chapter 5; O'Brien, chapter 7) allows students to take responsibility and speak out about what they observe rather than being part of the culture that supports rape. O'Brien describes his approach to effect a cultural shift in the thinking of student athletes, both male and female. In the MVP Program, for example, students are being taught how to be aware and critical of the myths and stereotypes—our cultural "conventional wisdom"—about sexual assault, rather than being the passive recipients and purveyors of them.

INTERVENTIONS

The Campus Sexual Assault Victims' Bill of Rights, part of the Higher Education Amendments of 1992 (Public Law 102-325, section 486(c)), mandated that colleges and universities develop and distribute a sexual assault policy, design prevention programs, and develop protocols that should be followed after the occurrence of a sexual assault. Coupled with another bill, the federal Student Right-to-Know and Campus Security Act (Public Law 101-542), which mandates the collection and publication of data about crimes, these directives have renewed attention on sexual assault on campuses across the nation and have stimulated the emergence of many programs and procedures that would otherwise not have been developed. The model programs described in chapters 4, 5, 6, 7, and 9 recognize the multifarious nature of sexual assault and base their educative, procedural, and treatment interventions on this understanding.

Taken together the themes presented above have dramatically altered the format and content of workshops designed to curb the incidence of campus sexual assault. As illustrated by the programs that several of our chapter authors have described, trends in program development are remarkably consistent across the nation. How information is presented and disseminated during awareness-building workshops has gone through a radical evolution, necessitated by the shift in our understanding that woman are not solely responsible for preventing sexual violence—the first theme outlined above. Hence, gender inclusiveness is now the rule, rather than the exception, and this established trend is evidenced throughout this volume. Both females *and* males must be educated. Peer-led interventions (see Fouts & Knapp, chapter 5) may be found to be more impactful than those led by authority figures. Rather than consisting of lectures and warnings, workshops are designed to have attendees become active participants in the process, talking about their attitudes, feelings, and experiences related to rape (chapters 5 and 7). Maximizing participation by personalizing the subject matter appears to increase the students' investment in the process (see Giordano, chapter 8). Instead of being passive recipients of information, participants in workshops are being challenged to critically evaluate cultural stereotypes and to learn to speak up and intervene when others are at risk for being victimized. Also, the mediums through which students and members of the campus community are being reached are becoming increasingly varied. Educational materials and channels for communication are more sophisticated than the traditional brochure or handout. Videos, posters, classroom presentations, role-plays, interactive theater, and the like increase the students' involvement in the process of learning. And this involvement appears to lead to increased knowledge about the facts of sexual assault (see especially chapters 4, 5, 7, 8, and 9).

Another clear message throughout the chapters is that interventions must be tailored to specific populations. Although the information shared is the same, the format and the manner in which this information is conveyed varies across audiences. For example, new students who do not have much experience on a college campus (chapter 5) benefit from a different approach than returning students. Whether male athletes and fraternity members commit more sexual assaults or whether the media attention creates this belief, the reality is that assaults do occur with alarming frequency within each population. Binder (chapter 6) and O'Brien (chapter 7) provide suggestions as to how to challenge these specific group cultures that contribute to sexual assault.

Although there is debate across the United States about banning fraternities and sororities to curb the problem of sexual assault, Binder challenges college administrators to utilize the characteristics of Greek organizations for changing the overall culture of the campus toward sexual assault. His is a comprehensive educational approach that includes such specific recommendations as stating clear policies and sanctions, monitoring social events, and anticipating where problems could occur (such as with big and little sister programs, which he asserts should not be allowed). His practical, how-to descriptions are assets for any staff member working with Greek students, and his approach embodies a philosophy that should be carefully considered by campus administrators.

Another population addressed in this volume is gay, lesbian, bisexual, and transgendered students. Traditionally, rape has been considered as an act committed almost exclusively by heterosexual men against women. Sexual violence in the sexual minority community has been largely ignored, which makes the information provided by Tuel in chapter 9 vital to developing interventions appropriate to all levels of prevention—primary, secondary, and tertiary. Equally important for programmatic efforts is training for university administrators and staff to increase their sensitivity to these victims of sexual assault in the provision of after-care services.

IMPLICATIONS

It is essential that campus administrators across all functional areas work to actively change the environment on college and university campuses to effectively reduce the incidence of sexual assault. As both Ottens (chapter 1) and Funderburk (chapter 11) argue, the impact on the victims and environment is profound. Only treating the victims is a necessary, but not sufficient, approach to this problem (see Funderburk, chapter 11). We must take the bull by the horns and be incessantly proactive in our approach, reaching all segments of the university environment. Campus professionals must be trained to counter their own rape myths and cultural stereotypes so that they never are able to contaminate the appropriate treatment of a victim of sexual assault.

O'Brien (chapter 7) speaks eloquently to the desirability of student athletes assuming the mantle of role-model in preventing sexual assault. This manifests itself, in a significant way, when student athletes act in dignified and respectful ways to intervene when they are witnesses to violent acts perpetrated against women. This dignity and respect must also be actively displayed by all who come in contact with an individual who has been assaulted, whether that be a university judicial officer (see Pearson, chapter 10), a counselor (see Funderburk, chapter 11), a police officer (see Zorza, chapter 3), or another campus administrator.

Although alcohol remains the primary rape-facilitating drug, the emergence in the last several years of the use of other substances, especially gamma hydroxybuterate and Rohypnol, is alarming and calls for increasing primary prevention efforts such as educational campaigns and complicates the recovery process (tertiary prevention) for the victims. Potential sexual predators in any locale with access to the Internet can call up recipes for the manufacture of these drugs. The risk that this poses to targets of assaults is virtually unprecedented. The use of these drugs is insidious, and, if it was not previously understood, points to the premeditated nature of many sexual assaults on college campuses. We cannot ignore this threat, and Zorza (chapter 3) is to be commended for putting the threat into bold relief.

Pearson in chapter 10 reminds the reader of the university's responsibility to alleged perpetrators and victims. He raises our awareness of the manifold intricacies that must be considered at the various decision points when sexual assault cases are pursued through the university judicial process. While he walks us through the process, we are reminded of how complicated it can be to maintain a posture of fairness to both parties involved in the case. How a campus judicial affairs office proceeds with a sexual assault allegation depends on the way sexual assault is defined in the university's code of student conduct, and these definitions vary widely from institution to institution. Judicial officers must make difficult decisions such as whether a victim advocate is utilized as a victim's advisor, given that advocating may be beyond the scope of the advisor's expertise and thus may jeopardize the integrity of the judicial process. How the victim might testify is another point of potential conflict and differential interpretation. Pearson's chapter is a must read for anyone involved with the issue of campus sexual assault. Without the wisdom and knowledge that Pearson imparts, it is easy for well-intentioned individuals to be critical of university judicial proceedings—until one understands the complexity of the issues.

Pearson also points out that as institutions intentionally design awareness-building and education programs such as those profiled in this book (see, especially, Fouts & Knapp, chapter 5), and when institutions' expertise improves at handling sexual violations, the number of sexual assaults reported will rise. This does not suggest an increase in the actual number of assaults; rather, it should more likely reflect the fact that given a caring, concerned campus environment and an enlightened student population, victims will be more willing to come forward, confident that they will be treated with respect and without blame.

It is our hope that the contents of this book provide college personnel with both a framework within which to act and concrete examples of programs that can be put in place to change the culture within institutions of higher learning, to provide educational opportunities for all students about the pernicious effects of all forms of campus sexual violence, and to aid in the recovery of the victims. This serious problem needs active intervention and its presence on campuses cannot be ignored.

REFERENCES

Brownmiller, S. (1975). *Against our will: Men, women and rape.* New York: Simon and Schuster.

Federal Bureau of Investigation Uniform Crime Reports. (1995). Washington, DC: Department of Justice.

Koss, M. P., Gidycz, C. A., & Wisniewski, N. (1987). The scope of rape: Incidence and prevalence of sexual aggression and victimization in a national sample of higher education students. *Journal of Consulting and Clinical Psychology, 55,* 162–170.

Warshaw, R. (1988). *I never called it rape.* New York: Harper & Row.

Index

295

Springer Publishing Company

Ending Spouse / Partner Abuse
A Psychoeducational Approach for Individuals and Couples

Robert Geffner, PhD, with **Carol Mantooth,** MS

"By offering eclectic interventions together with a balanced, non-judgmental therapeutic stance, Ending Spouse/Partner Abuse *heralds the future of anti-violence counseling."*
—Behavioral Science Book Service

This clinician's manual and workbook contains a 26-session treatment plan to reduce wife/partner maltreatment. Geffner and Mantooth describe an abuse intervention model that incorporates various theories of psychotherapy. The techniques of this model have been implemented by abuse help centers for over a decade.

The authors include comprehensive weekly counseling sessions that address how to initiate the therapeutic relationship; communicate and express feelings; teach self-management and assertiveness techniques; discuss intimacy issues; and implement a relapse prevention program. Each session contains brief intervention regimens, handouts, and homework assignments. The flexible modification of materials in the manual benefit the trained clinician with specific client needs.

For therapists and counselors who treat domestic partner abuse. Workbook available in English and Spanish.

Partial Contents:
I. Foundations and Brief Interventions • II. Communicating and Expressing Feelings • III. Self-Management and Assertiveness • IV. Intimacy Issues and Relapse Prevention Monthly Sessions

1999 400pp. 0-8261-1269-2 soft
1999 400pp. 0-8261-1289-7 soft
www.springerpub.com

536 Broadway, New York, NY 10012-3955 • (212) 431-4370 • Fax (212) 941-7842

Springer Publishing Company

The Heart of Intimate Abuse

Linda G. Mills, PhD, LCSW, JD

"The Heart of Intimate Abuse *decisively shows that the best answers to domestic violence ... are within those human beings willing to consider the roles of culture, fear, religion, and most of all, love.*"
—**Gavin de Becker,** author of *The Gift of Fear*

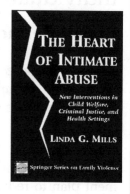

This startling analysis of patterns of violence in intimate relationships suggests that every abusive relationship has a paradoxical "heart" of its own. This dynamic emotional field must be understood in order for family violence interventions to be successful.

Mills takes a critical view of broad current case practices in criminal justice, social work, and medical systems, especially those that meet family violence with coercive interventions such as mandatory arrest—strategies which often ignore the interpersonal bonds hidden within abusive relationships. Mills introduces new intervention strategies which build on the emotional strengths of the battered woman as an individual, and go to the heart of her abusive relationship to find an intervention that works. Here at last is a bold vision of the core causes of intimate abuse on which professionals and policymakers can build strategies—a new ground of theory that at last reaches the heart of the problem of family violence.

Partial Contents: The Criminal Justice System's Response to Domestic Violence • The Public Child Welfare System's Response to Domestic Violence • The Health Care System's Response to Domestic Violence • Engaging the Battered Mother: Empowerment and Affective Advocacy • Systems Strategies for Working with Battered Mothers and Their Children • Empowerment and Affective Strategies I: Meetings in Criminal Justice • Empowerment and Affective Strategies II: Meetings in Public Child Welfare • Empowerment and Affective Strategies III: Meetings in Health Care • Treating Domestic Violence • An Empowerment Model for Battered Women and Their Children

Springer Series on Family Violence
1998   296pp   0-8261-1216-1   *hardcover* • *www.springerpub.com*

536 Broadway, New York, NY 10012-3955 • (212) 431-4370 • Fax (212) 941-7842

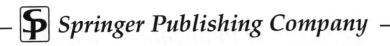
Springer Publishing Company

Battered Women and Their Families, 2nd Edition
Intervention Strategies and Treatment Programs
Albert R. Roberts, PhD, Editor

"This encyclopedic handbook includes the latest policies, assessment protocols and scales, and clinical practices. ...A landmark achievement. Every clinical social worker, nurse specialist, and physician should read this book. [It] is the first comprehensive book to examine domestic violence from a multi-cultural perspective. This brilliantly written and all inclusive resource provides new clinical knowledge and practice wisdom to alleviate the emotional pain and trauma of battered women and their children. I have been searching for a book like this for years."
—**Jesse J. Harris,** PhD, BCD, ACSW
Professor and Dean, School of Social Work
University of Maryland, Colonel Retired

Already an acclaimed success, this new edition of *Battered Women and Their Families* continues to focus on both the basic and advanced clinical techniques and strategies beneficial to chronically battered women and their children.

Partial Contents: I. Overview, Crisis Intervention and Short-Term Treatment • Crisis Intervention and Cognitive Problem-Solving Therapy with Battered Women: A National Survey and Practice Model, *A.R. Roberts and S. Burman* • The Stress-Crisis Continuum: Its Application to Domestic Violence, *P.V. Valentine, A.R. Roberts and A.W. Burgess* • **II. Children and Adolescents from Violent Homes** • Crisis Intervention with Traumatized Child Witnesses in Shelters for Battered Women, *P. Lehmann and B.E. Carlson* • Integrating Domestic Violence Assessment into Child Protective Services Intervention: Policy and Practice Implications, *L.G. Mills* • **III. Health Care and Welfare Policies and Practices with Battered Women** • Battered Women in the Emergency Room: Emerging Roles for the ER Social Worker and Clinical Nurse Specialist, *M.E. Boes* • Intimate Partner Violence: Intervention in Primary Health Care Settings, *B.E. Carlson and L.A. McNutt* • **IV. High-Risk Groups and Vulnerable Populations** • Elder Abuse: Protective and Empowerment Strategies for Crisis Intervention, *P. Brownell and I. Abelman* • **V. Cross-Cultural Issues, Policies and Practices with Battered Women** • Application of the Culturagram to Assess and Empower Culturally and Ethnically Diverse Battered Women, *P. Brownell and E.P. Congress*

Springer Series on Family Violence
1998   552pp   0-8261-4591-4   hardcover

Order Toll-Free: (877) 687-7476 • www.springerpub.com
536 Broadway, New York, NY 10012-3955 • (212) 431-4370 • Fax (212) 941-7842

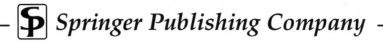 **Springer Publishing Company**

The Battered Woman Syndrome,
Second Edition
A Research Perspective   *New*

Lenore E. A. Walker, EdD

"Every psychologist and mental health professional who works with battered women needs to have Dr. Walker's new book on the shelf. Once again she has provided us with a synthesis of the literature on domestic violence and her own landmark research. Her work has provided the foundation for The Battered Woman Syndrome *in psychology and law, and with this new edition she continues to break new ground."* —**Dorothy W. Cantor**, Psy.D.
Former President, American Psychological Association

In this new edition of her groundbreaking book, Dr. Walker has provided a thorough update to her original findings on domestic abuse. The volume contains the latest on: the impact of exposure to violence on children, marital rape, child abuse, personality characteristics of different types of batterers, new psychotherapy models for batterers and their victims, and more.

Contents:
Part I. The Battered Woman Syndrome Study • Overview of the Battered Woman Syndrome Study • Psychosocial Characteristics of Battered Women, Batterers, and Non-Batterers • Behavioral Descriptions of Violence • The Lethal Potential • Sexual Issues for Battered Women • Impact of Violence in the Home on Children • Violence, Alcohol, and Drug Use • **Part II. Two Theoretical Perspectives** • Personality Characteristics and the Battered Woman Syndrome • Learned Helplessness and Battered Women • Walker Cycle Theory of Violence • **Part III. Implications for a Violence-Free Future** • Future Directions for Research • Psychotherapeutic Responses to Changing Violent Relationships • Legal Responses to Changing Violent Behavior • Conclusions • Appendixes

2000   352pp.   0-8261-4322-9   hard   www.springerpub.com

536 Broadway, New York, NY 10012-3955 • (212) 431-4370 • Fax (212) 941-7842

SP *Springer Publishing Company*

Crisis Intervention and Trauma Response
Theory and Practice

Barbara Rubin Wainrib, EdD
and **Ellin L. Bloch**, PhD

"The authors have eminently succeeded in developing effective and well-grounded theoretical approaches towards helping people in crisis situations . . . an important contribution to the field of crisis intervention . . . actively helps restore the feeling of self that has been damaged by trauma. I highly recommend this book."

—**Martin Symonds**, MD
Deputy Chief Surgeon (Psychiatrist), New York City
Police Department, Clinical Associate Professor of Psychiatry,
New York University-School of Medicine

"This book is very special in its integration of solid conceptualization and compassionate practice. Covering an unusually wide spectrum of crises and traumas, it places them in a context well-suited for the practice-oriented student. Through the use of well-integrated exercises and introspections, it successfully conveys the message that 'helping' is a personal—not just an academic—experience."

—**John A. Clizbe**, PhD
Management and Consulting Psychologist

Written in a lively and informative style, the book presents a successful general crisis response model for intervention. Using real-life case examples and exercises to develop techniques for building verbal and nonverbal skills, the authors encourage therapists to help clients cope by focusing on clients' inner strengths rather than on pathologies that need to be fixed.

The authors' down-to-earth approach to this topic will appeal to crisis intervention professionals, teachers, students, and volunteer workers.

Contents: • Crisis, Trauma, and You: Theories of Crisis and Trauma
• How We Respond to Crisis and Trauma
• Principles and Models of Intervention
• Assessment for Crisis and Trauma
• Suicide and Violence: Assessment and Intervention
• Putting It All Together: The Pragmatics

1998   224pp   0-8261-1175-0   softcover   www.springerpub.com

536 Broadway, New York, NY 10012-3955 • (212) 431-4370 • Fax (212) 941-7842